WESTERN STATE

WESTERN STATE TERRORISM

Edited by Alexander George

Polity Press

Copyright © this collection Polity Press 1991
Each chapter copyright © the author

First published 1991 by Polity Press
in association with Basil Blackwell

Editorial office:
Polity Press, 65 Bridge Street,
Cambridge CB2 1UR, UK

Marketing and production:
Basil Blackwell Ltd
108 Cowley Road, Oxford OX4 1JF, UK

ISBN 0-7456-0672-5
ISBN 0-7456-0931-7 (pbk)

British Library Cataloguing in Publication Data

A CIP catalogue record for this book is available from the British Library.

Typeset in 10 on 12 pt Times
by Colset Private Limited, Singapore
Printed in Great Britain by T.J. Press Ltd., Padstow, Cornwall

Contents

Contributors

Carmel Budiardjo Organizing Secretary of TAPOL, the Indonesia Human Rights Campaign; author of articles and books on Southeast Asia, including *The War Against East Timor* (with Liem Soei Liong)

Noam Chomsky Institute Professor of Linguistics at MIT; author of numerous essays and books on US foreign policy, most recently *Necessary Illusions*

Richard Falk Professor of International Relations at Princeton University; author of many articles and books on foreign affairs, including *Revolutionaries and Functionaries*

Alexander George Assistant Professor of Philosophy at Amherst College

Sean Gervasi A US economist who teaches in Paris, he worked for many years at the United Nations on Southern African questions and, from 1982 to 1984, was an adviser to the Ministry of Information in Maputo; he has written extensively on Southern African affairs

Edward S. Herman Professor of Finance at the University of Pennsylvania; author of many books and articles on US foreign policy, the media and terrorism, including *Manufacturing Consent* (with Noam Chomsky)

Gerry O'Sullivan Freelance writer and doctoral student at the University of Pennsylvania

Michael McClintock Researcher at Amnesty International (London); author of *The American Connection, Volume One: State Terror and Popular Resistance in El Salvador* and *Volume Two: State Terror and Popular Resistance in Guatemala*

Contributors

Bill Rolston Lecturer in Sociology at the University of Ulster; he has written extensively on Northern Ireland, including *Belfast in the Thirties: an Oral History* (with Ronnie Munck) and *Unemployment in West Belfast: the Obair Report* (with Mike Tomlinson)

Sybil Wong Executive Director of the Berkshire Forum

Acknowledgements

I have had more than a little help from my friends. I extend my deep gratitude to all of them. Thanks also to Wolfson College (Oxford) and to Amherst College for their support.

Alexander George

1

Introduction

Terrorism is one of the major long-lived foreign policy issues covered and debated in the wide-circulation media. For at least the past decade, terrorism has been a dominant topic, eliciting substantial reporting, analysis, and commentary. The Reagan administration entered office declaring that terrorism was one of the most important challenges the United States faced in foreign affairs. This declaration set the framework within which most discussions of terrorism have proceeded ever since. Terrorism, on this conception, targets primarily the West and is perpetrated by fanatical groups supplied, if not controlled, by a handful of lawless states and perhaps ultimately the Soviet Union.

The articles in this collection argue in different ways and with different emphases that this conception is a *mis*conception. There is no doubt that terrorists have mounted operations against citizens, property, and installations of the United States and the West. There is also little doubt that some of these operations have been supported in varying degrees by foreign governments. The misconception consists in thinking that such operations constitute the bulk of terrorist atrocities in the world today. One reason it is very difficult not to think this is because the term "terrorism" has been virtually appropriated by mainstream political discussion to signify atrocities targeting the West. This makes it difficult to consider whether there might be (very substantial) acts of terrorism other than those typically focused on by the media, academics, and government spokespersons.

The plain and painful truth is that on any reasonable definition of terrorism, taken literally, the United States and its friends are the major supporters, sponsors, and perpetrators of terrorist incidents in the world today. Again, this is not to deny that the West is sometimes the victim of terrorism or that the Soviet Union and its satellites are to some degree

1

responsible for some terrorist actions. It is to affirm – what should surely be of greatest concern to citizens of the West – that many, probably most, significant instances of terrorism are supported, if not organized, by the US, its partners, and their client states.

Some of the essays in this volume seek mainly to establish what might be called the fundamental thesis about terrorism: that its primary manifestations are supported, or directly carried out, by Western governments. Others examine questions that immediately follow: (1) Why is the thesis true, that is, in whose interest is it that the West, and the US in particular, substantially sponsor mass terrorism? (2) How has this situation arisen and what are the forces that keep it in place? (3) What is the ideological framework of assumptions within which most discussions of terrorism (in the mainstream media and academic scholarship) take place, and which functions are served by it? (4) Which mechanisms render this framework the dominant one (indeed, for all practical purposes, the only one)?

Recent events in El Salvador provide supporting (and in equal measure shameful) evidence for this central thesis. On November 11, 1989, the Farabundo Marti National Liberation Front (FMLN) launched its most substantial offensive yet against the government of El Salvador. In the week that followed, some 1,000 non-combatants were killed or wounded, most of them victims of indiscriminate aerial bombardment by the Salvadoran military. The *New York Times* reported that "According to relief officials, the great majority of wounded people that had been treated thus far received their injuries from the Government's aerial bombardments. And the officials assert that at least four-fifths of the casualties processed so far have been civilians."[1] "In addition," reports the human rights group Americas Watch, "the Army created an untenable and unfair situation for residents by placing many areas under a 24-hour curfew and then bombing the curfewed areas, sometimes without warning."[2] That the Salvadoran military has the competence to avoid indiscriminate bombardment when it wants to was illustrated by the markedly different fashion in which it attempted to retake the Sheraton-El Salvador in the wealthy district of Escalón. According to Americas Watch,

> In contrast to its behavior in poor neighborhoods, the Salvadoran army surrounded the hotel and tried to attack the guerrillas from the air, but showed considerable restraint to protect the residences and civilians in the wealthy neighborhoods. Also in stark contrast with its attitudes of the preceding days, the Salvadoran Army agreed to a short truce to allow the guests, including the armed US soldiers, to leave the place unharmed.[3]

This deliberate exercise of indiscriminate mass terror was accompanied by highly selective acts of violence, most notoriously the murder on November 16 of six Jesuit priests, their cook and her 15-year-old daughter (the latter two presumed to be witnesses to the killings of the priests). Some of the priests were among the country's most prominent liberal intellectuals and human rights advocates: Father Ignacio Ellacuría, rector of the Central American University (UCA); Father Ignacio Martín Baró, vice-rector of the UCA; Father Segundo Montes, head of the UCA's human rights institute. Their murder has had the presumably intended effect of paralyzing the country with fear: if even the most renowed proponents of a negotiated settlement can be gunned down, then no one is safe.

The Bush administration throughout has provided the terroristic Salvadoran regime with support of every kind. At the same time human rights groups and the archbishop of San Salvador, Arturo Rivera y Damas, were charging that the eight were victims of the Salvadoran armed forces, US Secretary of Defense Dick Cheney was assuring the press and Congress that no evidence existed to implicate the army.[4] Bush himself attempted to deflect responsibility for the killings away from the Salvadoran regime:

> Asked if he believed Mr Cristiani's [President of El Salvador] assurances that the Salvadoran government was not involved, Mr Bush said, "Absolutely, I believe it."
>
> "If renegade forces were involved on the left or on the right, they should be brought to justice," Mr Bush said, although he offered no evidence for the insinuation that leftists were behind the killings.[5]

In a by now familiar fashion, atrocities perpetrated by those we support are chalked up either to the "terrorist" left or to "right-wing death squads" beyond the control of the Salvadoran military.

Thus when, on January 7, Cristiani admitted that members of the military were responsible for the killings,[6] he was lauded as a man of "great courage" (Marlin Fitzwater, the president's spokesman) and presented as struggling heroically against "his foes on the extreme left and the extreme right" (*New York Times*).[7] This is the usual fiction that serves to obscure the plain fact that Cristiani heads a regime whose military is conducting a campaign of terror against its own citizens of a level of savagery that is perhaps unmatched in the world today.[8] Cristiani's January 13 announcement of the arrests of a colonel and several lower-ranking officers and enlisted men had its evidently intended effect: mollification of an easily placated and complicitous US Congress. The Salvadoran military also understood the point of the arrests and their

3

irrelevance to the situation within El Salvador. It should come as no surprise then that, according to one assessment, "The arrests have had no appreciable impact on the overall level of military violence; death squad killing and disappearances have not abated, and ongoing repression has forced the popular movement to continue functioning semi-clandestinely."[9] The campaign of aerial bombardment also continues. To take one example among many: on February 11, the air force bombed a refugee resettlement camp killing at least six people (five of them children) and wounding many others. The *New York Times* reports that

> Witnesses and religious workers said they were killed when the air force bombed and rocketed the village, about 50 miles northeast of the capital. An American nun who lives there said that on Sunday morning she saw three army helicopters, flying at tree-top level, fire at least 15 rockets at the area. An hour later two A-37 Dragonfly jets dropped at least eight bombs in the immediate vicinity, she said.[10]

It goes without saying that for every eminent figure killed there are dozens of unpublicized instances of torture and murder of teachers, peasants, trade unionists, and charity, relief, and church workers.[11] Foreigners are not immune to the violence and terror of the Salvadoran military. Americas Watch reports the detainment and torture of French, Japanese, and US citizens. Representatives of the US government provide little protection for its citizens incarcerated and brutalized by the military it supplies. According to Americas Watch, "From scores of interviews with Americans living in El Salvador, we can affirm that US Embassy staff have frequently been rude to American detainees under these circumstances, and taken the part not of the US citizens in custody but of their notorious captors." Instead of seeking to support abused US citizens, "consular officials rush to cast doubts on the credibility of the testimony of American citizens who claim mistreatment in the hands of the Salvadoran police."[12] It is instructive to contrast US silence over, or even complicity in, the violence directed against some of its own citizens with its condemnation of the rebels' capture of the Sheraton Hotel with no reported maltreatment of civilians. Administration officials quickly denounced the takeover as an "outrageous act of terrorism." And Marlin Fitzwater, the president's spokesman, declared that "these Marxist guerrillas have shown their true colors," adding that they had "embarked on a despicable road of violence by threatening civilians, Americans, and innocent citizens of all nations who may be in their path" – none of whom were harmed, as just noted, unlike the "civilians, Americans, and innocent citizens of all nations" who are tortured and killed by the military we train and supply.[13]

Our support for the terror extends far beyond misleading and false statements by government spokesmen. The Salvadoran government and army survive only through a massive influx of aid from Washington, totalling $4.6 billion dollars over the past decade. US military aid (by now some $1 billion dollars) is essential for keeping in power military and security forces largely responsible for the deaths of 70,000 civilians in the past ten years. The US has unfailingly supplied the tools of terror and repression to the Salvadoran military, as well as training in their use. The massacres of November 1989 were no exception: in September 1989, as Salvadoran state repression against popular movements was intensifying, the liberal senator Christopher Dodd joined Jesse Helms in sponsoring a bill to provide the Salvadoran military with $90 million in military assistance, to show that "we appreciate and support what he [Cristiani] is doing and we stand behind him".[14] An alternative proposal linking aid with progress on human rights and peace negotiations was opposed by Dodd and fellow liberal Democrat John Kerry, and subsequently defeated 68 to 32. Dodd's measure was approved by an even wider margin. When, on November 15, as the bloodbath was getting under way, the Salvadoran government requested extra arms and ammunition from the United States, the Bush administration rejected appeals to link military assistance to a serious investigation into the murders of the Jesuit priests and instead promised to hasten delivery of the military aid allocated for the 1990 fiscal year. Shortly afterwards, a weak bill introduced in the House of Representatives to suspend 30 percent of military aid to El Salvador until the regime undertook an honest inquiry into the killings was defeated in both the House and the Senate.[15] As of this writing, the Bush administration is seeking a $50 million increase in aid to El Salvador next year: "I know of his [Cristiani's] commitment to democracy," Bush declared, "And I have been very impressed with the courage he has shown in going after those who have broken the law in his country. And that's been a shining example to all of us."[16]

Clearly, these all too familiar events raise many important questions, some of them formulated in general terms above. This is especially so because US actions in El Salvador are not isolated and egregious aberrations from a fundamentally freedom- and justice-loving foreign policy:[17] similar patterns have been, and are being, played out in other parts of Central and South America, Africa, the Middle East, and South East Asia. Taken together, these give a good, if depressing, indication of the substantial involvement of the West in the most serious instances of terrorism today.

In a volume of this length, it is of course impossible to touch on more than a few issues relevant to what I have called the fundamental thesis about terrorism. This situation is compounded by the fact that some

5

contributors have sought to document their claims at length. I have encouraged this, for it is not only in healthy contrast to much standard work on terrorism but also of value in countering the incredulity and hostility with which honest discussions of Western support of terrorism and violence usually meet. (I urge all interested readers, be they sympathetic to or skeptical of the views presented here, to consult the works referenced; they form an important part of the case for the fundamental thesis and related claims.)

Naturally, the following essays differ in their particular focus as they approach the cluster of issues dealing with Western state-sponsored terrorism. Noam Chomsky, in his contribution, distinguishes between a propagandistic and a literal approach to the study of terrorism. Taking official US definitions of terrorism literally, he provides an overview of some of the major terrorist atrocities of the 1980s, especially in the Middle East and Central America, and earlier in Cuba and Lebanon. He argues that the US and a family of supported "mercenary states" bear major responsibility for terrorist violence today.

In their chapter, Edward S. Herman and Gerry O'Sullivan articulate what they call "the Western model and semantics of terrorism", which serves to downplay, if not totally obscure, the West's significant role in spawning international violence. They examine how this model is suggested by government spokespersons, wide-circulation media, and members of the "terrorism industry." This last consists in a network of terrorism "experts," think tanks, research institutes, and security firms, whose activities the authors investigate in detail, as well as the links among them and between this network and governmental agencies.

My chapter presents an analysis of terrorology, the academic study of terrorism, focusing in particular on ideological assumptions that commonly guide and motivate work in the field and on expository techniques that subtly strengthen the hold of such guiding tenets on the minds of both author and reader.

Richard Falk examines the roots of recent US foreign policy, arguing that historical and cultural factors have made the resort to violence and terrorism merely another acceptable policy option to be assessed according to the usual cost-benefit analyses. He pays special attention to developments since 1945, which have led, he argues, to an increased and more systematic US reliance on terrorism.

Michael McClintock pursues these themes, uncovering, in particular, the roots of much current and recent mass state terrorism in the military counterinsurgency doctrines first devised and implemented by the Kennedy administration. He traces the history and substance of these doctrines, their increasing importance in foreign military training, and the nature of their application, as well as its human cost, in Vietnam, Central America, and elsewhere.

The US is not the only Western nation to employ terrorism as a tool of foreign policy. Bill Rolston examines the British state's use of repression and violence in its attempts to control the situation in Northern Ireland. He also contributes to a thesis prominent in many of these essays: that Western governments, media and "experts" have so systematically warped terms like "terrorism," "violence," etc. as to make it very difficult to arrive at an accurate assessment of our governments' actions and of those of their designated enemies.

Of course wealthy Western nations also contribute to terrorism through their support – financial, military, and diplomatic – of Third World regimes founded on violence. While a number of these are discussed in these essays, Indonesia well deserves the dubious honor of a special chapter. Carmel Budiardjo examines the grisly history of the Suharto regime and its friendly relations to the US, from its birth and consolidation amid one of the major bloodbaths of this century, to its genocidal campaign in East Timor.

Finally, Sean Gervasi and Sybil Wong provide an analysis and historical overview of South Africa's decade-long "secret" war against the front-line states, in particular, Angola, Lesotho, Mozambique, and Zimbabwe. In addition, they argue that the US has played a major and varied role in supporting the terrorization of the peoples of southern Africa that has led to tremendous economic damage and human suffering.

Though far from comprehensive, these essays taken together give an accurate indication of the substantial involvement of the West in the most serious instances of terrorism today. This fact is not easy to assimilate. While humans typically have little difficulty seeing through the rationalizations of their fellow creatures, the actual motivations for one's own actions tend to vanish behind a cloud of self-deception. Similarly, our capacity for objectivity as regards the conduct of nations diminishes as the object of analysis more nearly approaches our own state. This is especially so in a democratic society, whose citizens have some say in the behavior of their government and hence some responsibility for the consequences of its actions. For with responsibility often comes self-justification, and with self-justification, blindness. Yet until we face the facts and take responsibility, our world will remain one of blood and lies.

Towards the end of his life, after having witnessed one world war and the warning signs of another, Freud wrote that he believed our knowledge of the human mind might one day be applied to entire societies to yield "a pathology of cultural communities." He speculated whether such a future inquiry might "be justified in reaching the diagnosis that, under

7

the influence of cultural urges, some civilizations, or some epochs of civilization – possibly the whole of mankind – have become 'neurotic'."[18] I fear we in the US are already there. Whether attainment of sanity in the near future is possible is uncertain. It is clear, however, that the first difficult steps will require much honesty about ourselves.

Alexander George
Amherst, Massachusetts

Notes

1 Mark A. Uhlig, "Salvadoran Army Continues Attack," *New York Times* (November 19, 1989). This and a number of other news reports cited here are quoted in the excellent *Carnage Again: Preliminary Report on Violations of War by Both Sides in the November 1989 Offensive in El Salvador* (November 24, 1989), Americas Watch. This assessment was widely confirmed by both the US and the international press; e.g., the *Independent* (London) reported that "Most civilian casualties appear to have been caused by army bombardments and mortar rounds" (Chris Norton (November 16, 1989), p. 12).

2 Americas Watch, *Carnage Again*, pp. 58–9, citing Richard Boudreaux, "Salvadorans Flock to Shelters as Fighting Ebbs," *Los Angeles Times* (November 19, 1989).

3 Americas Watch, *Carnage Again*, pp. 10–11.

4 See, e.g., Americas Watch, *Carnage Again*, p. 14; "Central America in Flames," *Amnesty Action* (November/December 1989), p. 3. Lindsey Gruson, "Salvador Bishop Links Military to Killing of Six," *New York Times* (November 20, 1989); Americas Watch, *Carnage Again*, p. 80.

5 Robert Pear, "House Rejects Curb on Salvador Aid," *New York Times* (November 21, 1989).

6 Apparently members of the US-trained Atlacatl Battalion using US-supplied weapons. Most of the nine Salvadoran soldiers subsequently ordered detained had received training from the US government and five of them had visited the US to take courses, including Special Forces and Commando Operations classes (Michael K. Frisby, "US Reportedly Trained 9 Salvadorans Linked to Priest Killings," *Boston Globe* (April 25, 1990)). The Atlacatl is already infamous for a number of particularly heinous atrocities, incidentally demonstrating the civilizing influence US training is often touted as having. For some instances, see Michael McClintock, *The American Connection, Volume One: State Terror and Popular Resistance in El Salvador* (Zed Books, 1985), pp. 307–10.

7 "Brave Stand for Justice in El Salvador," *New York Times* (January 9, 1990). It is worth recalling that not one Salvadoran officer has yet been convicted of a human rights violation in this now decade-long civil war. It is no surprise that as of this writing "Western diplomats and Salvadoran officials here [in

San Salvador] say the investigation into the murder of six Jesuit priests has all but come to end [sic] since the arrest in January of eight members of the army" (Robert Pear, "Salvador Accused on Jesuit Inquiry," *New York Times* (May 1, 1990)).

8   According to one summary,

Cristiani has escalated state terror against popular groups in El Salvador since he took office. The National Union of Salvadoran Workers (UNTS) reports that in the first three months after ARENA took over executive power, there were 317 civilians assassinated, 62 disappeared, over 400 captured by the security forces, and more than 100 women sexually assaulted while in detention. According to this same group, over 140 of its members were seized by the military and police in the period during and immediately after the September 13-15 peace talks in Mexico City. Eight of the 11 members of the executive board of the National Trade Union Federation of Salvadoran Workers (FENASTRAS) have been arrested under ARENA rule, and their protests and demonstrations have been broken up violently. In a press conference in late September, members of FENASTRAS claimed that of 64 people detained by the National Police during their protest march on September 18, eight were raped while in custody. The National University has been periodically attacked by gunfire which has wounded significant numbers, and over a dozen faculty and students have been arrested, with several murdered or disappeared. The office of the Union of Earthquake Victims (UNADES) has been ransacked and its officials arrested and abused. (Terry Allen and Edward S. Herman, "El Salvador 1989: Elections Under State Terror," *CovertAction Information Bulletin*, 33 (Winter 1990), p. 51, citing references from numerous human rights organizations.)

9   Kate Thompson, "Jesuit Case Cover-Up Designed to Guarantee US Aid," *Alert!* (CISPES), 8, no. 1 (February 1990).
10   Lindsey Gruson, "Homecoming is Tragic for Salvador Refugees," *New York Times* (February 14, 1990); "6 Said to Die in Salvador Air Force Raid," *New York Times* (February 12, 1990).
11   For instances of military-related threats, detentions, bombings, attacks, torture, and outright killings, see Americas Watch, *Carnage Again*.
12   Americas Watch, *Carnage Again*, pp. 37, 83-4.
13   Quoted in the *New Yorker* (December 11, 1989), p. 43. Our role in the terror may be even more direct than this. Noam Chomsky has drawn attention to the fact that in November 1989

Salvadoran army deserter Cesar Vielman Joya Martinez was informing reporters and congressional aides in Washington about his participation in torture and murder operations conducted by the special forces group GC-2 of the Salvadoran army's First Brigade, with the certain knowledge of its US advisers, who "had control of the department".... Joya Martinez claimed that his orders were issued by the Salvadoran Joint Chiefs of Staff and sent to the commanders of the Brigade, that he had seen orders for

9

72 executions from April through July, and that he had taken part in 8 of these death squad murders. The victims were first almost beaten to death during interrogation, then their throats were usually slit and their bodies were thrown over a cliff into the Pacific Ocean or buried in secret cemeteries, he said, giving a detailed account, many parts of which were independently confirmed. Among the First Brigade officers he implicated were its former commander, who is now the Vice-Minister of Defence, and the current commander of the elite Belloso battalion. They and others cited are "leaders and operators of the so-called death squadrons. . . .," he charged. (Noam Chomsky, "The Mortal Sin of Self-Defense," *Zeta Magazine* (December 1989), p. 14.)

The Bush administration promised an investigation – whose outcome will likely be irrelevant to, if not dictated by, our continued support for the homicidal regime. (For further information about apparent US involvement in the activities and training of Salvadorean death squads, see David Kush, "Death Squads in El Salvador: A Pattern of US Complicity," *Covert Action Information Bulletin*, 34 (summer 1990).)

The hypocritical double standard of the Bush administration as concerns the safety of US citizens in El Salvador is also not an aberration. Chomsky and others have drawn attention to the fact that, while Bush made much of the alleged danger to US lives as a justification for invading Panama, he expressed no concern for the kidnapping, just a few weeks earlier, of Diana Ortiz, an American nun, and her torture and sexual abuse by the Guatemalan police. Nor did Bush have anything to say a week or so after the invasion when US-supplied Contras murdered Sisters Maureen Courtney (from Milwaukee) and Teresa Rosales in Nicaragua. (See Noam Chomsky, "The Tasks Ahead IV: Post-Cold War Cold War," *Z Magazine* (March 1990), p. 14.)

14 Quoted in Allen and Herman, "El Salvador 1989: Elections Under Stale Terror," p. 51.

15 There is reason to believe that US officials have attempted to impede investigation into the murders of the Jesuit priests. Thus far, the only witnesses to have come forward have insisted that FBI agents sought to intimidate them during interrogations. Lucia Barrera de Cerna and her husband Jorge have charged that

they were repeatedly accused of lying by both American and Salvadoran investigators, and Mr Cerna said that at one point one of the FBI agents threatened them with deportation, saying that his testimony would determine whether they could stay in the United States. The couple also said that they were so scared and pressured during the interrogation in Miami, where they were kept incommunicado for several days, that they retracted their testimony and said that neither of them had seen anything on the night that the killings took place.

A report issued by the Lawyers Committee for Human Rights concludes that investigators "treated an obviously frightened and traumatized woman more like a criminal suspect than a potential cooperating witness with useful information." The Rev. Paul S. Tipton, president of the Association of Jesuit Colleges and Universities, noted the predictable, and hence the likely intended, consequence of this intimidation: "the mistreatment of the Cernas effectively has neutralized the only witness who has come forward, and it means probably no other witness will come forward" (Elaine Sciolino, "FBI Discounts Salvador Inquiry Role," *New York Times* (December 19, 1989)).

The US has made its position clear in other ways; for example, by publicizing the identity of the Salvadoran Army officer who provided information leading to the arrest of army men implicated in the killings. Ignoring their own pledges to protect the identity of anyone coming forward with information about the murders, US officials released the name of the informant, Colonel Carlos Armando Aviles, who was subsequently detained by the Salvadoran military. According to one report, "Several Salvadoran officials assert that the lesson of the incident is that it is dangerous to help the United States in delicate cases and that American promises to protect sources are worthless. 'Believe me, that message has been heard,' said an official with knowledge of the case" (Lindsey Gruson, "Washington Criticized for Identifying Army Informant in Salvador Killings," *New York Times* (January 19, 1990)).

16 Maureen Dowd, "Bush Seeks a Rise in Aid to Salvador," *New York Times* (February 2, 1990).

17 Though we are reassured of this all the time, whatever the facts. To choose one example among many: "When the Reagan Administration's policy of support for El Salvador began in the early 1980s," we are informed, "the goal was honorable. It was to establish democracy and thereby bring peace to a repressive country" ("The Sheraton Siege," *Time* (December 4, 1989), p. 51). Given the easily obtainable historical record to the contrary, this statement gives a good indication of the high level of political indoctrination among the mainstream pundits.

18 Sigmund Freud, *Civilization and its Discontents*, ed. and trans. James Strachey, (W.W. Norton & Co., 1962), p. 91.

2

International Terrorism: Image and Reality

Noam Chomsky

There are two ways to approach the study of terrorism. One may adopt a *literal approach*, taking the topic seriously, or a *propagandistic approach*, construing the concept of terrorism as a weapon to be exploited in the service of some system of power. In each case it is clear how to proceed. Pursuing the literal approach, we begin by determining what constitutes terrorism. We then seek instances of the phenomenon – concentrating on the major examples, if we are serious – and try to determine causes and remedies. The propagandistic approach dictates a different course. We begin with the thesis that terrorism is the responsibility of some officially designated enemy. We then designate terrorist acts as "terrorist" just in the cases where they can be attributed (whether plausibly nor not) to the required source; otherwise they are to be ignored, suppressed, or termed "retaliation" or "self-defense."

It comes as no surprise that the propagandistic approach is adopted by governments generally, and by their instruments in totalitarian states. More interesting is the fact that the same is largely true of the media and scholarship in the Western industrial democracies, as has been documented in extensive detail.[1] "We must recognise," Michael Stohl observes, "that by convention – and it must be emphasised *only* by convention – great power use and the threat of the use of force is normally described as coercive diplomacy and not as a form of terrorism," though it commonly involves "the threat and often the use of violence for what would be described as terroristic purposes were it not great powers who were pursuing the very same tactic."[2] Only one qualification must be added: the term "great powers" must be restricted to favored states; in the Western conventions under discussion, the Soviet Union is granted no such rhetorical license, and indeed can be charged and convicted on the flimsiest evidence.

Terrorism became a major public issue in the 1980s. The Reagan administration took office announcing its dedication to stamping out what the president called "the evil scourge of terrorism," a plague spread by "depraved opponents of civilization itself" in "a return to barbarism in the modern age" (Secretary of State George Shultz). The campaign focused on a particularly virulent form of the plague: state-directed international terrorism. The central thesis attributed responsibility to a Soviet-based "worldwide terror network aimed at the destabilization of Western democratic society," in the words of Claire Sterling, whose highly-praised book *The Terror Network* became the Bible of the administration and the founding document of the new discipline of ter-rorology. It was taken to have provided "ample evidence" that terrorism occurs "almost exclusively in democratic or relatively democratic societies" (Walter Laqueur), leaving little doubt about the origins of the plague. The book was soon exposed as a worthless propaganda tract, but the thesis remained intact, dominating mainstream reporting, commentary, and scholarship.

By the mid-1980s, concern over international terrorism reached the level of virtual frenzy. Middle-East/Mediterranean terrorism was selected by editors as the lead story of 1985 in an AP poll, and a year later the tourism industry in Europe was badly hit as Americans stayed away in fear of Arab terrorists infesting European cities. The plague then subsided, the monster having been tamed by the cool courage of the cowboy, according to the approved version.

Shifting to the literal approach, we first define the concept of terrorism, and then investigate its application, letting the chips fall where they may. Let us see where this course leads.

1 The Concept of Terrorism

Concepts of political discourse are hardly models of clarity, but there is general agreement as to what constitutes terrorism. As a point of departure we may take the official United States Code:

> "act of terrorism" means an activity that – (A) involves a violent act or an act dangerous to human life that is a violation of the criminal laws of the United States or any State, or that would be a criminal violation if committed within the jurisdiction of the United States or of any State; and (B) appears to be intended (i) to intimidate or coerce a civilian population; (ii) to influence the policy of a government by intimidation or coercion; or (iii) to affect the conduct of a government by assassination or kidnapping.[3]

13

Noam Chomsky

The concept is not precisely delimited. First, the boundary between international terrorism and aggression is not always clear. On this matter, let us give the benefit of the doubt to the United States and its clients: if they reject the charge of aggression in the case of some act of international violence, we will take it to fall under the lesser crime of terrorism. There is also disagreement over the distinction between terrorism and retaliation or legitimate resistance, to which we return.

US sources also provide more succinct definitions of "terrorism." A US Army manual on countering terrorism defines it as "the calculated use of violence or threat of violence to attain goals that are political, religious, or ideological in nature. This is done through intimidation, coercion, or instilling fear." Still simpler is the characterization in a Pentagon-commissioned study by noted terrorologist Robert Kupperman, which speaks of the threat or use of force "to achieve political objectives without the full-scale commitment of resources."[4]

Kupperman, however, is not discussing terrorism; rather, low intensity confict (LIC), a central doctrine of the Reagan administration. Note that as the description indicates and actual practice confirms, LIC – much like its predecessor "counterinsurgency" – is hardly more than a euphemism for state-directed international terrorism, that is, reliance on force that does not reach the level of the war crime of aggression.

The point is recognized within the scholarly discipline, though with the usual doctrinal twist. One leading Israeli specialist observes that "state-sponsored terrorism is a form of low-intensity conflict that states undertake when they find it convenient to engage in 'war' without being held accountable for their actions" (Professor Yonah Alexander).[5] Alexander restricts his attention to the Kremlin conspiracy to destabilize the West with "surrogate groups," offering such examples as "an extensive PLO training programme ... provided for Nicaragua." In this conception, "the PLO, which maintains a special relationship with Moscow," serves its Soviet master by passing on the "specialized training" in terrorism it acquires in the Soviet Union to Nicaragua, which is therefore able to conduct LIC against the United States and its interests. He also suggests ways in which "the Eastern Bloc's sincerity must be tested;" for example, "Showing willingness to stop propaganda campaigns linking the US and its allies to terrorism."

As the examples illustrate, it would take a fertile imagination to conjure up a thought so outlandish as to ruffle the composure of the fraternity, as long as doctrinal purity is preserved.

2 Terrorism and the Political Culture

There are many terrorist states in the world, but the United States is unusual in that it is *officially* committed to international terrorism, and on a scale that puts its rivals to shame. Thus Iran is surely a terrorist state, as Western governments and media rightly proclaim. Its major known contribution to international terrorism was revealed during the Iran–Contra inquiries: namely, Iran's perhaps inadvertent involvement in the US proxy war against Nicaragua. This fact is unacceptable, therefore unnoticed, though the Iranian connection in US-directed international terrorism was exposed at a time of impassioned denunciation of Iranian terrorism.

The same inquiries revealed that under the Reagan Doctrine, the US had forged new paths in international terrorism. Some states employ individual terrorists and criminals to carry out violent acts abroad. But in the Reagan years, the US went further, not only constructing a semi-private international terrorist network but also an array of client and mercenary *states* – Taiwan, South Korea, Israel, Saudi Arabia, and others – to finance and implement its terrorist operations. This advance in international terrorism was revealed during the period of maximal anguish over the plague, but did not enter into the discussion and debate.

The US commitment to international terrorism reaches to fine detail. Thus the proxy forces attacking Nicaragua were directed by their CIA and Pentagon commanders to attack "soft targets," that is, barely defended civilian targets. The State Department specifically authorized attacks on agricultural cooperatives – exactly what we denounce with horror when the agent is Abu Nidal. Media doves expressed thoughtful approval of this stand. *New Republic* editor Michael Kinsley, at the liberal extreme of mainstream commentary, argued that we should not be too quick to dismiss State Department justifications for terrorist attacks on farming cooperatives: a "sensible policy" must "meet the test of cost-benefit analysis," an analysis of "the amount of blood and misery that will be poured in, and the likelihood that democracy will emerge at the other end." It is understood that US elites have the right to conduct the analysis and pursue the project if it passes their tests.[6]

When a Contra supply plane was shot down in October 1986 with an American mercenary on board, it became impossible to suppress the evidence of illegal CIA supply flights to the proxy forces. The Iran–Contra hearings ensued, focusing much attention on these topics. A few days after they ended, the Central American presidents signed the Esquipulas II peace agreement. The US undertook at once to subvert it.

The agreement identified one factor as "an indispensable element to achieving a stable and lasting peace in the region," namely, termination of any form of aid "to irregular forces or insurgent movements" on the part of "regional or extraregional" governments. In response, the US moved at once to escalate the attacks on soft targets in Nicaragua. Right at the moment when indignation over Washington's clandestine operations peaked, Congress and the media kept their eyes scrupulously averted from the rapid increase in CIA supply flights to several a day, while cooperating with the White House program of dismantling the unwanted accords, a goal finally achieved in January 1988, though further steps were required to subvert a follow-up agreement of the Central American presidents in February 1989.[7]

As supply and surveillance flights for the proxy forces increased, so did violence and terror, as intended. This too passed largely unnoticed, though an occasional reference could be found. The *Los Angeles Times* reported in October 1987 that "Western military analysts say the contras have been stashing tons of newly airdropped weapons lately while trying to avoid heavy combat . . . Meanwhile, they have stepped up attacks on easy government targets like the La Patriota farm cooperative . . ., where several militiamen, an elderly woman and her year-old grandson died in a pre-dawn shelling." To select virtually at random from the many cases deemed unworthy of notice, on November 21, 1987, 150 Contras attacked two villages in the southern province of Rio San Juan with 88-mm mortars and rocket-propelled grenades, killing six children and six adults and injuring 30 others. Even cooperatives of religious pacifists who refused to bear arms were destroyed by the US terrorist forces. In El Salvador too, the army attacks cooperatives, killing, raping, and abducting members.[8]

The decision of the International Court of Justice in June 1986 condemning the United States for the "unlawful use of force" and illegal economic warfare was dismissed as an irrelevant pronouncement by a "hostile forum" (*New York Times*). Little notice was taken when the US vetoed a Security Council resolution calling on all states to observe international law and voted against General Assembly resolutions to the same effect (with Israel and El Salvador in 1986; with Israel alone in 1987). The guiding principle, it appears, is that the US is a lawless terrorist state and *this is right and just*, whatever the world may think, whatever international institutions may declare.

A corollary is the doctrine that no state has the right to defend itself from US attack. The broad acquiescence in this remarkable doctrine was revealed as Reagan administration agitprop floated periodic stories about Nicaraguan plans to obtain jet interceptors. There was some criticism of the media for uncritically swallowing the disinformation, but a more significant fact was ignored: the general agreement that such behavior on the part of Nicaragua would be entirely unacceptable. When the tale was concocted to divert attention from the Nicaraguan elections of 1984, Senator Paul Tsongas of Massachusetts, with the support of other leading doves, warned that the US would have to bomb Nicaragua if it obtained vintage 1950s MiGs, because "they're also capable against the United States," hence a threat to its security – as distinct, say, from US nuclear missiles on alert status in Turkey, no threat to the USSR since they are purely for defensive purposes.[9] It is understood that jet interceptors might enable Nicaragua to protect its territory from the CIA supply flights needed to keep the US proxy forces in the field and the regular surveillance flights that provide them with up-to-the-minute information on the disposition of Nicaraguan troops, so that they can safely attack soft targets. Understood, but scarcely mentioned.[10] And it seems that no one in the mainstream released the open secret that Nicaragua would happily accept French planes instead of MiGs if the US had not pressured its allies to bar military aid so that we might cower in fear of "the Soviet-supplied Sandinistas."

The same issue arose in August 1988, when congressional doves effusively supported the Byrd Amendment on "Assistance for the Nicaraguan Resistance." Three days before, the Contras had attacked the passenger vessel *Mission of Peace*, killing two people and wounding 27, all civilians, including a Baptist minister from New Jersey who headed a US religious delegation. The incident was unmentioned in the Senate debate on the Byrd Amendment. Rather, congressional doves warned that if the Nicaraguan army carried out "an unprovoked military attack" or "any other hostile action" against the perpetrators of such terrorist atrocities, then Congress would respond with vigor and righteousness by renewing official military aid to them. Media coverage and other commentary found nothing odd or noteworthy in this stance.

The message is clear: no one has the right of self-defense against US terrorist attack. The US is a terrorist state *by right*. That is unchallengeable doctrine.

Accordingly, organization of a terrorist proxy army to subdue some recalcitrant population is a legitimate chore. On the right, Jeane Kirkpatrick explained that "forceful intervention in the affairs of another nation" is neither "impractical" nor "immoral"[11] – merely illegal, a crime for which people were hanged at Nuremberg and Tokyo with ringing declarations that this was not "victor's justice" because, as Justice Robert Jackson proclaimed, "If certain acts and violations of treaties are crimes, they are crimes whether the United States does them or whether Germany does them. We are not prepared to lay down a rule of criminal conduct against others which we would not be willing to have invoked

17

against us."[12] Countering any such thoughts, Irving Kristol explains that "The argument from international law lacks all credibility." True, "a great power should not ordinarily intervene in the domestic affairs of a smaller nation," but this principle is overcome if "another great power has previously breached this rule." Since it is "beyond dispute" that "the Soviet Union has intervened in Nicaragua" by providing arms and technicians "in both the military and civilian spheres," then the US has the right to send its proxy army to attack Nicaragua. By the same argument, the Soviet Union has a perfect right to attack Turkey or Denmark – far more of a security threat to it than Nicaragua is to the United States – since it is "beyond dispute" that the US provides them with assistance, and would do far more if the USSR were to exercise the right of aggression accorded it by Kristol's logic.

Kristol might, however, counter this argument too by invoking a crucial distinction that he has drawn elsewhere in connection with the right of forceful intervention by the United States: "insignificant nations, like insignificant people, can quickly experience delusions of significance," he explained. And when they do, these delusions must be driven from their minds by force: "In truth, the days of 'gunboat diplomacy' are never over . . . Gunboats are as necessary for international order as police cars are for domestic order." Hence the US is entitled to use violence against Nicaragua, an insignificant nation, though the USSR lacks this right in the case of Turkey or Denmark.[13]

The overwhelming endorsement for US-directed international terrorism should not be obscured by the wide elite opposition to the Contra war. By 1986, polls showed that 80 percent of "leaders" opposed aid to the Contras, and there was vigorous debate in Congress and the media about the program. But it is important to attend to the terms of the debate. At the dissident extreme, Tom Wicker of the *New York Times* observed that "Mr Reagan's policy of supporting [the Contras] is a clear failure," so we should "acquiesce in some negotiated regional arrangement that would be enforced by Nicaragua's neighbors" – if they can take time away from slaughtering their own populations, a feature of these terror states that does not exclude them from the role of enforcing regional arrangements on the errant Sandinistas, against whom no remotely comparable charge could credibly be made. Expressing the same thought, the editors of the *Washington Post* saw the Contras as "an imperfect instrument," so that other means must be sought to "fit Nicaragua back into a Central American mode" and impose "reasonable conduct by a regional standard," the standard of Washington's terror states. Senate Majority Whip Alan Cranston, a leading dove, recognized that "the Contra effort is woefully inadequate to achieve . . . democracy in Nicaragua" (the US aim by doctrinal fiat, whatever the facts may be),

so the US must find other means to "isolate" the "reprehensible" government in Managua and "leave it to fester in its own juices." No such stric-
tures hold for Washington's murderous clients.[14]

In short, there is little deviation from the basic terms of Michael
Kinsley's "sensible policy." The questions have to do with efficacy, not
principle. The state has the right to use violence as deemed appropriate.

The motivation for the resort to international terrorism has been can-
didly explained. High administration officials observed that the goal of
the attack against Nicaragua was "forcing [the Sandinistas] to divert
scarce resources to the war and away from social programs." This was
the basic thrust of the 1981 CIA program endorsed by the administration.
As outlined by former CIA analyst David MacMichael in his testimony
before the World Court, this program has as its purpose: to use the proxy
army to "provoke cross-border attacks by Nicaraguan forces and thus
serve to demonstrate Nicaragua's aggressive nature," to pressure the
Nicaraguan Government to "clamp down on civil liberties within
Nicaragua itself, arresting its opposition, demonstrating its allegedly
inherent totalitarian nature and thus increase domestic dissent within the
country," and to undermine the shattered economy. Discussing the
strategy of maintaining a terrorist force within Nicaragua after the huge
CIA supply operation was theoretically cancelled by Congress in
February 1988 (and the proxy forces largely fled, revealing – though not
to articulate opinion – how little resemblance they bore to indigenous
guerrillas), a Defense Department official explained:

> Those 2000 hard-core guys could keep some pressure on the Nicaraguan
> government, force them to use their economic resources for the military,
> and prevent them from solving their economic problems – and that's a plus
> . . . Anything that puts pressure on the Sandinista regime, calls attention
> to its lack of democracy, and prevents the Sandinistas from solving their
> economic problems is a plus.

Viron Vaky, Assistant Secretary of State for Interamerican Affairs in the
Carter administration, observed that the principal argument for the terrorist attack is that "a longer war of attrition will so weaken the regime,
provoke such a radical hardening of repression, and win sufficient support from Nicaragua's discontented population that sooner or later the
regime will be overthrown by popular revolt, self-destruct by means of
internal coups or leadership splits, or simply capitulate to salvage what
it can." As a dove, Vaky regards the conception as "flawed" but in no
way wrong.[15]

The terrorist forces fully understand their directives, as we learn from
one of the most important defectors of the 1980s, the head of intelligence

of the main contra force (FDN), Horacio Arce, whose *nom de guerre* was "Mercenario;" talk of "democrats" and "freedom fighters" is for home consumption. Sandinista defectors are eagerly exploited by the White House and the media, and the Contras generally received extensive coverage. But Contra *defectors* are another matter, particularly when they have unwelcome tales to relate. Arce was ignored in the US when he defected in late 1988. In interviews in Mexico before returning to Managua to accept amnesty, Arce described his illegal training in an air-force base in the southern United States, identified by name the CIA agents who provided support for the Contras under an AID cover in the US Embassy in Tegucigalpa, outlined how the Honduran army provides intelligence and support for Contra military activities, and discussed the immense corruption of the proxy forces and their sale of arms to the Honduran arms bazaar, where they then reach Salvadoran guerrillas. He then explained: "We attack a lot of schools, health centers, and those sort of things. We have tried to make it so that the Nicaraguan government cannot provide social services for the peasants, cannot develop its project . . . that's the idea." The success of the US training is amply confirmed by the record.[16]

The contra war easily qualifies as "state-sponsored terrorism," as former CIA director Stansfield Turner testified before Congress in April 1985. But one might argue that it should be termed outright aggression. That might be taken to be the import of the 1986 World Court decision. Let us, however, continue to give the US the benefit of the doubt, thus assigning its actions against Nicaragua to the category of international terrorism.

3 International Terrorism in the 1980s

During the 1980s, the primary locus of international terrorism has been Central America. In Nicaragua the US proxy forces left a trail of murder, torture, rape, mutilation, kidnapping, and destruction, but were impeded because civilians had an army to defend them. No comparable problems arose in the US client states, where the main terrorist force attacking the civilian population *is* the army and other state security forces. In El Salvador, tens of thousands were slaughtered in what Archbishop Rivera y Damas in October 1980, shortly after the operations moved into high gear, described as "a war of extermination and genocide against a defenseless civilian population." This exercise in state terror sought "to destroy the people's organizations fighting to defend their fundamental human rights," as Archbishop Oscar Romero warned shortly before his assassination, while vainly pleading with President Carter not to send aid

20

to the armed forces who, he continued, "know only how to repress the people and defend the interests of the Salvadorean oligarchy."[17] The goals were largely achieved during the Reagan administration, which escalated the savagery of the assault against the population to new heights. When it seemed that the US might be drawn into an invasion that would be harmful to its own interests, there was some concern and protest in elite circles, but that abated as state terror appeared successful, with the popular organizations decimated and "decapitated." After elections under conditions of violence and repression guaranteeing victory to privileged elements acceptable to the US, the issue largely passed below the threshold.

Little notice was taken of the significant increase in state terror after the Esquipulas II accords; or of an Amnesty International report entitled *El Salvador: "Death Squads" – A Government Strategy* (October 1988), reporting the "alarming rise" in killings by official death squads as part of the government strategy of intimidating any potential opposition by "killing and mutilating victims in the most macabre way," leaving victims "mutilated, decapitated, dismembered, strangled or showing marks of torture . . . or rape." Since the goal of the government strategy is "to intimidate or coerce a civilian population" (that is, terrorism, as officially defined in the US Code), it is not enough simply to kill. Rather, bodies must be left dismembered by the roadside, and women must be found hanging from trees by their hair with their faces painted red and their breasts cut off, while domestic elites pretend not to see as they continue to fund, train, and support the murderers and torturers.

In the same years, a massacre of even greater scale took place in Guatemala, also supported throughout by the United States and its mercenary states. Here too, terror increased after the Esquipulas II peace agreement in order to guard against steps towards democracy, social reform, and protection of human rights called for in the accords. As in El Salvador, these developments were virtually ignored; the assigned task at the time was to focus attention on Nicaragua and to express vast outrage when Nicaragua occasionally approached the *lesser* abuses that are regular practice in the US client states. Since the goal is to restore Nicaragua to "the Central American mode" and ensure that it observes the "regional standards" satisfied by El Salvador and Guatemala, terror in client states is of no real concern, unless it becomes so visible as to endanger the flow of aid to the killers.[18]

Notice crucially that all of this is *international* terrorism, supported or directly organized in Washington with the assistance of its international network of mercenary states.

Well after the 1984 elections that were hailed for having brought democracy to El Salvador, the church-based human rights organization

21

Socorro Juridico, operating under the protection of the archdiocese of San Salvador, described the results of the continuing terror, still conducted by "the same members of the armed forces who enjoy official approval and are adequately trained to carry out these acts of collective suffering," in the following terms:

> Salvadoran society, affected by terror and panic, a result of the persistent violation of basic human rights, shows the following traits: collective intimidation and generalized fear, on the one hand, and on the other the internalized acceptance of the terror because of the daily and frequent use of violent means. In general, society accepts the frequent appearance of tortured bodies, because basic rights, the right to life, has absolutely no overriding value for society.[19]

The same comment applies to the societies that oversee these operations, or simply look the other way.

4 Before the Official Plague

International terrorism is, of course, not an invention of the 1980s. In the previous two decades, its major victims were Cuba and Lebanon.

Anti-Cuban terrorism was directed by a secret Special Group established in November 1961 under the code name "Mongoose," involving 400 Americans, 2,000 Cubans, a private navy of fast boats, and a $50 million annual budget, run in part by a Miami CIA station functioning in violation of the Neutrality Act and, presumably, the law banning CIA operations in the United States.[20] These operations included bombing of hotels and industrial installations, sinking of fishing boats, poisoning of crops and livestock, contamination of sugar exports, etc. Not all of these actions were specifically authorized by the CIA, but no such considerations absolve official enemies.

Several of these terrorist operations took place at the time of the Cuban missile crisis of October–November 1962. In the weeks before, Raymond Garthoff reports, a Cuban terrorist group operating from Florida with US government authorization carried out "a daring speedboat strafing attack on a Cuban seaside hotel near Havana where Soviet military technicians were known to congregate, killing a score of Russians and Cubans;" and shortly after, attacked British and Cuban cargo ships and again raided Cuba, among other actions that were stepped up in early October. At one of the tensest moments of the missile crisis, on November 8, a terrorist team dispatched from the United States blew up a Cuban industrial facility after the Mongoose operations had been officially suspended. Fidel Castro alleged that 400 workers had been killed in this operation, guided by "photographs taken by spying planes." This terrorist act, which might have set off a global nuclear war, evoked little comment when it was revealed. Attempts to assassinate Castro and other terror continued immediately after the crisis terminated, and were escalated by Nixon in 1969.[21]

Such operations continued after the Nixon years. In 1976, for example, two Cuban fishing vessels were attacked in April by boats from Miami, the main center of anti-Cuban terrorism worldwide. A few weeks later, the Cuban embassy in Portugal was bombed with two killed. In July, the Cuban mission to the UN in New York was bombed and there were bombings aimed at Cuban targets in the Caribbean and Colombia, along with the attempted bombing of a pro-Cuban meeting at the Academy of Music in New York. In August, two officials of the Cuban embassy in Argentina were kidnapped and Cubana airline offices in Panama were bombed. The Cuban embassy in Venezuela was fired upon in October and the embassy in Madrid was bombed in November. In October, CIA-trained Cuban exiles bombed a Cubana civilian airliner, killing all 73 aboard, including Cuba's gold medal-winning international fencing team. One of the agents of this terrorist operation, Bay of Pigs veteran Luis Posada Carriles, was sprung from the Venezuelan jail where he was held for the bombing; he mysteriously escaped and found his way to El Salvador, where he was put to work at the Ilopango military airbase to help organize the US terrorist operations in Nicaragua. The CIA attributed 89 terrorist operations in the US and the Caribbean area for 1969–79 to Cuban exile groups, and the major one, OMEGA 7, was identified by the FBI as the most dangerous terrorist group operating in the US during much of the 1970s.[22]

Cuba figures heavily in scholarly work on international terrorism. Walter Laqueur's standard work (see note 1) contains many innuendoes about Cuban sponsorship of terrorism, though little evidence. There is not a word, however, on the terrorist operations *against* Cuba. He writes that in "recent decades . . . the more oppressive regimes are not only free from terror, they have helped to launch it against more permissive societies." The intended meaning is that the United States, a "permissive society," is one of the victims of international terrorism, while Cuba, an "oppressive regime," is one of the agents. To establish the conclusion it is necessary to suppress the fact that the US has undeniably launched major terrorist attacks against Cuba and is relatively free from terror itself; and if there is a case to be made against Cuba, Laqueur has signally failed to present it.

Turning to the second major example of the pre-Reagan period, in southern Lebanon from the early 1970s the population was held hostage with the "rational prospect, ultimately fulfilled, that affected populations would exert pressure for the cessation of hostilities" and acceptance of Israeli arrangements for the region (Abba Eban, commenting on Prime Minister Menachem Begin's account of atrocities in Lebanon committed under the Labor government, in the style "of regimes which neither Mr Begin nor I would dare to mention by name," Eban observed, acknowledging the accuracy of the account).[23] Notice that this justification, offered by a respected Labor party dove, places these actions squarely under the rubric of international terrorism (if not aggression).

Thousands were killed and hundreds of thousands driven from their homes in these attacks. Little is known because the matter was of no interest; PLO attacks against Israel in the same years, barbaric but on a far lesser scale, elicited great indignation and extensive coverage. ABC correspondent Charles Glass, then a journalist in Lebanon, found "little American editorial interest in the conditions of the south Lebanese. The Israeli raids and shelling of their villages, their gradual exodus from south Lebanon to the growing slums on the outskirts of Beirut were nothing compared to the lurid tales of the 'terrorists' who threatened Israel, hijacked aeroplanes and seized embassies." The reaction was much the same, he continues, when Israeli death squads were operating in southern Lebanon after the 1982 Israeli invasion. One could read about them in the London *Times*, but US editors were not interested. Had the media reported the operations of "these death squads of plainclothes Shin Beth [secret police] men who assassinated suspects in the villages and camps of south Lebanon," "stirring up the Shiite Muslim population and helping to make the Marine presence untenable," there might have been some appreciation of the plight of the US Marines deployed in Lebanon. They seemed to have no idea why they were there apart from "the black enlisted men: almost all of them said, though sadly never on camera, that they had been sent to protect the rich against the poor." "The only people in Lebanon they identified with were the poor Shiite refugees who lived all around their base at the Beirut airport; it is sad that it was probably one of these poor Shiites . . . who killed 241 of them on 23 October 1983." If any of these matters had been reported, it might have been possible to avert, or at the very least to comprehend, the bombing in which the Marines were killed, victims of a policy that "the press could not explain to the public and their information officers could not explain to the Marines themselves."

In 1976, Syria entered Lebanon with US approval and helped implement further massacres, the major one at the Palestinian refugee camp of Tel Al-Zaater, where thousands were murdered by Syrian-backed Christian forces with Israeli arms.[24]

Without proceeding further, it is clear that the plague of state-directed international terrorism was rampant well before it was converted into a major issued by the "public diplomacy" of the Reagan administration.

5 The Canon: Retail Terrorism

Wholesale terrorism of the kind reviewed here has largely been excluded from the discussion of "the evil scourage of terrorism." Let us then turn to the smaller-scale acts of terror that fall within the canon.

Here too, the record goes back well before the 1980s, though the literature is too selective to be very useful. To mention a few examples not found in Laqueur's standard source, while he refers to the use of letter-bombs and "a primitive book bomb" used by approved villains, there is no mention of the sophisticated book-bomb used by Israeli intelligence to kill General Mustapha Hafez in Gaza in 1956 at a time when he was responsible for preventing Palestinian Fedayeen from infiltrating to attack Israeli targets.[25] Laqueur's review of the use of letter-bombs does not include the testimony of Ya'akov Eliav, who claims to have been the first to use letter-bombs when he served as a commander of the terrorist group headed by the current prime minister of Israel, Yitzhak Shamir (Lehi, the "Stern gang"). Working from Paris in 1946, he arranged to have 70 such bombs sent in official British government envelopes to all members of the British cabinet, the heads of the Tory opposition, and several military commanders. In June 1947, he and an accomplice were caught by Belgian police while attempting to send these letter-bombs, and all were intercepted.[26]

The standard record of hijacking and bombing of airliners also avoids some important topics, among them the US refusal of requests from communist countries in the 1950s to return "persons who hijacked planes, trains, and ships to escape" (State Department legal adviser Abraham Sofaer, who notes that the policy was "reexamined" from the late 1960s – when the US and its allies were targeted). Sofaer's comment understates the case. A Tass report condemning the *Achille Lauro* hijacking accused Washington of hypocrisy because two men who hijacked a Soviet airliner, killing a stewardess and wounding other crew members, were given refuge in the United States, which refused extradition.[27]

The first airplane hijacking in the Middle East also falls outside the canon: Israel's hijacking of a Syrian airways civilian jet in 1954, with the intent "to get hostages in order to obtain the release of our prisoners in Damascus," who had been captured on a spy mission in Syria (Prime Minister Moshe Sharett). Sharett accepted the "factual affirmation of the US State Department that our action was without precedent in the history of international practice." In October 1956, the Israeli air force shot down an unarmed Egyptian civilian plane, killing 16 people including four journalists, in a failed attempt to assassinate Field Marshall Abdul Hakim Amar, second to President Nasser, at a time when the two countries were not in a state of war. This was a preplanned operation, thus unlike Israel's downing of a Libyan civilian airliner with 110 killed as it was lost in a sandstorm two minutes flight time from Cairo, towards which it was heading. This February 1973 action look place while Israeli airborne and amphibious forces were attacking Tripoli in northern Lebanon, killing 31 people (mainly civilians) and destroying classrooms, clinics, and other buildings in a raid justified as preemptive.[28] All of this was (and is) dismissed as insignificant, if even noticed. The reaction to Arab terrorism is quite different.

Turning to the 1980s, consider 1985, when media concern peaked. The major single terrorist act of the year was the blowing up of an Air India flight, killing 329 people. The terrorists had been trained in a paramilitary camp in Alabama run by Frank Camper, where mercenaries were trained for terrorist acts in Central America and elsewhere. According to ex-mercenaries, Camper had close ties to US intelligence and was personally involved in the Air India bombing, allegedly a "sting" operation that got out of control. On a visit of India, Attorney-General Edwin Meese conceded in a backhanded way that the terrorist operations originated in a US terrorist training camp.[29] Any connection of a terrorist to Libya, however frail, suffices to demonstrate that Qaddafi is a "mad dog" who must be eliminated.

In the Middle East, the main center of international terrorism according to the canon, the worst single terrorist act of 1985 was a car-bombing in Beirut on March 8 that killed 80 people and wounded 256. "About 250 girls and women in flowing black chadors, pouring out of Friday prayers at the Imam Rida Mosque, took the brunt of the blast," Nora Boustany reported three years later: "At least 40 of them were killed and many more were maimed." The bomb also "burned babies in their beds, "killed a bride buying her trousseau," and "blew away three children as they walked home from the mosque" as it "devastated the main street of the densely populated" West Beirut suburb. The target was the Shi'ite leader Sheikh Fadlallah, accused of complicity in terrorism, but he escaped. The attack was arranged by the CIA and its Saudi clients with the assistance of Lebanese intelligence and a British specialist, and specifically authorized by CIA director William Casey, according to Bob Woodward's account in his book on Casey and the CIA.[30]

Even under its chosen conventions, then, it seems that the United States wins the prize for acts of international terrorism in the peak year of the official plague. The US client state of Israel follows closely behind. Its Iron First operations in Lebanon were without parallel for the year as sus-

26

tained acts of international terrorism in the Middle East, and the bombing of Tunis (with tacit US support) wins second prize for single terrorist acts, unless we take this to be a case of actual aggression, as was determined by the UN Security Council.[31]

In 1986, the major single terrorist act was the US bombing of Libya – assuming, again, that we do not assign this attack to the category of aggression. This was a brilliantly staged media event, the first bombing in history scheduled for prime-time TV, for the precise moment when the networks open their national news programs. This convenient arrangement allowed anchormen to switch at once to Tripoli so that their viewers could watch the exciting events live. The next act of the superbly crafted TV drama was a series of news conferences and White House statements explaining that this was "self-defense against future attack" and a measured response to a disco bombing in West Berlin ten days earlier for which Libya was to blame. The media were well aware that the evidence for this charge was slight, but the facts were ignored in the general adulation for Reagan's decisive stand against terrorism, echoed across the political spectrum. Crucial information undermining the US charges was suppressed from that moment on. It was later conceded quietly that the charges were groundless, but they nevertheless continued to be aired and the conclusions that follow from this belated recognition were never drawn.[32]

For 1986 too the United States seems to place well in the competition for the prize for international terrorism, even part from the wholesale terrorism it sponsored in Central America, where, in that year, Congress responded to the World Court call for an end to the "unlawful use of force" by voting $100 million of military aid to the US proxy forces in what the administration gleefully described as a virtual declaration of war.[33]

6   Terror and Resistance

Let us turn now to several contentious questions about the scope of terrorism, so far avoided.

Consider the boundary between terrorism and legitimate resistance. Sometimes, nationalist groups are prepared to describe their actions as terrorism, and some respected political leaders decline to condemn acts of terrorism in the national cause. An example particularly relevant to current discussion is the pre-state Zionist movement. Israel is the source of the 1980s "terrorism industry" (then transferred to the US for further development), as an ideological weapon against Palestinians.[34] The PLO is anathema in the United States. A special act of Congress, the Anti-Terrorism Act of 1987, "prohibits American citizens from receiving any assistance, funds, or 'anything of value except informational materials' from the PLO," which is not permitted to establish offices or other facilities to further its interests.[35] Palestinian violence has received worldwide condemnation.

The pre-state Zionist movement carried out extensive terror against Arab civilians, British, and Jews, also murdering UN mediator Folke Bernadotte (whose killers were protected after the state was established). In 1943, current Prime Minister Yitzhak Shamir wrote an article entitled "Terror" for the journal of the terrorist organization he headed (Lehi) in which he proposed to "dismiss all the 'phobia' and babble against terror with simple, obvious arguments." "Neither Jewish morality nor Jewish tradition can be used to disallow terror as a means of war," he wrote, and "We are very far from any moral hesitations when concerned with the national struggle." "First and foremost, terror is for us a part of the political war appropriate for the circumstances of today, and its task is a major one: it demonstrates in the clearest language, heard throughout the world including by our unfortunate brethren outside the gates of this country, our war against the occupier." As has been widely observed in Israel, the British occupation was far less repressive than Israel's rule in the occupied territories and faced a much more violent resistance.

British philosopher Isaiah Berlin recalls that Chaim Weizmann, first president of Israel and considered one of the saintly figures of the national movement,

> did not think it morally decent to denounce either the acts [of Jewish terrorism] or their perpetrators in public . . . he did not propose to speak out against acts, criminal as he thought them, which sprang from the tormented minds of men driven to desperation, and ready to give up their lives to save their brothers from what, he and they were equally convinced, was a betrayal and a destruction cynically prepared for them by the foreign offices of the western powers.[36]

The archives of the mainstream Zionist resistance group, Haganah, contain the names of 40 Jews killed by Menachem Begin's Irgun and Lehi. Yitzhak Shamir's personal assassination of a Lehi associate is a famous incident. The official Irgun history, while recalling with admiration many acts of terror against Arab civilians, also cites the murder of a Jewish member who, it was feared, would give information to the police if captured. Suspected collaborators were a particular target. The Haganah Special Actions Squads carried out "punitive actions" against Jewish informers. A Haganah prison in Haifa contained a torture chamber for interrogation of Jews suspected of collaboration with the British. In a

1988 interview, Dov Tsisis describes his work as a Haganah enforcer, "following orders, like the Nazis," to "eliminate" Jews interfering with the national struggle, "particularly informers." He also rejects the familiar charge that the murderous bombing of the King David Hotel was carried out by the Irgun alone, identifying himself as the special representative of Haganah commander Yitzhak Sadeh, who authorized it. He was later recommended by Moshe Dayan to replace him as commander of an elite unit. Anti-Nazi resisters also describe the murder of collaborators, throughout Europe. Israel Shahak, one of Israel's foremost civil libertarians and a survivor of the Warsaw ghetto and the concentration camps, recalls that "before the Warsaw ghetto revolt, . . . the Jewish underground, with complete justification, killed every Jewish collaborator that they could find." He recalls a vivid childhood memory from February 1943, "when I danced and sang together with other children around the body [of a murdered Jewish collaborator], with blood still flowing from his body, and to the present I have no regrets about that; on the contrary."[37]

While frank avowal of terrorism of the Shamir variety can occasionally be found, the more normal pattern is for actions undertaken against oppressive regimes and occupying armies to be considered resistance by their perpetrators and terrorism by the rulers, even when they are non-violent. What the Western democracies considered to be resistance in occupied Europe or Afghanistan, the Nazis and the USSR branded terror – in fact, terror inspired from abroad, therefore international terrorism. The US took the same position towards the South Vietnamese who bore the brunt of the US attack.

On similar grounds, South Africa takes strong exception to the international conventions on terrorism. Specifically, it objects to UN General Assembly Resolution 42/159 (December 7, 1987) because, while condemning international terrorism and outlining measures to combat it, the General Assembly:

> *Considers* that nothing in the present resolution could in any way prejudice the right to self-determination, freedom and independence, as derived from the Charter of the United Nations, of peoples forcibly deprived of that right . . ., particularly peoples under colonial and racist regimes and foreign occupation or other forms of colonial domination, nor . . . the right of these peoples to struggle to this end and to seek and receive support [in accordance with the Charter and other principles of international law].[38]

While this provision is endorsed by virtually the entire world community, South Africa is not entirely alone in opposing it. The resolution passed 153 to 2, with the United States and Israel opposed and Honduras

Noam Chomsky

alone abstaining. In this case, the stand of the US government won wide approval in the United States. Across the spectrum of articulate opinion in the US, it is implicitly taken for granted that the South African position is correct, indeed beyond controversy.

The issue came to a head in late 1988 in connection with the Israel-Palestinian conflict. In November, the Palestine National Council (PNC) declared an independent Palestinian state alongside of Israel, endorsing the UN terrorism resolution and other relevant UN resolutions. Yasser Arafat repeated the same positions in subsequent weeks in Europe, including a special session of the UN General Assembly convened in Geneva when he was barred from New York, in violation of legal obligations to the United Nations, on the grounds that his presence there would pose an unacceptable threat to the security of the United States. The reiteration by the PNC and Arafat of the UN terrorism resolution was denounced in the United States on the grounds that the Palestinian leadership had failed to meet Washington's conditions on good behavior, including "Rejection of terrorism in all its forms" without qualification. The qualification in question is the one endorsed by the world community with the exception of the US and Israel (and South Africa).

The editors of the *New York Times* ridiculed the PNC endorsement of international conventions on terrorism as "the old Arafat hedge." Anthony Lewis, who is at the outer limits of tolerable dissent on these matters, wrote that Arafat was progressing, but not sufficiently: "the United States says correctly that the PLO must unambiguously renounce all terrorism before it can take part in negotiations," and this proper condition had not yet been met. The general reaction largely fell within these bounds.

The reasoning is straightfoward. The PLO had refused to join the US, Israel, and South Africa off the spectrum of world opinion, and therefore merits either derision (from the hardliners) or encouragement for its limited but insufficient progress (from the dissidents).

When the US became isolated diplomatically, by December 1988, Washington moved to a fall-back position, pretending that Arafat had capitulated to US demands, though his position had not changed in any substantive way – for years, in fact. With Arafat's capitulation to US demands now official, by US stipulation, he could be rewarded by discussions with the US Ambassador in Tunis. As was underscored by Israeli Defense Minister Yitzhak Rabin, the US–PLO discussions were designed to deflect diplomatic pressures for settlement and to grant Israel a year or more to suppress the Palestinian uprising (Intifada) by "harsh military and economic pressure" so that "they will be broken."[39]

The issue of terrorism versus resistance arose at once during the US–PLO discussions. The protocols of the first meeting were leaked and

30

published in the *Jerusalem Post*, which expressed its pleasure that "the American representative adopted the Israeli positions," stating two crucial conditions that the PLO must accept: the PLO must call off the Intifada, and must abandon the idea of an international conference. With regard to the Intifada, the US stated its position as follows:

> Undoubtedly the internal struggles that we are witnessing in the occupied territories aim to undermine the security and stability of the State of Israel, and we therefore demand cessation of those riots, *which we view as terrorist acts against Israel*. This is especially true as we know you are directing, from outside the territories, those riots which are sometimes very violent.[40]

Once this "terrorism" is called off and the previous conditions of repression restored, the US and Israel can proceed to settle matters to their satisfaction. Again, the resistance of an oppressed population to a brutal military occupation is "terror," from the point of view of the occupiers and their paymaster.

The same issue arose during the 1985 Iron Fist operations of the Israeli army in southern Lebanon. These too were guided by the logic outlined by Abba Eban, cited earlier. The civilian population was held hostage under the threat of terror to ensure its acceptance of the political arrangements dictated by Israel for southern Lebanon and the occupied territories. The threat can be realized at will. To cite only one case, while the eyes of the world were focused in horror on Arab terrorists, the press reported that Israel tank cannon poured fire into the village of Sreifa in southern Lebanon, aiming at 30 houses from which the Israeli Army claimed they had been fired upon by "armed terrorists," resisting their military actions as they searched for two Israeli soldiers who had been "kidnapped" in the "security zone" Israel has carved out of Lebanon. Kept from the American press was the report by the UN peace-keeping forces that the IDF "went really crazy" in these operations, locking up entire villages, preventing the UN forces from sending in water, milk, and oranges to the villagers subjected to "interrogation" by the Israeli Defense Forces (IDF) or its local mercenaries. The IDF then left with many hostages including pregnant women, some taken to Israel in further violation of international law, destroying houses and looting and wrecking others. Prime Minister Shimon Peres, lauded in the US as a man of peace, said that Israel's search "expresses our attitude towards the value of human life and dignity."[41]

To the Israeli high command, the victims of the Iron Fist operations were "terrorist villagers;" it was thus understandable that 13 villagers were massacred by militiamen of the Israeli mercenary forces in the incident that elicited this observation. Yossi Olmert of the Shiloah Institute,

Israel's Institute of Strategic Studies, observed that "these terrorists operate with the support of most of the local population." An Israeli commander complained that "the terrorist . . . has many eyes here, because he lives here." The military correspondent of the *Jerusalem Post* (Hirsh Goodman) described the problems faced in combating the "terrorist mercenary," "fanatics, all of whom are sufficiently dedicated to their causes to go on running the risk of being killed while operating against the IDF," which must "maintain order and security" despite "the price the inhabitants will have to pay."[42]

A similar concept of terrorism is widely used by US officials and commentators. The press reports that Secretary of State Shultz's concern over international terrorism became "his passion" after the suicide bombing of US Marines in Lebanon in October 1983, troops that much of the population saw as a military force sent to impose the "New Order" established by the Israeli aggression: the rule of right-wing Christians and selected Muslim elites. The media did not call upon witnesses from Nicaragua, Angola, Lebanon and the occupied territories, and elsewhere, to testify to Shultz's "passion," either then, or when they renewed their praise for his "visceral contempt tor terrorism" and "personal crusade" against it in explaining his refusal to admit Arafat to speak at the United Nations.[43]

Doubtless Syria too regards the Lebanese who resist its bloody rule as "terrorists," but such a claim would evoke the ridicule and contempt it merits. The reaction changes with the cast of characters.

7 Terror and Retaliation

The concept of retaliation is a useful device of ideological warfare. Throughout a cycle of violent interaction, each side typically perceives its own acts as retaliation for the terrorism of the adversary. In the Middle East, the Israeli–Arab conflict provides many examples. Israel being a client state, US practice adopts the Israeli conventions.

To illustrate, consider the hijacking of the *Achille Lauro* and the murder of Leon Klinghoffer in 1985, doubtless a vile terrorist act. The hijackers, however, regarded their action not as terror but as retaliation for the Israeli bombing of Tunis a week earlier, killing 20 Tunisians and 55 Palestinians with smart bombs that tore people to shreds beyond recognition, among other horrors described by Israeli journalist Amnon Kapeliouk on the scene. Washington cooperated by refusing to warn its ally Tunisia that the bombers were on their way, and George Shultz telephoned Israeli Foreign Minister Yitzhak Shamir to inform him that the US administration "had considerable sympathy for the Israeli action," the press reported.[44] Shultz drew back from this open approval when the UN Security Council unanimously denounced the bombing as an "act of armed aggression" (the US abstaining). Prime Minister Shimon Peres was welcomed to Washington a few days later, while the press solemnly discussed his consultations with President Reagan on "the evil scourge of terrorism" and what can be done to counter it.

For the US and Israel, the Tunis bombing was not terror or aggression but rather legitimate retaliation for the coldblooded murder of three Israelis in Larnaca, Cyprus. Secretary Shultz termed the Tunis bombing "a legitimate response" to "terrorist attacks," evoking general approbation.[45] The Larnaca killers, as Israel conceded, had probable connections to Syria but none to Tunis, which was selected as a target because it was defenseless; the Reagan administration selected Libyan cities as a bombing target a few months later in part for the same reason.

The perpetrators of the Larnaca atrocity, in turn, regarded their act not as terrorism but as retaliation. It was, they claimed, a response to Israeli hijackings in international waters for many years, including civilian ferries travelling from Cyprus to Lebanon, with large numbers of people kidnapped, over 100 kept in Israeli prisons without trial, and many killed, some by Israeli gunners while they tried to stay afloat after their ship was sunk, according to survivors interviewed in prison. These Israeli terrorist operations are sometimes marginally noted. Thus after a prisoner exchange in 1983, the *New York Times* observed in paragraph 18 of a front-page story that 37 of the Arab prisoners, who had been held at the notorious Ansar torture chamber in southern Lebanon, "had been seized recently by the Israeli Navy as they tried to make their way from Cyprus to Tripoli," north of Beirut. In 1989, the *Washington Post* ran a story on the release of Palestinian prisoners held under administrative detention, many "at the controversial Negev tent city prison of Ketziot," another torture chamber. The story mentioned incidentally that "Meanwhile, before dawn, the Israeli navy stopped a boat sailing from Lebanon to Cyprus and seized 14 people described as suspected terrorists," taking them to Israel for "interrogation." The Israeli peace organization Dai l'Kibbush reports that in 1986–7, Israeli military courts convicted dozens of people kidnapped at sea or in Lebanon of "membership in a forbidden organization" but no anti-Israel activity or plans; the Palestinians kidnapped allegedly belonged to the PLO, and the Lebanese to Hizballah and in at least one case to the major Shi'ite organization Amal, all legal in Lebanon.[46] By the same logic, British occupying forces could have sent agents to kidnap Zionists in the United States or on the high seas in 1947, placing them in prison camps without charge or convicting them of support for terrorism. These Israeli operations are little discussed and do not fall within the canon.

The concepts of terrorism and retaliation are supple instruments, readily adapted to the needs of the moment.

8   From Literalism to Doctrinal Necessity

This review of state-directed international terrorism suffers from a serious flaw: it has adhered to naive literalism and is thus irrelevant to contemporary debate over the plague of the modern age.

The review is, furthermore, very far from comprehensive. It barely scratches the surface even for Central America and the Middle East, and the plague is by no means limited to these regions. But it does suffice to raise a few questions. One stands out particularly: how is it possible for scholars and the media to maintain the thesis that the plague of the modern age is traceable to the Soviet-based "worldwide terror network aimed at the destabilization of Western democratic society?" How is it possible to identify Iran, Libya, the PLO, Cuba, and other official enemies as the leading practitioners of international terrorism?

The answers are not difficult to find. We must simply abandon the literal approach and recognize that terrorist acts fall within the canon only when conducted by official enemies. When the US and its clients are the agents, they are acts of retaliation and self-defense in the service of democracy and human rights. Then all becomes clear.

Turning finally to possible remedies for the plague, the standard literature offers some proposals. Walter Laqueur urges that "the obvious way to reliate" against international terrorism "is, of course, to pay the sponsors back in their own coin," though such legitimate response may be difficult for Western societies, which fail to comprehend that others do not share their "standards of democracy, freedom and humanism." Before those afflicted with incurable literalism draw the wrong conclusions, however, it should be stressed that legitimate response does not include bombs in Washington and Tel Aviv, given the careful way in which the concept of terrorism has been crafted.

The *New York Times* called upon an expert on terrorism to offer his thoughts on how to counter the plague. His advice, based upon long experience, was straightforward: "The terrorists, and especially their commanders, must be eliminated." He gave three examples of successful counterterrorist actions: the US bombing of Libya, the Israeli bombing of Tunis, and Israel's invasion of Lebanon. He recommends more of the same "if the civilized world is to prevail." The *Times* editors gave his article the title: "It's Past Time to Crush The Terrorist Monster," and they highlighted the words: "Stop the slaughter of innocents." They identify the author solely as "Israel's Minister of Trade and Industry." His name is Ariel Sharon.[47] His terrorist career, dating back to the early 1950s, includes the slaughter of 69 villagers in Qibya and 20 at the al-Bureig refugee camp in 1953; terrorist operations in the Gaza region and northeastern Sinai in the early 1970s including the expulsion of some ten thousand farmers into the desert, their homes bulldozed and farmlands destroyed in preparation for Jewish settlement; the invasion of Lebanon undertaken in an effort – as now widely conceded – to overcome the threat of PLO diplomacy; the subsequent massacre at Sabra and Shatila; and others.

Some might feel that the choice of Ariel Sharon to provide "the civilized world" with lessons on how to "stop the slaughter of innocents" may be a little odd, perhaps perverse, possibly even hypocritical. But that is not so clear. The choice is not inconsistent with the values expressed in action and the intellectual culture expressed in words – or in silence.

In support of this conclusion, we may observe that the remedy for international terrorism – at least, a substantial component of it – is within our grasp. But no action is taken to this end, and indeed the matter is never discussed and is even inconceivable in respectable circles. Rather, one finds accolades to our benevolent intentions and nobility of purpose, our elevated "standards of democracy, freedom and humanism," sometimes flawed in performance. Elementary facts cannot be perceived and obvious thoughts are unthinkable. Simple truths, when expressed, elicit disbelief, horror, and outrage – at the fact that they are voiced.

In a moral and intellectual climate such as this, it may well be appropriate for the world's greatest newspaper to select Ariel Sharon as our tutor on the evils of terrorism and how to combat it.

Notes

1 Among other sources, see Edward S. Herman, *The Real Terror Network* (South End, 1982); Herman and Frank Brodhead, *The Rise and Fall of the Bulgarian Connection* (Sheridan Square Publications, 1986); Noam Chomsky, *Pirates and Emperors* (Claremont, 1986; Amana, 1988); Alexander George, "The Discipline of Terrorology," this volume. Also the discussion of Walter Laqueur's *The Age of Terrorism* (Little, Brown and Co., 1987), in Noam Chomsky, *Necessary Illusions* (South End, 1989, pp. 278ff). See this book for references, where not cited here.
2 "States, Terrorism and State Terrorism," in Robert O. Slater and Michael Stohl, *Current Perspectives on International Terrorism* (Macmillan, 1988). Stohl concludes that "In terms of terrorist coercive diplomacy the USA has . . . been far more active in the Third World than has the Soviet Union." Other studies show a similar pattern. In her review of military conflicts since World War II, Ruth Sivard finds that 95 percent have been in the Third

World, in most cases involving foreign forces, with "western powers accounting for 79 percent of the interventions, communist for 6 percent"; *World
Military and Social Expenditures 1981* (World Priorities, 1981), p. 8.

3 United States Code Congressional and Administrative News, 98th Congress,
Second Session, 1984, Oct. 19, volume 2; par. 3077, 98 STAT. 2707 (West
Publishing Co., 1984).

4 *US Army Operational Concept for Terrorism Counteraction* (TRADOC
Pamphlet No. 525-37, 1984); Robert Kupperman Associates, *Low Intensity
Conflict*, July 30, 1983. Both cited in Michael Klare and Peter Kornbluh
(eds), *Low Intensity Warfare* (Pantheon, 1988), pp. 69, 147. The actual
quotation from Kupperman refers specifically to "the threat of force;" its use
is also plainly intended.

5 *Jerusalem Post* (August 4, 1988).

6 See Noam Chomsky, *The Culture of Terrorism* (South End, 1988), pp. 43,
77.

7 For details on the highly successful demolition job, see Chomsky, *Culture
of Terrorism* and *Necessary Illusions*. On the immediate destruction of the
Esquipulas IV accords of February 1989 by the White House and congressional doves with media cooperation, see Chomsky, "The Tasks Ahead: I",
Z magazine (May 1989).

8 Richard Boudreaux and Marjorie Miller, *Los Angeles Times* (October 5,
1988); Associated Press, November 21, 1987; Witness for Peace, *Civilian
Victims of the US Contra War* (February–July 1987), p. 5. Americas Watch,
The Civilian Toll 1986–1987 (August 30, 1987); Americas Watch Petition to
US Trade Representative (May 29, 1987).

9 *Boston Globe* (November 9, 1984), citing also similar comments by Democratic dove Christopher Dodd.

10 A search of the liberal *Boston Globe*, perhaps the least antagonistic to the
Sandinistas among major US journals, revealed one editorial reference to the
fact that Nicaragua needs air power "to repel attacks by the CIA-run contras,
and to stop or deter supply flights" (November 9, 1986).

11 Jeane Kirkpatrick, "US Security and Latin America," *Commentary* (January
1981), p. 29.

12 Cited by Stohl, "States, Terrorism and State Terrorism."

13 Irving Kristol, "Why a Debate Over Contra Aid?," *Wall Street Journal* (April
11, 1986); Kristol, "Where Have All the Gunboats Gone?," *Wall Street Journal* (December 13, 1973).

14 See Chomsky, *Necessary Illusions*, p. 60.

15 Julia Preston, *Boston Globe* (February 9, 1986); MacMichael, see Chomsky
Culture of Terrorism; Doyle McManus, *Los Angeles Times* (May 28, 1988);
Vaky, see Chomsky, *Necessary Illusions*.

16 Ibid., pp. 204–5.

17 Rivera y Damas quoted in Ray Bonner, *Weakness and Deceit* (Times Books,
1984), p. 207; Romero quoted in Jenny Pearce, *Under the Eagle* (Latin
America Bureau, 1981).

18 For documentation on these matters, see Chomsky *Necessary Illusions*.

19 LADOC (Latin American Documentation), *Torture in Latin America*

(LADOC, 1987), the report of the First International Seminar on Torture in Latin America (Buenos Aires, December 1985), devoted to "the repressive system" that "has at its disposal knowledge and a multinational technology of terror, developed in specialized centers whose purpose is to perfect methods of exploitation, oppression and dependence of individuals and entire peoples" by the use of "state terrorism inspired by the Doctrine of National Security." This doctrine can be traced to the historic decision of the Kennedy administration to shift the mission of the Latin American military to "internal security," with far-reaching consequences.

20 Raymond L. Garthoff, *Reflections on the Cuban Missile Crisis* (Brookings Institution, 1987), p. 17.

21 Ibid., pp. 16f, 78f, 89f, 98. See the references of note 1. Also Bradley Earl Ayers, *The War that Never Was* (Bobbs-Merrill, 1976); Warren Hinckle and William Turner, *The Fish is Red* (Harper & Row, 1981); William Blum, *The CIA* (Zed Books, 1986); Morris Morley, *Imperial State and Revolution* (Cambridge University Press, 1987); Taylor Branch and George Crile, "The Kennedy Vendetta: Our Secret War on Cuba," *Harper's* (August 1975).

22 See Noam Chomsky, *Towards a New Cold War* (Pantheon, 1982), pp. 48–9; see Chomsky, *Culture of Terrorism*, p. 40; Stohl, "States, Terrorism and State Terrorism."

23 *Jerusalem Post* (August 16, 1981); see Chomsky, *Fateful Triangle* (South End, 1983), Chapter 5, sections 1, 3.4, for further quotes, background, and description.

24 Charles Glass, "No News is Bad News," *Index on Censorship* (January 1989). See Chomsky, *Fateful Triangle*, pp. 184f, and sources cited.

25 Ehud Ya'ari, *Egypt and the Fedayeen* (Hebrew) (Givat Haviva, 1975), pp. 27f, a study based on captured Egyptian and Jordanian documents. At the same time, Salah Mustapha, Egyptian military attaché in Jordan, was severely injured by a letter-bomb sent from East Jerusalem, presumably from the same source; ibid.

26 Israeli military historian Uri Milshtein, *Hadashot* (December 31, 1987), referring to Eliav's 1983 book *Hamevukash*.

27 Sofaer, *Foreign Affairs*, Summer 1986; *New York Times* (October 12, 1985).

28 See Chomsky, *Pirates and Emperors*, pp. 92–3, 108; *Ha'aretz* (April 5, 1989).

29 Leslie Cockburn, *Out of Control* (Atlantic Monthly Press, 1987), p. 26; Chomsky, *Pirates and Emperors*, p. 136.

30 Boustany, *Washington Post Weekly* (March 14, 1988); Woodward, *Veil: The Street Wars of the CIA 1981–1987* (Simon & Schuster, 1987), pp. 396f.

31 For a review of the Iron Fist operations and the Tunis bombing, see Chomsky, *Pirates and Emperors*, chapter 2.

32 For details, see Chomsky, *Pirates and Emperors*, chapter 3; Chomsky, *Necessary Illusions*, pp. 272–3; and sources cited.

33 James LeMoyne, "Week in Review," *New York Times* (June 29, 1986).

34 See Edward S. Herman, *The Terrorism Industry* (Pantheon, 1990); Herman and Gerry O'Sullivan, "'Terrorism' as Ideology and Cultural Industry," this volume.

35 Lawrence Harke, "The Anti-Terrorism Act of 1987 and American Freedoms:

A Critical Review," *University of Miami Law Review,* 43 (1989), pp. 667f.

36 Shamir, "Terror," *Hazit* (August 1943); parts reprinted in *Al Hamishmar* (December 24, 1987). Berlin, *Personal Impressions* (Viking, 1981), p. 50.

37 See Chomsky, *Fateful Triangle,* pp. 164–5n.; Gafi Amir, *Yediot Ahronot Supplement* (August 14, 1988); Israel Shahak, "Distortion of the Holocaust," *Kol Ha'ir* (May 19, 1989).

38 Text appears as Appendix III, *State Terrorism at Sea,* EAFORD Paper 44, Chicago, 1988.

39 For details, see Chomsky, *Necessary Illusions*; also Chomsky, "The Trollope Ploy," *Z Magazine* (March 1989); Chomsky, "The Art of Evasion: Diplomacy in the Middle East," *Z Magazine* (January 1990).

40 Emphasis in *Jerusalem Post.* See references of preceding note. The unacceptability of an international conference follows from the opposition of the US and Israel to a political settlement of the kind supported by most of the world community.

41 See Chomsky, *Pirates and Emperors,* p. 69.

42 Ibid., pp. 63f.

43 Don Oberdorfer, "The Mind of George Shultz," *Washington Post Weekly* (February 17, 1986); *New York Times* (November 28, 1988).

44 Bernard Gwertzman, *New York Times* (October 7, 1985).

45 Bernard Gwertzman, *New York Times* (October 2, 1985).

46 See *Pirates and Emperors,* pp. 51f., 87f.; note 35 above; Linda Gradstein, *Washington Post* (April 6, 1989); "Political Trials," Dai l'Kibbush, Jerusalem, August 1988, published in *News from Within* (December 14, 1988).

47 *New York Times* (September 30, 1986).

3

"Terrorism" as Ideology and Cultural Industry

Edward S. Herman and Gerry O'Sullivan

1 Introduction

"Terrorism" has become a widely used word in the West over the past several decades. In conventional analyses, this is explained as a result of increased terrorist activity, which, in turn, is based in part on the ability of terrorists to get their messages across by means of violent acts in the "open" West, in part on Soviet sponsorship and troublemaking.

An alternative view, rarely encountered in mainstream publications (but to be spelled out in this chapter), is that both the supply of terrorist activity and the demand for publicity regarding terrorism can be explained mainly in terms of Western interests and policy, not by the actions and plans of the "terrorists." In this version, the primary terrorism is Western in origin, displayed, for example, in the operations of the South African government in its repressions at home and in Namibia, and its cross-border attacks directly or through proxy terrorist forces in Angola, Lesotho, Mozambique, Kenya, and Zimbabwe; in Israeli policy on the West Bank, and its Iron Fist attacks and sponsorship of the South Lebanese army in Lebanon; and in the US organization and support of the Contras and a terrorist army in El Salvador, and its long-term training and support of military and police forces throughout its sphere of influence under an "insurance policy" strategy.[1]

Much of the "terrorism" discussed in the West is responsive to this primary Western violence. On the demand side, in this alternative perspective, it is the West and Western interests that have pushed "terrorism" to the forefront, not the terrorists. They have done this because they wanted to use terrorism as an ideological instrument of propaganda and control.[2] This mission of "terrorism" has been accomplished with outstanding success.

Edward S. Herman and Gerry O'Sullivan

In order to use terrorism for Western purposes it was necessary to define the word, develop a model of terrorism, and select facts in accord with Western needs. The West has long had mass media that serve such a function well.[3] The unique feature of Western agitation over terrorism during the last decade or so has been the development of a body of institutes, think tanks, and associated experts whose business has been to get across the desired messages. This can be regarded as a cultural "industry" in the economic sense, as the production and sale of an informational-perspectival output is well developed, and located in a set of identifiable individuals and institutions.

The economic framework is also appropriate because these institutions and associated experts meet a "demand" for intellectual-ideological service by states and other powerful interests, analogous to the demand for tanks by the army or advertising copy by the producers of soap. This is a market system, and intellectual service is responsive to market forces. Ideas, and those who produce them, can be bought and subsidized by those with the need and resources to provide the effective demand. Neither the African National Congress (ANC) nor the Mutual Support Group of Guatemala can fund databanks or theoretical analyses of the state terrorism that has killed scores of thousands in their countries and has posed an ongoing threat to the survivor populations. Western governments and business firms *do* underwrite such intellectual efforts, and they want data and analyses pertinent to *their* needs in confronting their perceived enemies, who are rebels and restive underclasses, rather than right-wing governments engaging in large-scale torture and killings, or Western-organized and funded insurgents attacking disfavored states. The definitions, models of "terrorism," and appropriately selective focus of attention follow accordingly.[4]

The terrorism "industry" comprises government officials and bodies, government and quasi-private think tanks and analysts, and private security firms. It is a multinational industry, with close ties between government and private sponsors, institutes, and experts in and between the United States, Israel, Great Britain, and to a lesser extent Canada, West Germany, France, South Africa, South Korea, Taiwan, and other members of the "free world". This multinational spread reflects a commonality of state interest, along with an intent on the part of some states to influence opinion in other countries (e.g., the Israeli effort to mobilize US opinion against the Palestinian cause). It is manifested in the internationalization of institutes, conferences, publications, expert and media citations of authorities, and standardized definitions and agendas.

The services of the terrorism industry have been very much needed in the West to cover over its own activities and crimes. During the past 40 years the Western states – including South Africa and Israel, as well as

40

the great powers – have had to employ intimidation on a very large scale to maintain access, control, and privileged positions in the Third World, in the face of the nationalist and popular upheavals of the "post-colonial" era. This has been a *primary* terrorism, in two senses: first, it has involved far more extensive killing and other forms of coercion than the "terrorism" focused upon in the West (see table 3.1); and second, it represents the efforts by the powerful to preserve undemocratic privileges and struc-

Table 3.1 Killings by state and non-state terrorists: numbers and orders of magnitude

Type of killing	Numbers killed	Fraction or multiple of PLO killings (entry 3)
Non-state		
German: Red Army Faction, Revolutionary Cells, and all other non-state, January 1970–April 1979[a]	31	0.1
Italian: Red Brigades and all other non-state, 1968–82[b]	334	1.2
PLO: Israelis killed in all acts of terror, 1968–81[c]	282	1.0
World: all "international terrorists," CIA global aggregate, 1969–80[d]	3,368	11.9
Single incidents of state terror		
El Salvador: Rio Sumpul, May 14, 1980[e]	600+	2.1+
South Africa: Kassinga refugee camp, May 4, 1978[f]	600+	2.1+
Guatemala: Panzos, May 29, 1978[g]	114	0.4
Israel: Sabra Shatila, September 16–18 1982[h]	1,900–3,500	6.7–12.4
Larger dimensions of state terror		
Argentina: 1976–82 "disappeared"[i]	11,000	39.0
Chile: 1973–85[j]	20,000+	70.9+
Dominican Republic: 1965–72[k]	2,000	7.1
El Salvador: Matanza I, 1932[l]	30,000	106.4
El Salvador: Matanza II, 1980–5[m]	50,000+	177.3+
Guatemala: Rios Montt pacification campaign, March–June 1982[n]	2,186	7.8
Guatemala: 1966–85[o]	100,000+	354.6+
Indonesia: 1965–6[p]	500,000+	1,773.0+
Indonesia: invasion and pacification of East Timor, 1980–5[q]	200,000+	709.2+

Edward S. Herman and Gerry O'Sullivan

Table 3.1 Killings by state and non-state terrorists: numbers and orders of magnitude

Type of killing	Numbers killed	Fraction or multiple of PLO killings (entry 3)
Libya: external assassinations of Libyans, 1980–3[r]	10+	0.04 +
Cambodia: Pol Pot era, 1975–8[s]	300,000 +	1,063.8+
US-sponsored Contras: civilians in Nicaragua, 1981–7[t]	3,000 +	10.6 +
South Africa and proxies: in Angola and Mozambique, 1980–9[u]	1,000,000 +	3,546 +

[a] H. J. Horchem, "Political Terrorism: The German Perspective," in Ariel Merari (ed), *On Terrorism and Combatting Terrorism* (University Publications of America, 1985), p. 63.

[b] V. S. Pisano, *Terrorism and Security: The Italian Experience*, Report of the Subcommittee on Security and Terrorism, Senate Judiciary Committee, 98th Cong., 2nd Sess., November 1984, p. 63.

[c] B. Michael, *Ha'aretz* (July 16, 1982), citing official police statistics. Some of the 282 were killed by Israeli forces in attempts to free hostages by force.

[d] CIA, *Patterns of International Terrorism: 1980* (CIA, June 1981), p. vi.

[e] M. McClintock, *The American Connection, vol. 1, State Terror and Popular Resistance in El Salvador* (Zed Books, 1985), p. 306.

[f] R. Leonard, *South African at War* (Lawrence Hill, 1983), p. 67.

[h] The Lebanese government claims that it recovered 762 bodies and 1,200 were privately buried by relatives: N. Chomsky, *The Fateful Triangle* (South End, 1983), p. 370. In a careful study, Amnon Kapeliouk estimates 3,000–3,500 murdered; *Sabra and Shatila: Inquiry into a Massacre* (Association of Arab-American University Graduates, 1984), pp. 62–3.

[i] J. Simpson and J. Bennett, *The Disappeared and the Mothers of the Plaza* (St Martins, 1985), p. 7.

[j] Amnesty International, *Report on Torture* (Farrar, Straus & Giroux, 1975), p. 252.

[k] C. M. Gutiérrez, *The Dominican Republic: Rebellion and Repression* (Monthly Review Press, 1972), p. 11.

[l] R. Armstrong and J. Shenk, *El Salvador: The Face of Revolution* (South End, 1982), p. 30.

[m] Central America Historical Institute.

[n] Amnesty International, Special Briefing, "Guatemala: Massive Extrajudicial Executions in Rural Areas under the Government of General Efrain Rios Montt," (July 1982), p. x.

[o] "Bitter and Cruel . . .," report of a mission to Guatemala by the British Parliamentary Human Rights Group (October 1984); C. Krueger and K. Enge, *Without Security or Development: Guatemala Militarized*, report submitted to the Washington Office on Latin America, (June 6, 1985).

[p] Amnesty International, *Political Killings by Governments* (Amnesty International, 1983), p. 34. This is a conservative estimate.

[q] N. Chomsky, *Towards a New Cold War* (Pantheon, 1982), pp. 341 and 470 (citing Father Leoneto Vierra do Rego and Father Francisco María Fernández).

[r] Amnesty International, *Political Killings by Governments*, pp. 69–77.

[s] Ibid., p. 24.

[t] H. Sklar, *Washington's War on Nicaragua* (South End, 1988), p. 393.

[u] P. Johnson and D. Martin, *Frontline Southern Africa* (Four Walls Eight Windows, 1988), p. 467 and sources used there.

tures from the threat of encroachment and control by popular organizations and mass movements. In this perspective, the actions of the ANC constitute a derivative and provoked response to a South African state terrorism which is primary in the two senses just noted.[5] Similarly, before July 1979 the Sandinistas fought against a primary terrorism in the form of the US-sponsored Somoza regime, which employed large-scale violence in support of a system of wholly undemocratic privelege.[6]

Although the West is the main source of primary terror in recent decades, it has been remarkably successful in deflecting the terrorist charge onto its victims. It has done this by constructing a model and semantics that serve its ends, and through the capacity of the terrorism industry and Western mass media to impose these on Western and even victimized populations.

2   The Western Model and Semantics of Terrorism

THE BASIC WESTERN MODEL

The basic model describing the nature and sources of terrorism, expounded by Western leaders and the members and experts of the terrorism industry, contains the following main elements:

1   The West is an innocent target and victim of terrorism. It stands for decency and the rule of law. In the words of former US Secretary of State George Shultz, speaking at the 1984 Jonathan Institute Conference in Washington, DC: "In our foreign policies we try to foster the kind of world that promotes peaceful settlement of disputes, one that welcomes change without violent conflict. We seek a world in which human rights are respected by all governments, a world based on the rule of law."[7] It follows that the United States (and by association, its allies) does not engage in or support terrorism in any way, shape or form.

2   The West only responds to other people's use of force.[8] Argentina, for example, while engaging in "deplorable" killings during the years from 1976 to 1983, was only responding to the actions of others – it was, in Shultz's words, a "deliberately provoked response – to a massive campaign of terrorism." The deplorable state killings were thus not "terrorism" – Schultz carefully avoids using the word for Argentine state policy – and the fault lies with those who deliberately provoked the Argentine government.

3   While terrorists have varying motives, "They are attempting to impose their will by force . . . designed to create fear." In contrast with the West, terrorists do not adhere to "civilized norms of conduct."

43

4   In those cases where the West supports insurgents who use force, this is done "in behalf of democracy against repressive regimes," as in the US support of the Nicaraguan Contras. Furthermore, insurgents supported by the West do not kill innocent civilians. "The contras in Nicaragua do not blow up school buses or hold mass executions of civilians."

5   Democracies are especially hated by and vulnerable to terrorists, and the aim of terrorists is "to undermine institutions, to destroy popular faith in moderate government. In Lebanon, for example, state-sponsored terrorism has exploited existing tensions and attempted to prevent that nation from rebuilding its democratic institutions." By contrast, "The number of terrorist incidents in or against totalitarian states is negligible."

6   Underlying these varied efforts to undermine democracies is Soviet support: "But in many countries, terrorism would long since have passed away had it not been for significant support from outside. The international links among terrorist groups are now clearly understood; and the Soviet link, direct or indirect, is also clearly understood."

This is clearly a "patriotic" model, in which all virtues are ascribed to oneself and one's friends and clients, all villainy is attached to the enemy. It reiterates a litany of myths and fabrications which have been built up to justify Western interests and policy. Thus, first and foremost, the West is solely a victim of the intimidation of others – its own struggle against change which threatens Western interests and its role as primary terrorist are ignored and denied, and the West is portrayed as a promoter of peaceful change and the rule of law.[9] In Lebanon, the 1982 US-supported Israeli invasion and attempt to foist a minority government on a victimized population is cast as *Lebanon*'s "rebuilding its democratic institutions!" The populace resisting this external aggression and imposed political settlement are "terrorists."

It is also part of the myth structure of the Western model that, while the West is continously under siege from "terrorism," the East is free of this scourge. This myth is derived in part by inference from the further myth that "terrorism" is a product of Soviet conspiratorial efforts to destabilize the "democracies." It also rests in part on the claim that Western-supported insurgencies are always in the interest of "democracy" and against "repressive governments," and that these preferred insurgents never blow up buses. When fact is allowed to intrude into this fictional tale,[10] and when we also admit state and state-sponsored terrorism that has been directed against countries like Cuba, Mozambique, Angola, Nicaragua, and Vietnam, the claim that the West is a unique victim of terrorists turns out to be not only a falsehood, but one that turns the truth

44

on its head. The reality is that the Eastern bloc and radical states have been subjected to far greater levels of terrorist violence than "the democracies."[11]

Where Shultz does admit deplorable state killings – e.g., in Argentina, in an earlier period – as noted, he makes this strictly responsive and provoked by others, thus removing any onus from the West. The fact that many thousands were tortured and killed who had no connection with the guerrillas is irrelevant to Shultz, who establishes the legitimacy of Argentine state actions by provocation, and then ignores what took place thereafter. Many commentators have pointed out that the Argentine guerrilla movement was essentially wiped out by 1977, but that the state system of torture and killings continued to flourish, and that a large part of the state assault was directed against the labor movement, in keeping with the new economic policy introduced by the army. Simpson and Bennett claim that "a third of the victims of the Dirty War were ordinary workers or trade unionists," and that "Trades union leaders were prime targets for victimization."[12] The National Commission on Disappeared Persons, appointed by President Alfonsin to look into the deaths of thousands during the military regime, concluded that "The armed forces responded to the terrorists' crimes *with a terrorism infinitely worse than that which they were combatting.*"[13] This point is not admissible in the Western model: the response is not terrorism, whatever its scale, quality, or intimidating purpose and effects.

We may observe also that although the Argentine military regime used torture on a large scale, as do Israel and South Africa, and although torture and disappearances grew geometrically in the US sphere of influence with the US investment in arms and training as an "insurance policy," Shultz speaks of "civilized norms of conduct" (as well as adherence to the "rule of law") as characterizing Western behavior, but violated by "terrorists."[14]

Shultz's association of terrorism with external support and ultimately the Soviet Union deflects attention from the indigenous and Western-based primary-terrorism roots of many insurgent struggles and a great deal of retail terrorism. His claim that the international links among terrorist groups, and the Soviet link, are "now clearly understood" is false – this is the clear position of the South African and Israeli governments and the right wing of the terrorism industry, but a number of the Western establishment's "moderate" experts contend that the links among the terrorist groups are tenuous and that the Soviet Union is not directing them to any clear end.[15] Even the CIA and Defense Intelligence Agency denied Soviet coordination and sponsorship of international terrorism in 1981, and only produced the requisite line after they were ordered to do so by CIA head William Casey.[16] The Soviet Union does often aid national liberation movements and insurgencies. By merging these with ad hoc terrorist groups that the Soviet Union does *not* aid, Western ideologues can make the Soviet Union the sponsor of "international terrorism."

The model just described, expounded by the US Secretary of State, expresses official US views and policy on terrorism and reflects Western establishment interests. The model's biases are enormous, and it is grounded in myth and fabricated evidence. This was to be expected from an official spokesman of the Reagan administration and US government. What is more interesting, and the main focus of the present chapter, is the extent to which such a self-serving official model is accepted in all its essentials by the private sector of the terrorism industry and by the Western mass media. Shultz's version of the Western model is in no sense "extreme" – it represents an approximately mean position in the spectrum of terrorism industry opinion.

We may classify expert opinion as follows: first is the view, which we will call "moderate establishment," that accepts the essential features of the Western model, postulating the West as the primary victim of terrorism and adapting questions accordingly, but expressing reservations about Soviet coordination and sponsorship,[17] the illegitimacy and external (Soviet) roots of liberation movements, and the desirability of preemptive attacks on terrorists. A second view, which we will call "right-wing establishment," asserts clear Soviet control and/or coordination of international terrorists, claims that national liberation and (frequently) other dissident movements – animal liberation, environmental, peace – originate or fall under the control of international Communism, and urges that the West must resist such subversion by preemptive measures. Third is the "dissident" view, one which regards the Western model as biased in favor of Western interests by its premises, which rule out the possibility that the West may be the terrorist, or the sponsor as well as the victim of terrorism. In this dissident view the Western model is therefore not an appropriate basis for an objective analysis of terrorism. Of the 32 leading Western terrorism experts whose views we will discuss further below, only one falls into the third category; the other 31 experts work within the confines of the Western model. These experts thus disagree and debate, but with the single exception do not challenge the basic view that the West is the victim, not a primary source, of terrorism.

THE "THEATRE" OF TERRORISM

Another important element of Western expert opinion on terrorism is a focus on the role of the media as a "theatre" of terrorism.[18] In this view, the West is especially vulnerable to terrorism because the "free" Western media are inclined to feature heavily the drama of terrorist incidents and claims, thereby giving terrorists an outreach they could not otherwise command. This encourages them to use this readily available "theatre" to get their messages across. Many of the experts who stress the importance of media access and publicity also contend that the media treat terrorists with excessive sympathy, further encouraging their terrorist activities.[19]

One of the merits of this approach from the standpoint of the Western establishment is that it roots terrorism in Western freedom itself, with the West portrayed as an unfair victim of its own virtues. The claim that this openness is "taken advantage of" by the closed East completes the circle of injustice. Right-wing analysts and journalists are especially fond of this argument because it allows them to laud Western "freedom" while urging the regretful necessity of curbing that freedom in order to fight fire with fire.

This way of looking at terrorism has the added advantage of deflecting attention from the deeper causes of terrorism, such as the real grievances of the terrorists and any antecedent behavior by the West, to control over terrorists' access to the media. Was the escalation of terrorism after 1982 a result of easy media access or was it a response to the invasion of Lebanon and the mass murders at Sabra and Shatila? It is clearly more comfortable for the Western establishment to have its experts focus on the West's "openness" as cause, rather than the prior and ongoing assaults on the "terrorists" and their families.[20]

During and after a number of terrorist incidents in the 1980s, the US media were attacked for allegedly giving too much publicity and sympathetic attention to the terrorists and interfering with official efforts to deal with them. The media were put on the defensive, and went to great pains to assure the public of their patriotism, detestation of terrorists, and devotion only to getting basic news to their readers. In this secondary debate over the media's role in fostering terrorism, the evidence on who manipulates the media and whose positions are favored and disfavored in media coverage is invariably distorted. The early Reagan administration used "terrorism" as a public relations device to mobilize support for its policies, and the increase in media attention to the subject that ensued would seem to have met a *government* demand for attention to "terrorism," not a demand of the "terrorists." The press and Western experts invariably fail to discuss this point; despite a clear Reagan strategic-PR emphasis, they pretend that only the terrorists have an interest in publicity about terrorism.

That terrorists get a good press is a fallacy regularly perpetrated by the terrorism industry experts.[21] While the media do occasionally convey some of the grievances of the terrorists and allow them to appear in a human light, media coverage of terrorist events is dominated by official condemnation of the attacks and a focus on the fate of the victims. Furthermore, once an incident has ended, the retrospectives of officials, victims, and media commentators are confined almost exclusively to recriminations, tales of terrorist abuse, and attacks on the media.[22]

THE SEMANTICS OF TERRORISM

The semantic adjustment to the Western need to turn the terrorism label away from the primary violence of the West and onto its victims and other lesser terrorists has assumed a number of forms. One is to confine terrorism to non-state actors using force to challenge governments, exempting government from its traditional high ranking as terrorist (with selected exceptions). The redefinition is often implicit in a system of murky word usage that allows the powerful to name their terrorists more or less at their own discretion. Notable here was the announcement of Secretary of State Alexander Haig early in 1981 that "terrorism" was going to replace "human rights" as the main foreign policy concern of the new Reagan administration. The press noted at the time that just what Haig meant by "terrorism" was unspecified and unclear,[23] but neither the press nor establishment experts engaged in any further analysis or critique. Both allowed the administration's specification of terrorists to prevail by simply following in its wake, discussing terrorism on the administration's terms, and failing to engage in critical analysis.

As the Reagan administration rushed into warmer relations with Argentina, Chile, Guatemala, and South Africa, it was obvious that the leaders of these states were not "terrorists" but were merely violating something called "human rights." Terrorists were evidently those who used violence in *opposing* governments, like the Red Brigades, the Baader-Meinhof gang, and national liberation movements such as the ANC and SWAPO. It was not feasible in the United States to openly describe the ANC and SWAPO as terrorist organizations on a regular basis, but the more extreme right-wing elements of the administration, such as UN Ambassador Jeane Kirkpatrick and her Deputy Ambassador Charles Lichtenstein, did not hesitate to so label them, especially when addressing friendly audiences.[24] Other right-wing experts of the terrorism industry also put the ANC and SWAPO in the terrorist category, again especially when addressing sympathetic audiences.[25] But while the ANC and SWAPO may sometimes be designated terrorist organizations by the Western terrorism industry and the mass media, neither refer to

South Africa as a "terrorist state;" Botha and De Klerk are never designated, like Gaddafi, "terrorist" commanders.

The importance of shifting attention from state to non-state terrorists may be seen in table 3.1, which shows the relative dimensions of killings by state and non-state actors. The grand total of victims of the terror favorites of the Western establishment – the PLO, Red Brigades, and Baader-Meinhof gang (the sum of the first-three entries) – is approximately equal to the numbers killed in the single Salvadoran army massacre at the Rio Sumpul river in 1980 or in the single South African attack on the Kassinga refugee camp in 1978. The Phalange – Israeli massacre at the Sabra and Shatila refugee camps involved more deaths than the multi-year total of all the Western favorites by a wide margin, and the same is true of the US-sponsored Contra massacres of Nicaraguan civilians. The civilian massacres by state terrorists in Argentina, Chile, El Savlador, Guatemala, Indonesia, and South Africa each exceeded not only the total of the favored trio but also the aggregate killings by all "international terrorists" in the pre-Casey CIA calculations for the entire globe, 1969–1980. It is obvious why the Reagan–Haig team and the Western terrorism industry and press have had to bypass state terror and focus on retail terror – state terror has been immense, and the West and its clients have been the major agents.

Another semantic device used to help sort out terrorists according to political convenience is the concept of "international terrorism." In a 1980 definition by the CIA, international terrorism is "Terrorism conducted with the support of a foreign government or organization and/or directed against foreign nationals, institutions, or governments."[26] This concept allows the Western terrorism industry to designate the Soviet Union and Libya as "sponsors" of international terrorism, as they aid the PLO, the ANC, and other movements and groups outside of their borders. It also makes the PLO and the ANC "international terrorist organizations," as they depend on and receive aid from the outside. Of course, the United States has aided Chile, Israel, and the governments of El Salvador and Guatemala, and has organized and funded the Contras and other "freedom fighters." Israel sponsored and aided the South Lebanese army of Saad Hadaad and his successor, Antoine Lahd; and South Africa has supported Savimbi and UNITA in Angola and RENAMO in Mozambique for years. All of these cases involve external support of terrorism and make the United States, Israel, and South Africa sponsors of international terrorism.

How does the West exempt itself from the charge of supporting international terrorism? It does this, first, by the previously mentioned exclusion of state terrorism, although the CIA definition does not suggest such an exclusion. By this definition, US aid to Chile, El Salvador, and others is not sponsorship of "international terrorism" – it is merely the sponsorship of wholesale terror. A second semantic device is the preferential use of "retaliation" and "counterterror," in which the West only responds to other people's terror, a point to which we return later. The third device is simple and crude selectivity of attention, and refusal to apply the same standards of evidence to Western- and non-Western-based violence. For example, the state exemption does not fit the Nicaraguan Contras, who could hardly be said to be "retaliating" to Sandinista violence. The United States organized and financed the Contras, supplied them with a terrorists' manual, and planned many of their actions in detail. The fit to the concept of sponsorship of international terrorism could not be more precise.[27]

Similarly, actions by Abu Nidal, whose dependence on Libya is surely no greater than the dependence of Haddad's and Lahd's South Lebanese army on Israel, are allocated to Gaddafi as the responsible party and supporter of "international terrorism;" actions by the Israeli proxies are not similarly treated, and we have never seen their cross-border operations referred to by the US mass media or Western terrorism experts as a case of "international terrorism." And when the Christian Phalange entered the Sabra and Shatila refugee camps under Israeli guidance and observation and slaughtered as many as 3,500 Palestinians, Israel was not immediately branded a leading terrorist state, although the Israeli role was much clearer than Gaddafi's role in airport bombings in Western Europe, and although this single massacre exceeded the toll of the PLO, Baader-Meinhof gang, and Red Brigades taken together.[28]

Playing dumb is also crucial in handling US relations with its repressive clients. If any arms and training of suitable terrorists are traceable to the Soviet Union, this is considered by Western experts and press as serious business and evidence of Soviet misbehavior. If, on the other hand, US client states torture and kill, if death squads and disappearances proliferate in the US sphere of influence, and if these follow a massive US investment in military aid and training clearly designed to influence the course of political events in the client states, the terrorism experts and mass media nevertheless fail to see a systematic connection and responsibility.[29]

Another important semantic device used to ensure that "terror" is applied only to rebels and other convenient terrorists is the preferential use of "retaliation" and "counterterror." The West and its clients only "retaliate" and engage in "counterterror" – its victims and other enemies terrorize. This choice of terminology is usually entirely arbitrary, as the victims and enemies also usually assert that they are responding to prior, Western terror. But this is disallowed in the West, without discussion. Israel has been provoking PLO terror by its own quite deliberate terror for many years in order to avoid having to negotiate with the Palestinians[30] - but this is not admitted into Western mainstream discourse, and the allocation of who retaliates and who terrorizes in this case reflects sheer bias.[31]

A final major semantic device has been to focus heavily on the attacking of *innocent civilians* as the essence of terrorism. In the words of Benjamin Netanyahu, "Terrorism is the deliberate and systematic murder, maiming, and menacing of the innocent to inspire fear for political ends."[32] The merit of this focus, from the standpoint of Western terrorologists and propagandists, is that it conjures up an image of victims of hijackings and shootings in airports, rather than the victims of Iron Fist bombings of Lebanese villages, South African scorched-earth attacks and murders in Angola, or Guatemalan and Salvadoran army massacres of peasants.[33] The main reason for the predominance of this imagery is the bias of the Western terrorism industry and media, which feature victimization in the West often, and do so with human detail and passion, while muting, suppressing, and treating impersonally and without indignation the evidence of victimization *by* the West.[34]

The favored imagery is also helped by the fact that people on hijacked planes or shot in airports appear to be the ultimate in "innocence," as it seems pure chance that they are victimized; they are not identified by or known to the terrorists and are therefore random victims. There is no doubt that these are innocent victims,[35] but the civilians killed by state terrorists in bombing raids are also innocent *and they are vastly more numerous than the highly publicized victims of hijackers and airport bombers.* Their innocence is compromised in the minds of Western publics, however, because - apart from the failure of the Western media to humanize them and show their suffering in any detail - the Western state terrorists who kill them rarely admit that they are deliberately attacking ordinary civilians. They are killing "suspected leftists," or attacking "nests of terrorists," and the United States was always bombing alleged "Vietcong bases" in South Vietnam. Any civilians killed in Western bombing or artillery attacks on enemy "nests" or "bases" are therefore either not "innocent" or they are "inadvertent" victims (not "deliberately murdered," in the Netanyahu version).

But this is fraudulent. Civilian populations do not cease being innocent because Western propaganda declares them to be "suspected leftists" or their homes to be "suspected enemy base camps."[36] Killings are not "inadvertent" if they are a systematic and inevitable result of calculated military policy.[37] Primary terrorists very commonly treat entire populations as not innocent, because the populations and their political spokespersons will not accept the terrorist state's will. The terms just cited - suspected leftists, nests of terrorists, enemy bases - are euphemisms that subtly justify attacks on civilian populations. But the Western terrorism industry and mass media refuse to make this explicit: they permit the victims of "friendly" state terrorism to be portrayed as "sympathizers" of "the terrorists," on the say-so of the *real* terrorists, if the victims are not ignored altogether.

3 The Terrorism Industry

The terrorism industry manufactures, refines, and packages for distribution information, analyses, and opinion on a topic called "terrorism." The industry comprises, first, a public sector of government agencies and officials, who establish "policy" and provide official opinions and selected facts on terrorist activity in speeches, press conferences, press releases, hearings, reports, and interviews. It includes, also, a private sector of think tanks and research institutes, security firms that deal in risk analysis and personal and property security and protection, and an associated body of terrorism "experts." The industry's experts are associated mainly with the institutes and think tanks, some of which are affiliated with academic institutions, but officials and analysts of security firms are also regarded as authorities on terrorism, particularly in its practical and control aspects.

There are important structural connections between the public and private sectors, with the latter often sponsored by and serving as a virtual arm of the former. The officials of security firms are frequently drawn from government security services, and they depend on their relationships and earlier ties for prestige, references, referrals, and informational support. Security firms are also sometimes vehicles for the implementation of covert state policy.[38] The institutes and their experts, who complement the government in producing, refining, and getting over the proper line, also move as in a revolving door between the nominally separate public and private spheres, and they are encouraged and supported by both government and the private corporate system.

THE GOVERNMENT SECTOR

Governments play a major role in the terrorism industry, both directly and indirectly. Directly, they fix policy, implement it, and explain and justify the policy to the public. When "terrorism" becomes a featured aspect of government policy and propaganda, as in the Reagan era in the United States, the government investment and role escalates. It is our view, also, that the Western establishment's intense focus on terrorism has not been based on any major terrorist threat, but rather has been contrived and the "threat" inflated for political purposes. Under these circumstances, the ideological and propaganda aspects of "terrorism" are actually the predominant features of "policy" on the subject, and the government propaganda effort will bulk large.[39]

Since the Nixon years, the US State Department has had an Office to Combat Terrorism (or some equivalent), and the CIA, Pentagon, and FBI have long had personnel allocated to "counterterrorism." Given the increased concern over terrorism in the 1980s, the funds allocated to this area have been greatly enlarged. By 1985 it was estimated that the government was spending $2 billion and employing 18,000 people to deal with terrorism, much of the activity being apparently slated for physical security.[40] In its much enlarged information-propaganda operation, the State Department now has an Ambassador-at-Large for Counter-terrorism, whose function is "to generate greater global understanding of the threat of terrorism and efforts to resist it."[41] He spends a great deal of time addressing a variety of audiences, including those provided by Voice of America and Worldnet (a government-owned TV network linking Washington to US Embassies and missions throughout the world).

The government also has played a very important *indirect* role in the production of information (and disinformation) on terrorism. It has encouraged and provided crucial support to the private sector of the industry, some of whose members qualify as quasi-governmental. The Rand Corporation, a "private" think tank sponsored by the US Airforce, has a section devoted to terrorism. The important Georgetown Center for Strategic and International Studies (CSIS) had as an early senior official Ray Cline, a former deputy director of the CIA, and there has been a steady interchange of personnel between the State Department and the CIA on the one hand and this nominally independent, quasi-academic body on the other. Many other accredited "private experts" have worked for military and intelligence organizations and maintain ongoing relationships with them. In Great Britain, Brian Crozier's Institute for the Study of Conflict was a creation of the CIA and British intelligence, and served as a propaganda organ for both (as well as for the the Confederation of British Industries).[42] The South African Terrorism Research Centre was organized as a nominally independent research organization, under the direction of Michael Morris, a long-time operative of the South African secret police.[43]

Such institutes and experts work in tandem with government agencies in supplying a proper perspective and suitable information on terrorism to the public. They are also important vehicles for specific pieces of government propaganda. This point is applicable to government – media relationships as well, where the government has long used selected reporters, papers, and magazines as vehicles for the placement of black propaganda.[44] The government also provides covert financial support as well as privileged information to its favorite institutes and experts, hiring them as consultants, subsidizing and distributing their writings, and giving them publicity in government-sponsored events (seminars, hearings, press releases, and press conferences).[45]

Allied governments within the "free world" are also regularly engaged in the manufacture and distribution of information and propaganda on "terrorism," and they all take essentially the same "free-world" line as that outlined by Shultz in 1984. Many of them sponsor and covertly support private-sector terrorism industries of their own.

The "free-world" system for combating "terrorism" includes many countries and agencies that are themselves premier terrorists. South Africa, Israel, and the Latin American National Security States have all been deeply concerned over "terrorism," which they identify with national liberation movements and any resistance to their own state terrorism. Authoritarian regimes in Taiwan and South Korea, with CIA assistance, sponsored the Asian Peoples' Anti-Communist League and World Anti-Communist League (WACL) in 1954 and 1966 respectively. WACL has fused together Reverend Moon's Unification Church (and CAUSA – Confederation of Associations for the Unification of the Americas – subsidiary), Nazi and neo-Nazi elements, and right-wing terrorists on a global basis. At a WACL meeting in Buenos Aires in 1980, the chairman was General Suarez Mason, a leader of the Argentine army during the Dirty War; others in attendance were Roberto D'Aubuisson and Sandoval Alarcon, leaders of the death squads of El Salvador and Guatemala respectively, Stefano delle Chiaie, the Italian terrorist, Luis Garcia Meza, the Bolivian head of state by grace of Argentina and the drug cartel, and other far rightists from the United States and elsewhere.

In the Western model of terrorism, the West stands for democracy and civilized values. In reality, it organizes and defends primary terrorism, which is implemented in part by South Africa, Israel, the National Security States and death squads of Latin America, and the Contras (who were serviced by WACL, under an explicit arrangement between Reagan and WACL chairman John Singlaub).[46] In the system of distributed functions, the experts talk about civilized values and the Baader-Meinhof gang; Botha, Shamir, Mejia Victores, Pinochet, D'Aubuisson, Suarez Mason, and WACL carry out more mundane services.

THE PRIVATE SECTOR INSTITUTES AND THINK TANKS

A prime function of the terrorism institutes and think tanks is to support individuals who will expound the proper views. By being brought to an institute which declares itself devoted to advancing knowledge and helping policy-makers on an "independent and non-partisan" basis (as all of these coopted and biased ventures do), the selected individuals are accredited as "experts." The funding and publicity given them by the institutes adds to their authority status. The institutes also hold conferences and seminars on terrorism, in which their own and other experts participate, giving outreach and publicity to their views. The Israeli government-sponsored Jonathan Institute has sponsored conferences as its primary operation, those held in July 1979 and June 1984 attracting worldwide attention to the issues as perceived by the Israeli government and terrorism establishment.

Many of the institutes and think tanks that are important components of the terrorism industry originated or grew rapidly as part of a major corporate offensive in the 1970s. John Saloma has described the development of a "conservative labyrinth" of foundations and private institutions designed to parlay corporate resources into coopting intellectuals, subsidizing sound views, providing for the networking of right-wing intellectuals, and establishing an intellectual hegemony of the right by sheer force of money and propaganda.[47] By the mid-1980s organizations like the Hoover Institution, American Enterprise Institute (AEI), the CSIS, and the Heritage Foundation each had annual budgets in excess of $10 million, and Heritage had become sufficiently affluent to be able to finance foreign progeny in Great Britain and elsewhere.

Some of the larger institutes that are part of the terrorism industry operate in many different spheres of intellectual activity and policy interest. The big four in the United States – Heritage, the CSIS, the AEI, and Hoover – are fairly diverse in their activities. As "terrorism" became a perceived area of policy interest these "conglomerates" entered that field, sponsored experts to deal with it, and provided support for their activities. Quite a few institutes specialize in terrorism more narrowly, and some are largely the vehicle for single individuals.

Many of the terrorism industry institutes operate on a shoestring, depending on research contracts with government and on consultancies with business firms wanting advice on political risk and security problems. Some, however, have gotten government money, and others get money from sources close to government. The ISC in Great Britain was started with CIA funding, but after exposure in the press the funding was transferred to Richard Mellon Scaife. Scaife has been an important funder for many institutions that comprise the "conservative labyrinth" in the United States, and, as with the Crozier operation, they may be regarded as serving a larger state interest whose funding as between government bodies and the corporate elite depends on convenience.

The large institutes in the United States obtain the bulk of their funding from a broad constituency of corporations and the corporate wealthy, with only modest financial aid from government. In 1986, the CSIS, for example, raised its $14 million mainly from 153 corporations and 92 foundations (mostly corporate based), including 26 companies heavily involved in supplying weapons to the Pentagon. The corporate establishment and military-industrial complex in particular find the CSIS a worthy investment.

Although the Heritage Foundation makes the CSIS look centrist by comparison, this is illusory. The CSIS has a strong right-wing bias, and its investigations, conferences, panels, and reports are frequently well geared to government and right-wing propaganda lines. In the early 1970s, the CSIS played an important role in the destabilization of the Allende regime in Chile. Its director of Latin American Studies, James Theberge, claimed to have uncovered a clandestine Korean communist guerrilla training camp at which Chilean leftists learned how to intimidate the "democratic opposition [which they allegedly did] during the electoral campaign of March 1973." These fabrications were planted in Chilean newspapers and military journals, all attributed to an institute in Washington, DC. Fred Landis pointed out that "it served the CIA well to have such non-news circulated by a friendly 'expert' and laundered through a reputable news organization like UPI."[48]

The CSIS also organized a conference on the Red threat to Italy, which was held just before the Italian elections of 1976. The panel included William Colby and Ray Cline, both from the CIA; John Connally, a member of the Foreign Intelligence Oversight Board; Claire Booth Luce, former ambassador to Italy; and Claire Sterling. The composition of this group points up the CSIS's close ties to government, its "action" mission, and its lack of connection to anything resembling objective scholarship. For this group the Italian scene presented a "national security" threat to the United States and called for forceful intervention.[49]

One day after the CSIS conference, an article co-authored by Sterling and Ledeen, entitled "Italy's Russian Sugar Daddies," appeared in the *New Republic*; it claimed that the Soviets were secretly funding the Italian Communist party through a network of import – export businesses. This essay, reprinted in the CIA-funded *Rome Daily American* and in *Il Borghese*, the official organ of the neo-fascist Movimento Sociala Italiano (MSI), was distributed to reporters from the United States at the request of the US Embassy.[50] It served to divert attention away from the fact that the United States itself was secretly funding centrist and right-wing parties in a massive interventionary operation.[51]

More recently, and illustrative of the continued non-scholarly, propagandistic, and right-wing bent of the CSIS, in 1984 a CSIS panel was organized on the alleged KGB-Bulgarian plot to kill the Pope. Long-time CIA official Paul Henze, as well as Arnaud de Borchgrave, Robert

Kupperman, Zbigniew Brzezinski, Max Kampelman, Ray Cline, and Marvin Kalb were members. The panel took the then still unadjudicated case as proven, assailed the US government for not proclaiming its truth, and peddled some extremely foolish right-wing claims of Soviet influence over the Western media.[52] This was a propaganda exercise of no intellectual content, designed to exploit the belief in Soviet guilt which had been encouraged by the US government, terrorism experts Sterling, Henze, and others, and the mass media.

The right-wing thrust and propaganda function of the CSIS is shown in the early role of Theberge and the conferences and panels discussed above. The CSIS's journal, *Washington Quarterly*, has been edited by Michael Ledeen, a long-time collaborator with Claire Sterling and closely tied to the Italian and Israeli secret services, and, more recently, to Haig and the Reagan administration. Ray Cline, a long-time CIA official with strong ties to WACL and other far-right governments and institutions, has been a major figure in CSIS activities. The fact that the CSIS appointed as an "Adjunct Scholar" Arnaud de Borchgrave – far-right journalist, editor of the Unification Church paper and magazine *Washington Times* and *Insight on the News*, and collaborator with Birchite John Rees – is indicative of the organizations concept of "scholarship."

The revolving door between the CSIS and the US intelligence agencies has been active, and Fred Landis's designation of the organization as an "ivory tower for old spooks" is apt. Ledeen, Walter Laqueur, and Edward Luttwak, another CSIS stalwart, have had very close relationships with Israel and Mossad, as well as with US government officials. The CSIS is a truly "multinational" member of the terrorism industry.

THE EXPERTS

The link between the institutes or think tanks and the mass media is provided by the large body of "experts" on terrorism, or "terrorologists," who publish books, articles, and monographs through the leading publishing houses, the mainstream press, and newsletters and journals issued by the various institutions which house them. With the aid of their sponsoring organizations, these experts attend one another's conferences and seminars, serve on the editorial advisory boards of one another's journals (such as *Terrorism* and *Conflict Quarterly*), review their colleagues' books, write forewords for each other, and cite one another copiously. By this mutually supportive network, these experts establish their facts as true and their very similar assumptions and opinions as mere common sense. They validate themselves and each other through an echo chamber.

In analysing the linkages and opinions of the terrorism experts our hypotheses are that: (1) the private sector experts will tend to be affiliated to governments currently or to have been so connected in the recent past; (2) they will often be associated with institutes and think tanks organized to push establishment views, many with a strong right-wing bias; (3) many of them will be linked directly or indirectly to the international ultra-right, exemplified by the Unification Church system and WACL; (4) many will be connected with private sector security firms; and (5) the experts will rarely if ever depart from the official Western model and line on terrorism, and, given the right-wing bias of the institutes, will in fact tend to expound the far-right version of the line.

Ultimately, we are most interested in those analysts of terrorism who are accredited as experts by the mass media, and who are thus allowed to define the issues and given access to the public. Experts also include those who are cited frequently by specialists in the field and mobilized as witnesses at hearings and participants in conferences. The list below gives first the 16 leading experts on terrorism, based on citations from a representative mass media sample of 135 news items on the subject.[53] It then lists 13 experts, based on number of citations to their work by other terrorism experts, as reported in Schmid's volumes on *Political Terrorism*.[54] There are five individuals common to lists A and B, so that the two together provide 24 separate experts. To this set of 24, we have added eight supplementary names, based on our judgment of their importance as measured by influence and outreach.

16 experts, based on citations in 135-media-item sample

Brian Jenkins	Paul Henze
Robert Kupperman	William Colby
Neil Livingstone	Uri Ra-Anan
Paul Wilkinson	Ariel Merari
Michael Ledeen	Joseph Churba
Lawrence Eagleberger	Fouad Ajami
Claire Sterling	Ray Cline
Yonah Alexander	Walter Laqueur

13 experts, according to expert citations in Schmid

Paul Wilkinson	E.V.Mickalous
Michael Crozier	Brian Jenkins
Walter Laqueur	Richard Clutterbuck
Ted Gurr	Yonah Alexander
E.V. Walter	J.B. Bell
M.C. Bassiouni	Margaret Crenshaw
Robert Kupperman	

Supplementary list of 8 major terrorism experts

Arnaud de Borchgrave   Robert Moss
Lord Alan Chalfont   Richard Pipes
Samuel Francis   Stepan Possony
Jeane Kirkpatrick   Maurice Tugwell

In table 3.2 the institutional connections of these experts are shown on an aggregated basis in rows 1 through 7, and some important characteristics of their opinions and perspectives can seen in rows 8 and 9. Columns 1 and 2 of the table provide this information for the 16 individuals who were the experts in our media sample. The third and fourth columns give similar data for a larger set of 32 leading experts on terrorism, which includes all of those in the first two columns, plus 16 others. It can be seen that the differences in connections and opinions between these two sets are small.

The table offers striking confirmation of our major hypotheses. First, we can see in entries 1–3 how closely the private experts are linked to

Table 3.2 Linkages and perspectives of the terrorism industry experts

Characteristic	Media 16		Big 32	
	No.	%	No.	%
1 US government link	11	68.8	20	62.5
CIA	(4)	(25.0)	(7)	(21.9)
2 British government link	1	6.3	6	(18.8)
Army/police	(1)	(6.3)	(6)	(18.8)
3 Net government affiliated	12	75.0	22	68.8
4 Institute/think tank	11	68.8	23	71.9
Big Four[a]	(5)	(31.3)	(13)	(40.6)
Moon related	(3)	(18.8)	(5)	(15.6)
Israel lobby related	(2)	(12.5)	(4)	(12.5)
5 Risk analysis/security	8	50.0	15	46.9
6 Journalist	1	6.3	5	15.6
7 Academic	5	31.3	13	40.6
8 Focuses on left and insurgent terror	16	100.0	31	96.9
9 Fit in classification by model:				
Moderate establishment	4	25.0	6	18.8
Right-wing establishment	10	62.5	20	62.5
Dissident	–	–	1	3.1
None[b]	2	12.5	5	15.6

[a] Heritage, Hoover, the AEI, and the CSIS.
[b] No model evident in published writings.

governments. Over two-thirds have had some US or British government affiliation in the recent past, and between a fifth and a quarter have had a CIA connection. Conferences on terrorism commonly include as major speakers both the private-sector experts and government officials, who operate collegially and whose views are hard to tell apart. William Casey, head of the CIA during much of the Reagan era, was the featured speaker at the 1985 conference on terrorism at the Fletcher School of Diplomacy, addressing the subject of "The International Linkages: What Do We Know?" Casey fitted in smoothly; the experts had no problems accommodating the activist head of an activist intelligence agency into the scholarly proceedings.

These linkages between government officials and the experts suggests the strong likelihood that the experts will adhere to a government party line; or, put another way, it points to a certain lack of independence on the part of these experts. This should raise questions about their suitability as sole sources for a supposedly independent – not to say adversarial – press. It is a striking fact that the media not only do not seem to have qualms about this lack of independence, they do not appear to be aware that this is a problem. The assumptions and truths of state officials are so taken for granted that a symbiotic relation between the state and the "independent" press is not seen to contaminate the press function. This even extends to an unquestioning (and often undisclosed) use of CIA, ex-CIA, and other state intelligence functionaries (Colby, Cline, Crozier, Henze, Moss, Tugwell, etc.), who are treated as presumably objective news sources and analysts. Only in other countries is government penetration and control of the press compromising to press integrity.

A second theme of this analysis of experts is that, in order to mobilize bias, the government and corporate elite have nurtured those with the proper views by providing them with financial support and institutes in which to work. It can be seen in entry 4 of table 3.2 that over two-thirds of the experts have been affiliated with institutes and think tanks. As we indicated earlier, these organizations have been funded and otherwise supported by dominant establishment institutions – corporations, corporate foundations, the government, and the wealthy heirs of the corporate system. This funding and support relationship is conspicuously true of the big four institutes – Heritage, Hoover, the CSIS, and the AEI – with which a very sizable fraction of the experts have been associated. We can see in entry 4 that between 30 and 40 percent of the experts have been affiliated with this leading foursome. It can also be seen that there are significant connections between the mainstream terrorism experts and Moon supported institutes and those affiliated with the Israeli lobby.

In entry 5 of table 3.2 we can also see that about half of the mainstream experts have been affiliated with private firms in the risk analysis and security business. This linkage tends to compromise them as experts on terrorism, partly because they sell their services to businesses and governments which have restricted views on the nature of terrorism. They also have a vested interest in "threat inflation," as their business is contingent on an adequate volume of terrorism for their clients to be protected against. Security business also ties the participants more closely to the government security establishment in an informational exchange and revolving door relationship.

Five of the establishment experts are journalists, and a larger number are academics. These relationships often overlap with ties to government and the institutes. Arnaud de Borchgrave, Brian Crozier, Robert Moss, and Claire Sterling are classed as journalists, but the first three have had important links to governments and institutes; Sterling has been funded by the *Reader's Digest*, which has had long-standing CIA connections,[55] and her links to western intelligence agencies, and to the various terrorism institutes and experts, have been collegial and mutually supportive.[56] Roughly one-third of the experts have had an academic connection (entry 7), but a great majority of these experts have also had links to governments, the institutes, and risk analysis firms. This is evident among the most prestigious experts, who are also most heavily cited by the media, like Laqueur and Wilkinson. The relatively sizable contingent of academics in columns 3 and 4 results from the fact that the sample of 32 includes those listed by Schmid as heavily cited by other experts, who refer to some of the more esoteric and quantitative literature by E. V. Walter, L. C. Bassiouni, Ted Gurr, and Martha Crenshaw. The first two have had only academic connections, and they have only rarely been cited in the media.

Turning to the views of the experts, we can see from entry 8 that virtually all of the experts focus on left and insurgent terror. In entry 9, it can be seen that only one of the 32 experts, namely M. C. Bassiouni, departs from the Western model of terrorism.[57] Similarly, looking at where the experts fit into our classification of terrorism models – dissident, moderate establishment, and right-wing establishment – all the experts for whom it is possible to make a judgment, except Bassiouni, adhere to the two establishment versions of the Western model. We may note, also, the right-wing domination of the expert pattern. Roughly two-thirds of the classifiable experts expound the extremist version of the establishment model, in which the Soviet Union directs or coordinates world terrorism, national liberation movements are generally tabbed as terrorist organizations or agents of world Communism, and hardline policies of national and international response are espoused.

The bias of the western experts is shown more directly and dramatically in table 3.3, which summarizes the topics covered in the major books of three of our terrorism experts – Laqueur, Sterling, and Wilkinson – plus the popular and oft-cited book, *The Terrorists: Their Weapons, Leaders, and Tactics*, by Christopher Dobson and Robert Payne. We have tallied the coverage by counting the references in the indexes of these books to a dozen Western and right-wing terrorists or operations, on the one hand, and a dozen non-Western or left-wing terrorists, on the other. It can be seen at the most cursory inspection that Western and right-wing terror is off the experts' agenda and is essentially suppressed. Neither Saad Hadaad, the Israeli proxy in Lebanon, nor Stefano Delle Chiaie, the major Italian terrorist, appear in the indexes of these four volumes; whereas the Baader-Meinhof gang is mentioned 115 times and Carlos 60 times. Overall, the dozen Western/right-wing terrorists or operations are addressed twice; the dozen non-state/left-wing terrorists are mentioned 733 times. Only approved terror and terrorists are discussed by these authors.

4 The Mass Media as Transmission Belt of the Terrorism Industry

The terrorism industry produces the Western "line" on terrorism and selects the appropriately supportive facts, and the mass media disseminate these to the public. The transmission process is smooth, as the mass media pass along the manufactured messages without further substantial processing, and function essentially as conduits. Although self-designated as "watchdogs" and described by their right-wing critics as "adversaries" to established power, the US mass media have raised no questions about the premises and agenda of the terrorism industry, and generally fail even to filter out or correct literal error.

The dominance of government and private-sector members of the terrorism industry in mass media sourcing is displayed clearly in table 3.4, which shows the distribution of source citations in a representative sample of 135 articles and news broadcasts on terrorism in the years 1978–85.[58] It can be seen that US government officials account for 42 percent of the citations in the sample articles; all Western governments account for 55 percent of the aggregate media sourcing. The 16 private-sector experts most often tapped by the media were cited 71 times, or 24 percent of all citations. Of these 16 non-government experts, 12 were former government officials, 12 were affiliated with one or more of the terrorism industry think tanks, and only one could be reasonably described as an

Table 3.3 References by terrorism industry experts to Western right-wing and non-Western left-wing terrorism[a]

Type of terrorism	Dobson–Payne	Laqueur	Wilkinson	Sterling
Western/right-wing				
Roberto D'Aubuisson	–	–	–	–
Stefano Delle Chiaie	–	–	–	–
Orlando Bosch-CORU	–	–	1	–
Luis Posada Carriles	–	–	–	–
Botha–South Africa	–	(2)[b]	(1)[b]	–
Operation Condor	–	–	–	–
Pinochet	–	–	–	–
Videla	(2)[b]	–	–	–
Sharon–Begin–Yaron	(1)[b]	–	(2)[b]	.
Saad Haddad	–	–	–	–
Contras–Reagan–North	–	1	(4)[b]	–
Tecos (Mexico)	–	–	–	–
Total	0	1	1	0
Non-western/left-wing				
Arafat-Fatah-PLO	22	26	10	51
Carlos	11	7	2	40
Abu Nidal	11	16	1	2
Marighela	8	8	6	11
Baader-Meinhof	34	19	4	36
Red Brigades	15	22	2	57
Tupamaros	5	19	6	22
Castro–Cuba	4	19	15	40
Gadaffi–Libya	18	21	13	34
Soviet Union	–	9	11	54
Weathermen	5	7	2	2
Black Panthers	1	2	–	3
Totals	134	175	72	352

[a] Based on citations from the indexes of books listed by author, namely: Christopher Dobson and Robert Payne, *The Terrorists: Their Weapons, Leaders and Tactics* (Facts on File, revised edn, 1982); Walter Laqueur, *The Age of Terrorism* (Little, Brown, 1987); Paul Wilkinson, *Terrorism and the Liberal State* (New York University Press, revised edn, 1986); Claire Sterling, *The Terror Network* (Holt, Rinehart, Winston/Reader's Digest, 1981).

[b] Means that while individual or group are listed in index, they are not treated as a terrorist in the text, but rather as a victim of terror or as somebody having to cope with terrorists.

independent source of information.[59] Government experts plus the 16 non-government (but largely government affiliated) experts account for 80 percent of all citations. As noted in table 3.4, a majority of the "other" sources are victims in terrorist incidents, who recount their experiences, fears and reactions to the media. The number of individuals used as sources by the media who contest in any way the "industry" premises and opinions (here classed as "dissidents") is exceedingly small.

The mass media's uncritical reliance on government and the private-sector experts of the terrorism industry as sources allows the Western model and line on terrorism to prevail in newsmaking as a matter of course and without significant dissent. It also causes the biased definitions and dichotomies of the Western model and line to seem entirely natural. In the words of Stuart Hall, "The dominant definition of the problem acquires, by repetition, and by the weight and credibility of those who propose and subscribe it, the warrant of 'common sense'."[60] The media also contribute to the institutionalization of an official line by the extreme superficiality of their news offerings. It is normal procedure to offer a brief summary of official claims without any discussion of word meaning and usage, analysis of any arbitrariness and illogic, or evaluation of factual claims.

As an illustration, on the Ted Koppel Nightline show of June 25, 1984, Israeli Ambassador to the United States Benjamin Netanyahu was invited by reporter Betsy Aaron to comment on the oft-cited incident which took place at Ma'alot in 1974 as an illustration of Arab–PLO terror. He said: "We had 20 school children massacred because we couldn't get to them

Table 3.4 Mass media sources in covering "terrorism"[a]

Source	Number of citations	Percent
US government officials	123	42.3
Other Western country officials	38	13.1
Private-sector "experts"[b]	71	24.4
Dissidents[c]	4	1.4
Other[d]	55	18.9
Total	291	100.0

[a] Based on a sample of 135 TV and press news reports on terrorism, 1978–86 (described in n. 58).

[b] The 16 terrorism industry authorities most frequently cited in our mass media sample: see list on p. 000.

[c] The only individuals in our sample who contested mainstream assumptions were two spokesmen for the ACLU and two Palestinian academics on the *McNeil–Lehrer Newshour*.

[d] The large category "other" includes mainly the "victims" of terrorist acts, especially hostages interviewed after their release.

in time, and the terrorists murdered them." In fact, most of the children died in an assault by Israeli troops and were killed by Israeli gunfire, as the Israeli government refused to negotiate in any way with the hostage-takers. Furthermore, the children were not small, but teenagers who were members of a paramilitary youth group (Gadna). The hostage-taking was "preceded by weeks of sustained Israeli napalm bombing of Palestinian refugee camps in southern Lebanon," with some 200 persons killed. Just two days prior to the episode reported to the Western public, an Israeli air attack on the village of El-Kjeir in Lebanon killed four civilians.[61] As we pointed out earlier, the Western media regularly suppress evidence of the primary terrorism, causing the responses of the victims to appear as seemingly unprovoked and inexplicably evil. This may result not merely from the suppression of context, but also by perpetrating literal fabrications that are not correctable (simple murder of innocents by the hostage-takers), as Betsy Aaron, Netanyahu, and Koppel do here.

In accord with the Western model and agenda, the US government and terrorism experts attend closely to and wax furious over Libyan support of Abu Nidal, but treat in a low key and without the slightest indignation Israel's support of Saad Haddad and South Africa's sponsorship of proxy armies in Angola and Mozambique. The mass media follow along without question, with news and comment structured accordingly. The terrorists are those whom the terrorism industry designates terrorists; they do this in accordance with a Western propaganda line and political agenda, and the mass media follow like lapdogs.

As we indicated earlier, the Western model of terrorism focuses on non-state actors, as too many Western client states would have to be condemned if the traditional meaning was allowed to prevail. In fact, a major purpose of the intensified Reagan era focus on "terrorism" was to deflect attention away from Argentina, Chile, Guatemala, and South Africa, and onto the Red Brigades and PLO. We can see in table 3.5 that the US mass media followed the Reagan agenda closely, just as the experts did (table 3.3). In our sample of news reports, non-state terrorists outnumbered state terrorists by 96 to 10. In the CBS news coverage of 1981, summarized in table 3.6, the ratio was 152 to 5, if we exclude Libya, which was the premier "terrorist" of 1981, as CBS news – along with the rest of the media – intently followed the career of the mythical Libyan "hit squad" late in that year.

Of the state terrorists identified by the media, all but one were non-Western states, as shown in table 3.5. In that single exceptional case, a news article cites *Arab* spokesmen declaring Israel's bombing of an Iraq reactor to be an act of terrorism. In other words, not a single article or broadcast in this media sample cited a Western source identifying a Western state or client as a terrorist state. Note that this was a period of mass

Table 3.5   State and non-state terrorism and terrorists and their political affiliations, as portrayed in the US mass media[a]

Category	No. of citations
State and non-state actors as terrorists	
Non-state	96
State	10
Political characteristics of state and non-state terrorists	
State.	
Non-Western	9
Western	1[b]
Non-state.	
Left-wing	60[c]
Right-wing	10
Unclear	28
States identified as sponsoring terrorism	
Western:	
United States	1[d]
Non-Western:	
Libya	31
Soviet Union	30
Iran	25
Syria	16
Cuba	11
North Korea	10
South Yemen	5
Iraq	2
Nicaragua	2

[a] Derived from sample of 135 news reports (see n. 58).

[b] A news article in the *New York Times* (June 9, 1981) features *Arab* accusations that the 1981 Israeli bombing of an Iraqi nuclear reactor was an act of international terrorism. When Israelis shot down a civilian Libyan aircraft in 1973, the only *Times* usage of words like "criminal" and "murderous" was in quotations from Arab sources. But those words were used often by the Western press in reference to the Soviet shooting down of Korean airlinear 007.

[c] The subtotals here do not add up to 96 because some articles cite both right-wing and left-wing terrorisms.

[d] In the last two paragraphs of a news article in the *Philadelphia Inquirer*, April 18, 1984, two reporters are quoted asking Reagan press officer Speakes whether the US support of the Contras does not constitute state sponsorship of terrorism, which he vigorously denied.

murder in Argentina and Guatemala, and massive internal repression and external attacks by South Africa, but these do not show up once as cases of state terrorism in the 135 sample articles and broadcasts. The CBS index for 1981 shows 45 non-Western and three Western cases of state terrorism, the latter including El Salvador, the only instance in which a

Table 3.6 Terrorists as seen by CBS-TV News in 1981[a]

Category	No. of appearances
State versus non-state actors as terrorists	
State	48
(State exclusive of Libya)	(5)
Non-state	152
Political classification of terrorists	
State:	
Libya	43
Soviet Union	2
Western states and clients	3[b]
Non-state:	
Left-wing	71
Right-wing	11
Unclear	70[c]
Names of states or groups engaged in or sponsoring terrorism	
Western or right-wing:	
El Salvador government	1[c]
US government	1[c]
Israel	1[c]
Jewish Defense League	1
Agca and Gray Wolves	6[d]
Non-Western and/or left-wing:	
Libya	43
Red Brigades	18
IRA	15
PLO	13
Weathermen	12
El Salvadoran rebels	6
Soviet Union	2
Black guerrillas of South Africa	2
Guatemalan rebels	1
Pro-Syrian group	1
Armenian	3
Puerto Rican rebels	2

[a] Based on an analysis of the titles of all the 1981 entries in the CBS index under the heading "Terrorism".

[b] The accusation against the Salvadoran government was made by the archibishop of El Salvador; the claim that the United States is engaged in terrorism was made by Khomeini; the allegation that Israel was a terrorist state cited in the CBS News index was by an Arab.

[c] The large number that were unclear was based in part on the ambiguity of index titles, although a very substantial number were hijackings and other terrorist acts that seemed to have no left-right political identification.

[d] In 1981, before Sterling and the Western media tied Agca to Bulgaria and the KGB, his political affiliations were identified as right-wing.

Latin America terror state is cited as a state terrorist. The disproportion is similarly large in press designation of Western and non-Western state sponsorship of terrorism, as can be seen in tables 3.5 and 3.6. This has nothing to do with the substance of terrorism; it reflects a political agenda running from Western states to the Western terrorism industry to the Western media, which exempts its own from an invidious designation.

5 Conclusions

The development, activities, and influence of the terrorism industry illustrate how the powerful dominate the Western mass media and public perceptions of reality through processes which appear entirely natural. The government and corporate wealthy nourish the institutes and think tanks that service and sponsor the suitable intellectuals and journalists, who convey the proper messages. The design is to give authoritative status to experts who will confirm and reinforce state propaganda, to occupy the informational space that might otherwise be entered by dissident voices, and thus to ensure closure of fact and opinion. These selected analysts are also pushed by major media enterprises, whose principals strive to advance conservative propaganda themes (*Reader's Digest*, *Time*, *Wall Street Journal*, and *New York Times*), and by the numerous right-wing syndicated columnists who aggressively propagandize these themes (William Buckley, Jr., George Will, Evans and Novak, Jeane Kirkpatrick, James Kilpatrick, William Rusher, Raymond Price, etc.). The industry messages quickly become common sense; alternative views appear eccentric and wild.

It is not considered relevant by the mass media, nor is it disclosed to the public, that the experts are coopted and reflect the views of the government and powerful vested interests. Thus even CIA assets with badly tarnished records as paid propagandists are advanced as unbiased experts and asked open-ended questions. This is encouraged by the fact that the truth of the government–state position is quickly established as beyond question, so that the function of experts is merely to clarify and elaborate on pre-established truths. This reflects an effective propaganda system.

In fact, the achievement of the terrorism industry is of a high order. In his book *Black Athena: The Afroasiatic Roots of Classical Civilization, Volume 1: The Fabrication of Ancient Greece 1785–1985*,[62] Martin Bernal shows how the classical scholars and intellectuals of the West, from the late eighteenth into the twentieth centuries, paralleling the subjugation of the black and other colonialized races by Western imperialism, succeeded in expunging from Western portrayals of Ancient

Greece the notion expounded by Herodotus (and traditional Greek scholarship) that classical Greece had been profoundly influenced by Asian and African cultures. In a great feat of ideologically based cleansing, the fount of Western civilization was purified and shown to have been of purely Aryan origin and free of alien influences. We believe that the conversion of the West into the victim of "terrorism" and its victims into the "terrorists" is, in light of the facts, an equal or greater achievement of Western scholarship and journalism.

Notes

1   In 1963, General Robert Porter explained to the US Congress that US aid and training programs in the Third World were "an insurance policy protecting our vast foreign investment" (Quoted in Jan Black, *United States Penetration of Brazil* (University of Pennsylvania Press, 1977), p. 228). For evidence that this political end was the basis of US aid and training programs, see Edward S. Herman and Gerry O'Sullivan, *The "Terrorism" Industry* (Pantheon Books, 1990), chapter 2, and sources cited there.

2   This demand was explicit in speeches by high Israeli leaders at the Jonathan Institute Conference of July 1979 and in Reagan and Haig pronouncements in 1981 in the United States. See Herman and O'Sullivan, *The "Terrorism" Industry*.

3   See W. Lance Bennett, *News: The Politics of Illusion* (Longman, 2nd edn, 1988); Mark Hertsgaard, *On Bended Knee: The Press and the Reagan Presidency* (Farrar Straus Giroux, 1988); Edward S. Herman and Noam Chomsky, *Manufacturing Consent: The Political Economy of the Mass Media* (Pantheon, 1988).

4   The academic analyst of terrorism Alex P. Schmid, in his compilation of the literature and expert opinion on the subject, *Political Terrorism* (North Holland Publishing Company, 1983), points out that of the 50 experts on terrorism who responded to his questionnaire, only one had generated original data on state terror, while 18 had done this for non-state terror (p. 274). He notes that "Given the ubiquity of rule by terror the uneven attention given to regime terrorism in contrast to insurgent terrorism by social scientists is depressing" (p. 174). The closest that Schmid comes to explaining this is his statement that: "The academic literature on terrorism has depended heavily on data provided by governments or thinktanks contracted by government agencies. Many authors have also sought to give advice and guidance to antiterrorist agencies of governments. The result has not been a happy one" (p. 180).

5   See I.E. Sagay, "State Terrorism in South Africa," United Nations Centre Against Apartheid, *Notes and Documents* (October 1984); Joseph Hanlon, *Beggar Your Neighbors: Apartheid Power in Southern Africa* (Catholic Institute for International Relations, 1986), pp. 1–2, 21–3; Richard Leonard, *South Africa At War* (Lawrence Hill & Co., 1983), chapter 2; Gervasi and

Wong's chapter in this book and works cited therein.

6 For a good summary, see Penny Lernoux, *Cry of the People* (Doubleday, 1980), pp. 81–107.

7 Shultz's statement was issued by the Bureau of Public Affairs of the US Department of State as Current Policy Release No. 589, "Terrorism: The Challenge to the Democracies" (June 24, 1984). The quotations in this section are all taken from this paper.

8 See under "The Semantics of Terrorism," below, the Orwellian use of "retaliation" in the West.

9 This is an audacious position, coming from a Reagan administration spokesman, whose government gave critical and maximum feasible support to South African aggression, and whose move to unilateralism and denial of the authority of the International Court of Justice is well known. On the abandonment of legality by this government, see Walter Karp, "Liberty Under Siege," *Harper's* (November 1985); "Special Issue on Domestic Surveillance," *CovertAction Information Bulletin*, No. 31 (Winter 1989); Eve Pell, *The Big Chill* (Beacon Press, 1984); and Noam Chomsky, *Culture of Terrorism* (South End, 1988).

10 The Nicaraguan Contras were organized by the CIA out of the remnants of Somoza's National Guard. In 1988, with US support, the leadership of the Contras was given over to Colonel Enrique Bermudez, a long-time leader of the National Guard. This did not cause the US mass media to question the "democratic" aim of the "resistance." Shultz's assertion that "The contras in Nicaragua do not blow up school buses or hold mass executions of civilians" will surely go down in history as a classic Big Lie, as the documentation of the murder of civilians as standard operating procedure of the Contras was already massive in 1984. See Reed Brody, *Contra Terror in Nicaragua* (South End, 1985), for 145 sworn affidavits on Contra atrocities against civilians, and other materials. See also Americas Watch's reports on human rights in Nicaragua, which support the same conclusion.

11 On the long-term terrorist assault on Cuba, see Warren Hinckle and William Turner, *The Fish is Red* (Harper & Row, 1981); on the attacks on Angola and Mozambique, Hanlon, *Beggar Your Neighbors*; on the issue more generally, Herman, *The Real Terror Network*, pp. 62–82, and William Blum, *The CIA: A Forgotten History* (Zed Books, 1986), *passim*.

12 Simpson and Bennett, *The Disappeared and the Mothers of the Plaza*, p. 189.

13 Quoted in ibid., p. 399. We have added the italics.

14 As this comes from a spokesman for the country that destroyed two Japanese cities with atom bombs and continues to refuse to pledge no first use of atomic weapons, a country that developed and used heavily in Vietnam napalm, phosphorus, and fragmentation bombs, and deposited 18 million gallons of defoliants on the Vietnamese countryside – among many other innovations and contributions – we can only marvel at the chutzpah of power.

15 See the Rand Corporation expert Brian Jenkins' review of Claire Sterling's *The Terror Network*, described as a "conjuror's" operation, *International Herald Tribune* (May 28, 1981); and the denunciation of Ray Cline's Soviet

network theory by a group of CIA analysts, in Jeff Stein, "Old Spies and Cold Peas," *Inquiry* (December 19, 1980), p. 20.

16 John Kelly, "Casey's Terrorism Math," *Counterspy* (June–August 1983), p. 9; Ralph McGehee, "Terrorism," *Zeta Magazine* (February 1988), p. 60; Bob Woodward, *Veil: The Secret Wars of the CIA 1981–1987* (Simon & Schuster, 1987), pp. 122–9.

17 The moderates view Soviet aid to terrorists as ad hoc and opportunistic, not a centrally coordinated operation designed to destabilize democracies everywhere.

18 In fact, some of the experts *define* terrorism as the use of violence in combination with a search for publicity for the violent event. See Brian Jenkins, *International Terrorism: A New Mode of Conflict* (Crescent, 1975), p. 4; Gabriel Weimann, "Mass Mediated Theater of Terror: Must the Show Go On?," in Peter Bruck (ed.), *The News Media and Terrorism* (Discussion Document Series, Carleton University, undated), pp. 1–2.

19 This applies to most of the experts who fall into the "right-wing establishment" category (Ledeen, deBorchgrave, Moss, Henze, Sterling, etc.), and some of the others. See the statement of Chalfont in n. 21 below.

20 The Western right-wing and most of the terrorism establishment furiously oppose any focus on "root causes" of terrorism, although they all enjoy taking cracks at the middle-class, alienated backgrounds of Baader-Meinhof and other Western retail terrorists. For Paul Johnson, speaking at the Jonathan Institute Conference of 1979, "The wrong approach is to see terrorism as one of the many symptoms of a deep-seated malaise in our society . . . It is an international offensive – an open and declared war on civilization itself" (in Benjamin Netanyhu (ed.), *International Terrorism: Challenge and Response* (Transaction Books, 1981), pp. 12 and 15). In more sophisticated analyses, root causes are dismissed as hard to pinpoint, and leading to inaction. The British Institute for the Study of Terrorism (IST) issued a document in 1988 on "Terrorism and Root Causes," emphasizing these points. Although IST spends a great deal of its effort on South Africa and the ANC, its illustrations of terrorism for the purpose of discussing root causes are drawn from advanced countries – the hang-ups of the alienated radicals. As regards South Africa and the ANC, IST does not mention root causes – only the Red connections of the ANC.

21 At the Jonathan Institute Conference of 1984, Lord Alan Chalfont asserted that a real problem of "the quality press" is "its tendency to adopt a position of magisterial objectivity between our society and those attacking it," and "to equate the actions of legitimate governments, such as that in El Salvador, in fighting terrorists and revolutionaries with the activities of the terrorists themselves" ("Lost in the Terrorist Theater," *Harper's* (October 1984), p. 56). This is a common neo-conservative formulation. The "legitimacy" of the Salvadoran government was itself a major achievement of the "quality press" in its service to "our" side, but Chalfont assumes that this legitimation was based on objective truth, so that further rallying behind this legitimized government is called for. His claim of the magisterial objectivity of the quality press between friends and enemies stands the truth on its head. See

the discussion of "Worthy and Unworthy Victims" in Herman and Chomsky, *Manufacturing Consent*, chapter 2.

22 See David L. Paletz, Peter Fozzard, and John Ayanian, "The I.R.A., the Red Brigades, and the F.A.L.N. in the New York Times," *Journal of Communication* (Spring 1982), pp. 162–71. See also Edward S. Herman and Gabriel Weimann, in Peter A. Bruck (ed.), "The News Media and Terrorism" (Discussion Document Series, Carleton University, 1988).

23 Haig's remarks "immediately raised two questions: What did Mr Haig mean by terrorism? What evidence did he have to support the charges against the Soviet Union? Neither question has been resolved" (Philip Taubman, "US Tries to Back Up Haig on Terrorism," *New York Times* (May 3, 1981)).

24 In an interview with the Johannesburg *Financial Mail* (November 18, 1983), Lichenstein said that "destabilization will remain in force until Angola and Mozambique do not permit their country to be used by terrorists to attack South Africa." It may also be noted that Lichenstein implies that South Africa and the United States operate on the same plan as regards destabilization.

25 Samuel Francis, Lord ALan Chalfont, Ray Cline, and Yonah Alexander do this directly; Claire Sterling and Paul Wilkinson do it indirectly, by giving heavy weight to these organizations' connection with leftists abroad and support by the Soviet Union. Chalfont, who was chairman of the Jonathan Institute Conference held in Washington, DC, in June 1984, did not cite the ANC as a terrorist organization in his introductory speech, as this conference attempted to get the basic Western message across to a large US audience, and calling the ANC a terrorist organization would not have gone over well with such an audience. But in his foreword to a monograph by Keith Campbell, *ANC: A Soviet Task Force?* (Institute for the Study of Terrorism, 1986), Chalfont alleges that "nothing could be further from the truth" than the claim that the ANC is a "straightforward nationalist movement" – it is a communist front organization using "the method of terrorism." This document was put out by the IST, which Chalfont chairs and which propagandizes heavily in favor of the apartheid regime of South Africa. This major theme of Chalfont's organization is disseminated only to congenial audiences, or surreptitiously.

26 CIA, *Patterns of International Terrorism, 1980*, p. ii.

27 Former CIA director Stansfield Turner testified before the House Subcommittee on Western Hemispheric Affairs on April 16, 1985, that US organization and support of the Contras would "have to be characterized as terrorism, as state-sponsored terrorism" (quoted in Peter Kornbluh, "The Covert War," in Thomas Walker (ed.), *Reagan Versus the Sandinistas* (Westview Press, 1987), p. 27).

28 In a remarkable display of dishonest apologetics for Western state terror, Paul Wilkinson mentions Sabra and Shatila as a case where Israel was *unable to protect* the Palestinians. See his *Terrorism and the Liberal State* (New York University Press, 2nd edn, 1986), p. 203.

29 In reviewing Sterling's *The Terror Network*, the London *Economist* (September 19, 1981), after noting Sterling's admission that direct links of

non-state terror to the Kremlin were not there, concludes: "The Soviet Union, as it were, merely puts the gun on the table and leaves others to wage a global war by proxy." Although the United States has put more guns on the table, with linkages and purpose clear, the inference made as regards the Soviet Union is never made for the United States by the terrorism industry, or in *The Economist*, or in the US mass media, by virtue of patriotic blinders and/or deliberate suppression.

30 See, e.g., Chomsky, *Fateful Triangle*, chapter 3.

31 An excellent illustration is provided below in the case of the massacre at Ma'alot.

32 *Terrorism: How the West Can Win* (Farrar, Straus & Giroux, 1986), p. 9.

33 Netanyahu, an Israeli rightist and former ambassador to the United States, does not discuss whether Israel kills innocent civilians deliberately. As an Israeli spokesman and propagandist he just rules this out by patriotic assumption, and gets away with this in the West. He also indulges in other blatant lies. For example, Netanyahu states that "the PLO . . . introduced airline hijacking as an international weapon" (*Terrorism: How the West Can Win*, p. 11) – when in fact Israel's 1954 hijacking of a Syrian plane to obtain hostages for bargaining preceded the existence of the PLO and was even described by the US State Department as a precedent-setting violation of international law. See Chomsky, *Fateful Triangle*, p. 77.

34 James Zogby describes the following case: in 1981 the Israelis bombed the Fukhani neighborhood of Beirut, killing 383 Lebanese and Palestinian civilians in a single day's action. The Palestinians responded by lobbing shells into Israeli settlements, killing one and wounding five. US network coverage from Israel "was vivid and deeply moving," with ambulances, wounded Israelis carried on stretchers, crying onlookers, and an interview of the mother of a victim. The same film was used twice. For the 383 victims of the Israeli attacks there was only a single showing – of rubble only. Zogby notes that "To be sure, casualty figures were announced. The reporters told their stories well, without the victims, and without the families of victims . . . And so, while Americans were given to see the anguish of Israel's six casualties, the hundreds of Lebanese and Palestinian victims remained invisible" ("Jewish Souls, Arab Bones," *Propaganda Review* (Summer 1988), p. 19).

35 Schmid notes, however, that "A tourist going to a place like Israel who becomes a victim is not so innocent in the eyes of a Palestinian observer. He might reason that the tourist is supporting the Israeli economy with hard currency and thereby indirectly strengthening his opponent. The tendency to see the world in terms of supporters or opponents only is likely to eradicate the category of innocents for terrorists" (*Political Terrorism*, p. 80). The power of rationalization is such that, as we discuss in the text, the civilian populations of the West's enemies are easily removed from the category of innocent if they support these enemies in any way; but tourists visiting Israel are never viewed in the West in the manner described by Schmid.

36 If airport bombing victims who had been buying tickets to visit Israel were

declared by terrorists to be "suspected supporters of Israel," this would not be considered in the West a valid basis for removing them from the category of "innocent" civilians.

37   If a retail terrorist throwing a bomb into a café regularly used by enemy military personnel were to contend that any non-military victims of the bomb were "inadvertent," this would not be accepted in the West, because there would be a high probability and risk that innocents would be hurt. The same logic applies to Israeli bombings of Lebanese villages, or targets in Tunis, or US B-52 raid of villages in Indochina.

38   For an extended analysis of the role of security firms in the terrorism industry, see Herman and O'Sullivan, *The "Terrorism" Industry*, chapter 6.

39   This point was actually suggested indirectly in the press, which noted in 1981 that "Some officials question whether terrorism is an appropriate focus for the foreign policy of the United States." This is followed by a sentence noting that a meaningful policy on the subject "has failed to crystalize," consistent with the hypothesis that it was "noise" and not real action that was the heart of the "policy" (Philip Taubman, "US Tries to Back Up Haig on Terrorism," *New York Times* (May 3, 1981)).

40   *Public Report of the Vice President's Task Force on Combatting Terrorism* (US Superintendent of Documents, February 1986), p. 10.

41   Ibid., p. 34.

42   Herman and O'Sullivan, *The "Terrorism" Industry*, chapter 5, under "The United Kingdom," and citations therein.

43   Gordon Winter, *Inside Boss* (Penguin, 1981), pp. 320–1.

44   A favorite trick of the CIA and State Department in Latin America has been the use of planted stories alleging *Cuban* subversion. See the case of Ecuador, described in detail by Philip Agee from his experience there as a CIA officer in that country, in *Inside The Company* (Bantam, 1975), pp. 104–322. More generally, see John Crewdson and Joseph Treaster, "The CIA's 3-Decade Effort to Mold the World's Views," "Worldwide Propaganda Network Built and Controlled by the CIA," and "CIA Established Many Links to Journalists in US and Abroad," *New York Times* (December 25–7, 1977); Brian Freemantle, *CIA* (Stein and Day, 1985), chapter 7; Blum, *The CIA, passim*.

45   For example, the US Army contracted with terrorism industry experts Yonah Alexander and Ray Cline to write a book on terrorism, and the Denton Subcommittee on Security and Terrorism published and distributed it. Another book on terrorism by Alexander and Cline was distributed free by the State Department to those writing for information on the subject. See Stephen Segaller, *Invisible Armies: Terrorism in the 1980s* (Harcourt Brace Jovanovich, 1987), p. 123.

46   See Herman and O'Sullivan, *The "Terrorism" Industry*, chapter 4, n. 49 and associated text.

47   John Saloma, *Ominous Politics: The New Conservative Labyrinth* (Hill and Wang, 1984). On the corporate fears and hostilities that generated the offensive, see Leonard Silk and David Vogel, *Ethics and Profits* (The Conference Board, 1976).

48   "Georgetown's Ivory Tower for Old Spooks," *Inquiry* (Sept. 30, 1979), p. 8.

49 Ibid., p. 7.
50 Ibid., p. 8.
51 *CIA: The Pike Report* (Spokesman Books, 1977), esp. pp. 192–4; Edward S. Herman and Frank Brodhead, *The Rise and Fall of the Bulgarian Connection*, (Sheridan Square Publications, 1986), p. 73.
52 See "The Georgetown Disinformation Center," in Herman and Brodhead, *Rise and Fall of the Bulgarian Connection*, pp. 245–7.
53 For a discussion of this sample, see n. 58.
54 Alex P. Schmid, *Political Terrorism* (North-Holland Publishing Company, 1983); Alex P. Schmid and Albert J. Jongman, *Political Terrorism* (North-Holland Publishing Company, revised and updated, 1988).
55 Fred Landis, "The CIA and the Reader's Digest," *CovertAction Information Bulletin*, 29 (Winter 1988), pp. 41–7.
56 See Herman and Brodhead, *Rise and Fall of the Bulgarian Connection*, pp. 143–6.
57 This is based on his contribution to the book which he edited, *International Terrorism and Political Crimes* (Thomas, 1974); his "Prolegomena to Political Violence," *Creighton Law Review*, 12 (1979); and his "Terrorism to Some is Heroism to Others," *USA Today* (July 29, 1983).
58 The sample includes the following: a random selection of 25 CBS news broadcasts on terrorism drawn from the CBS Index for the years 1981, 1983, and 1985; a random sample of 30 items on terrorism for the same years taken from the *Readers Guide* for the three news magazines, *Time*, *Newsweek*, and *US News and World Report*; 15 news broadcasts of the McNeil-Lehrer News Hour that dealt with terrorism in 1985–6; 33 randomly chosen articles on terrorism from the *New York Times*, 1981–5, plus seven major articles on terrorism (including two in the *New York Times Magazine* for 1978–84); 15 randomly chosen articles on terrorism from the *Philadelphia Inquirer*, 1981–5; and 10 other newspaper articles drawn at random from the News Index, also for 1981–5.
59 This was Fouad Ajami. The list of 16 is given on pp. 58–9.
60 "The Rediscovery of 'Ideology': the return of the Oppressed in Media Studies," in Michael Gurevitch, Tony Bennett, James Curran, and Janet Woolacott (eds), *Culture, Society and the Media* (Methuen, 1982), p. 81.
61 Edward Said, *The Question of Palestine* (Times Books, 1979), pp. 172, 249; David Hurst, *The Gun and the Olive Branch* (Faber and Faber, 2nd edn, 1984), pp. 329–30.
62 Rutgers University Press, 1987.

4

The Discipline of Terrorology

Alexander George

There is more than one way to win a debate. One method is to present arguments intended to persuade one's opponents of the truth of one's views. This is a risky business in general, for there is no guarantee that these arguments will be accepted, and even if they are, it might only be a short time before counter-arguments are formulated.

A far safer and more efficient way is to shift the framework of debate in such a way that *any* conclusion reached within it is in accord with one's views. Whether one wins or loses particular debates conducted within such a shrewdly chosen framework is then largely irrelevant, since the very act of debating will strengthen those presuppositions that are ultimately of greatest concern.

Most discussions within the booming discipline of terrorology, the "science of terrorism," serve just such a ground-shifting purpose. The ground in this case is the locus of responsibility for the most significant acts of international terrorism and violence. Whether this responsibility rests with Western states, and with the US in particular, is of course a question that should exercise concerned citizens of the West, since they have some influence over their own governments, while comparatively little, if any, elsewhere. In this asymmetry of influence, there lies a serious threat to those groups which manage the capitalist economies of the West and who recognize that most people would not condone the particular and general violence that goes hand in hand with the perpetuation of a "friendly" world order, that is, one permitting corporate penetration, exploitation of labour, access to raw minerals, etc.

The construction of the discipline of terrorology by intellectuals and others has been of great value here because of the extreme bias that pervades its assumptions about the actions of the US, its allies, and its clients - notwithstanding frequent explicit assurances to the contrary.

This bias reinforces the dogma that the West is the champion of liberal and humane values now under threat from irrational, or perhaps super-rational, groups seeking to undermine the international world order through force and terror. Once the debate about terrorism is accepted on these terms, the truth has been lost, for all the issues subsequently arising will obscure a fact that should surely be of cardinal importance to us all: that the death and suffering brought about by those typically branded as terrorists is small in number when compared with that wrought directly and indirectly by the great powers in their attempts to maintain and strengthen their positions of domination.

I would like to focus here on the participation of academics in this enterprise. Because they are trained to clothe their work in the trappings of objectivity, independence and scholarship, their contributions to this field are particularly effective in securing influence and respect for the view of the West as embattled defender of liberal values against the forces of evil. A good example is Paul Wilkinson's recent book, *Terrorism and the Liberal State*.[1] I shall focus on it because its author, unlike many in this area, is not a raving madman. On the contrary, Wilkinson's work is perhaps unrepresentative of the literature on terrorism precisely because of its moderation; the book has been praised as "by far the best general survey of the subject [of terrorism]" and its author judged "cool and objective."[2] Indeed Wilkinson, a professor at the University of Aberdeen, has become one of Britain's leading terrorologists and as such has had extensive access to the nation's mass media, including television and the major daily newspapers and weekly magazines.

Wilkinson seeks to provide a "scholarly analysis" of terrorism, a task that he believes requires "historical, philosophical, as well as scientific" approaches to the subject (pp. 54, 96). According to him, terrorism involves the "systematic use of murder and destruction, and the threat of murder and destruction, to terrorize individuals, groups, communities or governments into conceding to the terrorists' political aims" (p. 56). Although many refinements and improvements are of course possible, let us adopt this definition for the remainder. With it in mind, we might consider briefly a couple of the most impressive displays of terrorism of the past decade.

Since the early 1980s, some 70,000 Salvadorans have died at the hands of their government's security forces. The terror is indiscriminate: anyone involved in educational, health, church, union, press, or human rights activities at any level is a likely target. In the countryside, the government's campaign against its own citizens is completely unrestrained, with the most intensive campaign of aerial bombardment in the history of the Americas taking a large civilian toll. The bombing campaign, begun in late 1983, is a no-holds-barred operation designed to terrorize the entire rural population: incendiary bombs, Israeli-supplied napalm and US-supplied phosphorus, the use of AC-47s (of Vietnam fame), all choreographed with the aid of US intelligence gathered from Honduras-based US OV-1 planes overflying El Salvador.[3] Numerous towns and villages have been demolished; for example, La Escopeta, which, according to one journalist who visited it, is now a "ghost town." "Every structure," he reports, "appears to have been hit at least once by a bomb and many show signs of being strafed by machine-gun fire."[4]

In the West, this is typically redescribed as a war against the guerrillas, but those on the ground know differently. According to a report based on an interview with Lawrence Bailey, an ex-US Marine employed as a mercenary in El Salvador,

> there is a striking difference between news reports of the El Salvador war and what actually takes place in the field.
> The difference is the target of attack. "The army is not killing communist guerrillas, despite what is reported," he said. "It is murdering the civilians who side with them."
> "It's a beautiful technique," Lawrence Bailey said. "By terrorizing civilians, the army is crushing the rebellion without the need to directly confront the guerrillas," he said.
> Bailey contends that the massacres of civilians are not scattered human rights abuses in an otherwise traditional war.
> "Attacking the civilians is the game plan," he said. From the talks he has had with others in his political camp in El Salvador, and from what he has seen in the field, the strategy is clear. "Kill the sympathizers, and you win the war."
> "The murders," he concluded, "are not a peripheral matter to be cleaned up while the war continues, but rather, the essential strategy."[5]

We have in El Salvador, then, a clear case of mass terrorism directed by a state against its own citizens. In this case, the state and its military are being supported, supplied and trained by the US, Britain, and others.[6] Surely, this is the kind of state terrorism that should be of most interest to citizens of the West. Unfortunately, Wilkinson, a self-proclaimed "passionate opponent of terrorism" (p. 177), does not mention it. Indeed, the only reference to El Salvador in the entire book (there is no entry for it in the book's Index) comes in noting that "the State Department's dossier on the tragic situation in El Salvador underlines the importance of Cuba as a Soviet Proxy for the subversion of the vulnerable and unstable regimes in Central America" (p. 190). In typical fashion, the reader's gaze is directed away from the complicity and responsibility of his or her own government for "the tragic situation" and towards more convenient targets.

It is worth pausing for a moment at Wilkinson's mention of "the State Department's dossier." One cannot be quite sure which dossier he has in mind as he provides no reference (incidentally giving the reader a clue to Wilkinson's conception of "scholarly analysis"). It is likely, however, that he is alluding to the US "White Paper," released in February 1981, that cited "definitive evidence of the clandestine military support given by the Soviet Union, Cuba, and their Communist allies to Marxist-Leninist guerrillas now fighting to overthrow the established government of El Salvador."[7] Although accepted uncritically by most of the mainstream US press and by Congress for several months, the report was subsequently demolished by Jonathan Kwitney in a celebrated exposé in the *Wall Street Journal*, based in part on interviews with State Department personnel involved in the document's preparation, one of whom described it as "misleading" and "over-embellished."[8] Robert White, ambassador to El Salvador under Jimmy Carter, commented that "the only thing that ever made me think that these documents [upon which the 'White Paper' was based] were genuine was that they prove so little."[9]

Or perhaps Wilkinson would cite in evidence Orlando Tardencilla, a young Nicaraguan abducted from El Salvador. The US State Department presented him to the press in March 1982 and claimed that he had admitted to having been trained in Ethiopia and Cuba. Once before the press, however, he insisted that his confession had been made under torture and that he had been coerced into repeating the story in Washington: "an official in the US Embassy told me that they needed to demonstrate the presence of Cubans in El Salvador. They gave me an option: I could come here, or face certain death."[10]

None of this is discussed by Wilkinson, who merely asserts that the "State Department released a dossier to prove Soviet and Cuban involvement in terrorism in Central America" (p. 187). He grants that later CIA analyses in fact found no such link. The obvious conclusion is of course unacceptable, so Wilkinson draws a different one: "One had become aware that, since Vietnam and Watergate, the CIA had become dangerously run-down and inadequate as the intelligence arm of the leading Western power; but most people did not expect it to start operating as an agency of disinformation!" (p. 187). That Russia and its communist allies are somehow responsible for "the tragic situation" in El Salvador is just taken as an article of faith, requiring no evidence and not subject to refutation. That the US might bear some responsibility for the terror gripping El Salvador or, in still greater proportions, Guatemala is apparently an idea unworthy of serious consideration.[11]

Wilkinson claims that "there are only a few examples of terrorism being effective as the principal weapon" (p. 61). Keeping to the literal meaning of his own definition of "terrorism," we can see immediately that he is wrong by considering the terroristic violence unleashed by many govern-ments, such as El Salvador and Guatemala, on their largely defenseless populations. This violence has on the whole served despots well in their attempts to stifle dissent while they plunder their countries. This obvious fact is obscured only if we interpret terrorism as something typically targeting us in the West; that is, only if we lose sight of its literal meaning and substitute a convenient, Orwellian interpretation according to which terroristic actions can never be perpetrated *by us* but only *against us*.[12]

Throughout Wilkinson's book, terrorism is presented as the antithesis to the liberal state, thereby reinforcing the view that liberal states are con-stitutionally incapable of supporting or engaging in terrorism. Instead, they are "inherently vulnerable to terrorist crime" (p. 287), a "beleaguered minority" inhabiting "a hostile environment" (p. 184). It thus becomes difficult to consider seriously whether liberal states might in fact be linked to acts of terrorism more widespread and systematic than those attributed of Official Terrorists.

As one further example of this, consider briefly the recent book *Democracies against Terror: The Western Response to State-Sponsored Terrorism*, by Geoffrey M. Levitt.[13] The title immediately indicates the usual bias; the book (perhaps not unrelatedly) is hailed on its back cover as a "major contribution to the literature" (John F. Murphy, professor of law at Villanova University). Walter Laqueur in his Foreword confirms that "state-supported terrorism has been directed more often than not against Western governments."[14] And Levitt assures us of this regularly: "the United States and its allies have been among the chief targets of state-supported terrorism," "the United States is the most prominent terrorist target internationally," etc.[15] The theme, in short, is "terrorism as an anti-Western campaign".[16] Not the slightest shred of evidence is offered to support this assertion, however. Candidates for acts of US or Western terrorism are never considered. Throughout the book, US government officials and explanations are quoted without comment or critical analysis. Terms are chosen that reflect the ideological presumptions of the author. For example, discussing the June 1985 TWA hijacking, Levitt refers to the "terrorists" taking "hostages." However, in discussing one of their demands – the release of hundreds of hostages that Israel had seized in Lebanon and illegally removed to Israel – he writes only of the "release of all Arab detainees from Israeli prisons."[17] Levitt begins his book by observing correctly that "A state that makes its resources – financial, logistical, training, intelligence, and political – available for terrorism vastly enhances the striking power of terrorists. Of even more profound concern is the damage done by state-supported terrorism to the fragile international order."[18] That the author of these words cannot even consider whether his own state might be engaged in such activities reveals a level of political brainwashing that would be the envy of any Soviet propagandist.[19]

The point can be made even more clearly if we consider another recent major terrorist campaign: Indonesia's violent bid to gain control of the Portuguese territory of East Timor. This is a clear case of the "systematic use of murder and destruction" that Wilkinson spoke of, though one might argue that its scale really places it in the category of outright aggression. Begun in December 1975 and continuing to this day, the Indonesian aggression has resulted in the deaths of 100,000 to 200,000 of a Timorese population estimated in the mid-1970s at around 600,000. According to the head of the Catholic Church in East Timor, Indonesia's campaign has led to "the ethnic, cultural and religious extinction of the identity of the People of East Timor." Thirteen years have passed since Indonesia's invasion, Bishop Belo wrote in a recent letter to the Secretary General of the UN, "And we continue to die as a people and a nation."[20] Amnesty International reported in the mid '80s the arbitrary killing of hundreds of non-combatants, the extrajudicial execution of those surrendering to Indonesian forces, "disappearances," arbitrary arrests and detention without trial "on a massive scale," and forced resettlement in *campos de concentracao*, as they are generally called by the Timorese. Torture of detainees was widespread and officially condoned: Amnesty confirmed the existence of secret military manuals issued to troops which permitted torture and suggested how force may best be used during interrogations.[21] Deaths through massive aerial and naval bombardment, together with the consequent starvation, have taken thousands of lives.

Throughout this period, Wilkinson's own liberal state offered the Indonesian regime continuous and increasing military, financial, and diplomatic support. Sir John Ford, London's ambassador to Jakarta at the time of the invasion, reported in a telegram to the Foreign Office in July 1975:

> The people of Portuguese Timor are in no condition to exercise the right to self-determination. . . . The territory seems likely to become steadily more of a problem child, and the arguments in favour of its integration into Indonesia are all the stronger . . . Certainly as seen from here, it is in Britain's interest that Indonesia should absorb the territory as soon and as unobtrusively as possible, and that if it should come to the crunch and there is a row in the United Nations, we should keep our heads down and avoid taking sides against the Indonesian Government.[22]

As it turned out, Britain, along with most of the West, did keep its head down as the torture of this "problem child" was repeatedly raised before the United Nations. Five days after the Indonesian invasion, the General

Assembly voted on Resolution 3485, which strongly deplored the invasion and called upon Indonesia to remove its forces immediately so as to permit the East Timorese exercise of their right to self-determination. Britain abstained and, since Indonesia's fraudulent "annexation" of the territory in July 1976, continues to do so whenever similar resolutions reach the floor. This diplomatic support has proceeded in tandem with substantial financial aid and military support. Indeed, major arms sales help explain Britain's tacit acquiescence to the cataclysm.

The reader of Wilkinson's book will not learn any of this.[23] East Timor is not mentioned at all and Indonesia only once, in a passing reference to the "Indonesian Civil War of 1966" (p. 213), a curious description of what amounted to nothing less than a military-led "Communist" pogrom in which, according to Admiral Sudomo, head of the Indonesian state security apparatus, over 500,000 perished.[24] (Wilkinson offers an undocumented figure of 100,000.)

The ethnocidal campaign in Timor, which dwarfs anything discussed by Wilkinson, is obviously of no interest because it fails to conform to that picture of the world according to which the "beleaguered" Western democracies have their hands full struggling valiantly "to prevent the fall of the non-communist world by a thousand cuts" (p. 185). Our own crimes, those we perpetrate or organize or supply or encourage, are of no concern. In fact they do not even exist, since the terms "atrocity," "murder," "terror," etc. are not applicable to our actions or those of our friends, but are reserved instead for those of our enemies. Once this conception is conveyed, it will be impossible for citizens of the West to attain an accurate understanding of their governments' responsibility for substantial violence and terror in the real world. And such an understanding is of course a necessary prerequisite to working intelligently for meaningful change.

Wilkinson does, to be sure, mention state-sponsored terrorism. He writes that "some of the states most involved in this proxy war activity [against other states] . . . include the Soviet Union, East Germany, Czechoslovakia, Bulgaria, Romania, Cuba, Libya, Iran, North Korea, Yemen and Vietnam" (p. 215). The naive reader might be forgiven for wondering why the United States does not appear on this list, given its financing of the murderous UNITA forces operating against Angola,[25] or its creation and support for the Nicaraguan Contras, to mention just two relevant policies that should come quickly to mind. The Contras are a true proxy army, one that has killed thousands of civilians (the war's death toll as of early 1989 was over 29,000, more than half of them civilians), caused the displacement of hundreds of thousands of peasants, and severely damaged the Nicaraguan economy.[26] In June 1986, the International Court of Justice ruled that the US's actions were illegal.

Congress expressed its concern over the ruling by voting a couple of weeks later for Reagan's $100 million military aid package to the Contras. The administration reaffirmed its belief in the rule of law by vetoing a UN Security Council resolution calling on all states to observe international law (11-1, with three abstentions) and by voting against a General Assembly resolution calling for compliance with the Court's rulings (passed 94-3, with only Israel and El Salvador joining the US).[27] Facts being the merest irrelevancies however, the US remains a liberal, not a terrorist, state.

Wilkinson does elaborate somewhat on his grounds for the inclusion of Libya. He writes that "in September 1984 it was reported that Gaddafi boasted publicly of having sent troops and weapons to help the Sandinistas in Nicaragua" (p. 215). Wilkinson conveniently omits to mention what the Sandinistas (constituting an internationally recognized government with the consequent right to accept weapons from whomever they please) were being helped to do, namely, defend their country against a terrorist attack by the US-supported mercenary army. Here, in a neat twist typical of modern terrorology, we find that a weak nation defending itself against an armed attack by the hemispheric superpower has been transmogrified into a terrorist state. And the same naturally holds for those states abetting it in its crime of self-defense. Note also the double standard employed: Libya is singled out for its help to the Sandinistas, but not France or any of the many other nations that have provided or have sought to provide Nicaragua with financial or military aid. France, being a "liberal state," cannot by definition engage in terrorist activity. It is also useful, of course, to give the impression that Nicaragua is an international pariah in league only with such archetypes of state terror as Libya. Similarly, Britain is not included in Wilkinson's list of terrorist states in spite of its having sent weapons to help the Indonesians subjugate East Timor; nor of course is the US in spite of its long history of contributions to terrorist causes, the Contras being only a recent example.[28]

Wilkinson does refer to terrorist actions perpetrated, organized, or supported by Western states, but never under that description and always with attention to extenuating circumstances. Thus, "Incidents such as the 1985 sinking of *Rainbow Warrior*" (and the murder of a photographer) "underline the danger of acts of state terrorism by democracies' secret services if strict control is not maintained" (p. 129) – the suggestion being that if strict control *is* maintained, then such events just would not arise, since they rub against the grain of the liberal temperament. This is of a piece with Jeane Kirkpatrick's insistence that "the French clearly did not intend to attack civilians and bystanders and maim, torture, or kill."[29] This is claimed to be "clearly" so not on the basis of any facts, which indicate quite the contrary, but apparently on the basis of the dogma that

Alexander George

Western states are not constitutionally capable of committing terrorist acts, that these are possible only if the state relinquishes "strict control" over its agencies of force.

Wilkinson has a similar view of misdeeds of the CIA, dismissing them as errors, mistakes of judgment due to temporary lack of control, etc. Alluding to the CIA's terrorist campaign against Cuba, Wilkinson writes of a "large and ill-controlled" organization training groups who later pursued terroristic policies "in open defiance of the agency or government that once employed them." Wilkinson even finds it "ironic that many of those who have continued the terrorist war in defiance of the CIA were actually trained in small arms and explosives techniques by the Agency" (p. 130).

Though he fails to mention it, he must no doubt find similarly "ironic" the March 1985 car-bombing in Beirut that killed some eighty people and wounded two hundred, making it the single terrorist attack that claimed most lives in the Middle East in 1985. This attack, targeting a Shi'ite leader, was conducted by a Lebanese group that had been trained and supported by the CIA, with which it was working at the time of the bombing.[30]

And in Central America, of course, "ironies" abound, like the fact that Honduran military personnel trained in interrogation techniques by the CIA admit to participating in the murder of prisoners; or that one of the few survivors of a Honduran death squad attack is "able to identify an American CIA agent who was present during part of the interrogation" which consisted of "80 days of torture and sexual abuse."[31] No doubt Wilkinson would also find it "ironic" should those taught by the PLO, by Gaddafi's forces, by Iran, or by the KGB commit crimes publicly condemned by their trainers.

Wilkinson routinely applies a related double standard when discussing events in the Middle East. The distinction there is between "Arab terrorism" and Israeli "punishments for terrorism" (p. 158), perhaps a shade harsher than we would like to see, but retaliations all the same.[32] In a similar vein, Philip Windsor, an academic at the London School of Economics, writes of a "pattern of outrage and reprisal" in the Middle East – carried out by Arabs and Israelis, respectively, of course.[33] Windsor, incidentally, believes that "the Hashashin [are] the historical and etymological ancestors of today's assassins," i.e., of "their Shi'ite descendants;" he goes on to suggest that terrorism in the Middle East is special because of the long "terrorist tradition . . . in the political culture of the Arab world."[34] That Arabs might not have a monopoly on terrorism and that this fact might explain their resort to violence is a view that, on the standard conception, is hardly formulable and certainly not to be taken seriously.

84

Along the same lines, we find the observations of Clifton Bailey, a lecturer on Arab culture and history at Tel Aviv University. "In fighting the West, with its seemingly overwhelming might," he writes, "the Shi'ites have so far succeeded by wielding a weapon not found in the Western stockpile: the tribal disregard for human life" – as the survivors of Auschwitz, Dresden, Hiroshima, and Vietnam would all surely agree. Bailey sums up the conflict in these terms: "the danger that terror poses to the West is the ancient challenge of tribal barbarianism to civilization."[35] These comments are all the more frightening for being typical of informed, even scholarly, opinion on the Middle East.

Returning to Wilkinson's view of the CIA, let us briefly consider the presuppositions that it reveals, viz. that atrocities traceable to the agency are likely due to its "large and ill-controlled" nature. That Wilkinson, an intelligent person with the opportunity to consult the factual record, could take such a benign view of the CIA is simply incredible, and surely a great tribute to the efficacy of the system of indoctrination to which he is himself a willing contributor. Wilkinson has apparently forgotten, for example, the "ironic" episode of the CIA terror manual distributed to the Contras, which urged operatives "to neutralize carefully selected and planned targets,"[36] and the fact that "the CIA mined Nicaragua's harbors," according to Edgar Chamorro, a former leader of the Contras, to take two recent consequences of "ill-control" more or less at random.[37] Again, Wilkinson is not alone in finding US behavior ironical, as indeed it must appear, given his presuppositions about the benevolence and decency of liberal states. For example, Christopher Hill of the London School of Economics claims that US support for the Contras is the "final alarming irony."[38] That such presuppositions are mistaken and these "ironies" thoroughly predictable is, again, a possibility beyond contemplation.

Not surprisingly, these assumptions are even more pronounced as Wilkinson turns to the behavior of his own state, for which he is full of effusive praise:

> The British Army has achieved a truly impressive record in countering revolutionary war and major terrorist outbreaks around the world since 1945. British soldiers have shown enormous skill, courage and patience in carrying out these tasks, and their loyalty in carrying out instructions from the civil government has never been put in question. The army is steeped in the democratic ethos. (p. 159)

Wilkinson cites the British army's behavior in Northern Ireland as a particularly fine performance, proudly claiming that "it is doubtful whether any other army in the world could have performed the internal security role in Northern Ireland with such humanity, restraint and effectiveness" (p. 159).

We can gain some insight into Wilkinson's conception of "humanity and restraint" by considering the army's activities shortly after the introduction of internment without trial in August 1971 – in particular, the torture of internees by specially trained interrogators from the military and the Royal Ulster Constabulary. In the first mass media report of the torture, the *Sunday Times* quoted Patrick Shivers (never, incidentally, a member of the IRA) who, with the other victims, was "blindfolded by having a hood, two layers of fabric thick, placed over their heads. These hoods remained on their heads for up to six days." Shivers reported that he

> was taken into a room. In the room there was a consistent noise like the escaping of compressed air. It was loud and deafening. The noise was continuous. I then heard a voice moaning. It sounded like a person who wanted to die. My hands were put high above my head against the wall. My legs were spread apart. My head was pulled back by someone catching hold of the hood at the same time my backside was pushed in so as to cause the maximum strain on my body. I was kept in this position for four, or perhaps six hours until I collapsed and fell to the ground. After I fell I was lifted up again and put against the wall in the same position and the same routine was followed until I again collapsed. Again I was put up and this continued indefinitely. This treatment lasted for two or three days and during this time I got no sleep and no food. I lost consciousness several times.[39]

Clearly a model of "humanity and restraint:" the victims could, after all, have been executed Gibraltar-style.[40]

In September 1976, the European Human Rights Commission ruled that the sensory deprivation techniques used by the British Army in Northen Ireland involved torture. In January 1978, the European Court declared that, while the British Army was not guilty of torture *per se*, it had inflicted "intense physical and mental suffering and . . . acute psychiatric disturbance during interrogation," thereby contravening the European Convention on Human Rights.[41] Commenting on the evidence produced at the European Court case, journalist John Shirley wrote

> Between the introduction of internment and the imposition of direct rule in Northern Ireland, more than 170 people were systematically beaten up by members of the British Army and/or the Royal Ulster Constabulary. Most of these assaults occurred not idly (or even understandably) in the streets at the moment of arrest, but during interrogation at the Palace Barracks, Holly Wood, and elsewhere. Some of the victims sustained broken bones, injuries to the genital area, severe bruising and psychological

damage. Others claimed to have been drugged. A few . . . were given crude electric shocks. Like a number of the sensory deprivation victims, many, it would seem, were innocent of any terrorist involvement.[42]

It was not possible then, as it is now, simply to neglect these events, and so opinion-makers at the time had to justify them, leaving those who cared to look with some striking lessons on how easily defenders of the "liberal state" can become apologists for state terror. Thus we find *The Times* scrupulously drawing "a distinction between degrees of evil," while the *Guardian* virtually condoned torture by urging that "vigorous and tough interrogation must go on." "Discomfort of the kind revealed in this report [the Compton Report which confirmed that sensory deprivation and physical abuse had taken place], leaving no physical damage, cannot be weighed against the number of human lives which will be lost if the security forces do not get a continuing flow of information."[43] Others chose to take offence at these unfriendly charges. For example, the BBC World Service programme, *Ulster Today*, indignantly declared that "not since the days of hanging, drawing and quartering and the rack, has the word 'torture' tainted the Mother of Parliaments here in Britain." In reference to this, John Shirley noted:

> Britain holds the unenviable distinction of being the only European country to be accused before the Human Rights Commission *twice* for torturing people (the last time was in Cyprus). The techniques of sensory deprivation were not applied to *only* 14 men in Belfast *as long ago* as 1971, as the papers were so keen to emphasize. They have been used in varying combinations by British Army interrogators in almost every colonial campaign the UK has fought since the end of World War II.[44]

Wilkinson apparently does not find any of this relevant, and instead lauds the British security forces for carrying out their duty with "such humanity, restraint and effectiveness." Actually, it would be a mistake to think that Wilkinson has omitted anything germane to his concerns: since the domain of inquiry of modern terrorology is strictly confined to the atrocities of the enemy, the above considerations are completely irrelevant.

Not surprisingly, Wilkinson can bring himself to admit only that "in 1972 the initial rounding up [in Northern Ireland] of large numbers of suspects was handled so *clumsily* that it became a major propaganda weapon for the terrorists" (p. 161, italics added). Later, he writes that "in the light of the enormous personal stress and strain placed on every member of the RUC it would be surprising if *errors of judgement resulting in over-reaction* did not occasionally occur." "Why should we expect the RUC to be superhuman as well as brave and loyal?," he asks. Wilkinson can concede only that the RUC murder of Sean Downes in August 1984, when he was hit by a plastic bullet at a peaceful rally, "was an *operational blunder*" and really the "major responsibility" of the Provisional Sinn Fein, "which staged this propaganda demonstration to get just the publicity which, unfortunately, the RUC gave them." "*Mistakes* of this kind," he goes on to assure us, "inevitable in the terrible circumstances of the Province, should not be allowed to detract from the RUC's tremendous and devoted sacrifices in the battle to uphold the rule of law against the ruthless bombers and gunmen who have mown down so many of their brave colleagues and British soldiers" (p. 163, all italics added). "Murder," "torture," "brutality," "terror;" these words do not belong to the vocabulary terrorologists use to describe the behavior of their own states which can, at worst, act "clumsily," "blunder," make "mistakes," "over-react" through "errors of judgement," etc.[45] Naturally, there is no question of symmetry, no question of speaking in this way of the official enemy's atrocities, no question of explaining the context or pressures that might lead people to act in desperate and deplorable ways. The discipline of terrorology requires much discipline on the part of its practitioners.

All of this brings on quite a severe case of information deprivation. That is just the point, of course: a great threat to governing elites is that citizens of Western democracies might gain enough insight into their own state and the international order to become motivated to seek deep structural changes in the central institutions of their societies so as to render them more responsive to human needs and priorities. Should this occur, we have what Harvard professor Samuel Huntington called a "Crisis of Democracy:"

> The effective operation of a democratic political system usually requires some measure of apathy and non-involvement on the part of some individuals and groups. In the past, every democratic society has had a marginal population, of greater or lesser size, which has not actively participated in politics. In itself, this marginality on the part of some groups is inherently undemocratic, but it is also one of the facts which has enabled democracy to function effectively.[46]

Huntington finds that "some of the problems of governance in the United States today stem from an *excess of democracy* . . . Needed, instead is a greater degree of moderation in democracy." Unless this "excess" can be brought under control, there is the risk that the domestic population of industrially advanced Western democracies will demand that steps be taken toward a more just national and international order, a "crisis" of no small proportions for the world's elite. Huntington observes:

For a quarter of a century the United States was the hegemonic power in a system of world order. The manifestations of the democratic distemper, however, have already stimulated uncertainty among allies and could well stimulate adventurism among enemies . . . A decline in the governability of democracy at home means a decline in the influence of democracy abroad.[47]

We can cure this "democratic distemper" only if we recognize that "there are also potentially desirable limits to the extension of political democracy."[48]

Wilkinson, too, in spite of his praise for the virtues of the liberal state, expresses fear and loathing for the "excess of democracy" that sprang up in reaction to the US war against Indochina. According to him

The obscenities and stones hurled against liberal democratic institutions at the height of the student revolt in the late 1960s by the spoiled children of Western affluence and privilege dramatically shattered the illusion that the sole forces remaining to challenge liberal democracy in the West were fascism and communism. (p. 71)

(One wonders, incidentally, whether these remarks are part of Wilkinson's "historical, philosophical," or "scientific" reflections on terrorism.) There is even a suggestion that too much education might be at the root of the problem, since "much of the politically motivated terrorism in liberal democracies for the past decade has been committed by the spoilt children of affluence . . . from comfortably-off middle class homes with the 'advantages' of higher education" (p. 93).[49]

All this again echoes those academics disturbed by the "excess of democracy," those who find that "By now higher education is the most important value-producing system in society. That it works poorly or at cross-purposes with society [sic] should be a matter of greater concern."[50] And indeed it is, so much so that we can find an official in the UK's Department of Education and Science recently urging that Britons not be over-educated: "We are beginning to create aspirations which society cannot match . . . When young people . . . can't find work which meets their abilities and expectations, then we are only creating frustration with . . . disturbing social consequences. We have to ration . . . educational opportunities so that society can cope with the output of education . . . People must be educated once more to know their place."[51]

The discipline of terrorology is a useful part of that education, for it conveys a picture of the international role of the West that is as reassuring as it is false. Terrorology, in short, is the latest drug designed to eradicate the "Vietnam syndrome." This is a disease which afflicts those attempting to curb the state's destructive tendencies and to make it more responsive to the needs and aspirations of ordinary people, and consequently one which poses a mortal threat to those groups profiting most from the current "order." From the managers' point of view, the optimal condition of the domestic population is a contented ignorance that fosters "apathy and non-involvement," which in turn relieves the Crisis of Democracy.

Yet another way in which terrorology can help pull the domestic population into line is through fear. If the citizenry can be made to believe that the terrorist genuinely threatens the collapse of their world "by a thousand cuts," then they will be rendered more malleable and more concessive toward the demands of their political leaders. Democracy will then be able "to function effectively" again.[52] We should not be surprised, then, to find Wilkinson, in a veritable paean to violence, warning that

> political leaders and decision-makers may need to make tough and unpleasant decisions to safeguard the security of state and citizens. It is no good having people at the top who are so squeamish about the use of force, so soft and conscience-torn about killing or locking up terrorists, that they are paralysed into inaction. Fighting terrorism, as many families in Britain know to their heavy cost, requires both moral and physical courage of a high order.

He goes on to remark that "The moral courage of all citizens in a liberal democracy is put to severe test by prolonged acts of terrorism" – certainly true, though perhaps not quite in the sense Wilkinson intended. Moving into high rhetorical gear, he reminds us that "in such circumstances the patriotic ethic of loyal service to one's country and allegiance to the constitution must be the basis of public resistance to the petty tyranny of terror." He concludes portentously that "insofar as most Western liberal democratic societies have recently experienced a serious weakening of the ethic of authority, discipline and political obligation, we must recognize a more subtle and dangerous long-term vulnerability than any we have previously mentioned" (p. 109).

The message is clear: the phenomenon of terrorism proves that patriots must do all they can to combat that "serious weakening of the ethic of authority, discipline and political obligation" initiated by "spoilt children." In short, the Crisis of Democracy must be reversed, and the "governability of democracy" restored before Western civilization comes to an end. These views accord well with those of the leader of Wilkinson's "liberal state." Recently, Prime Minister Thatcher insisted that "We do sometimes have to sacrifice a little of the freedom we cherish in order to defend ourselves from those whose aim is to destroy freedom altogether."

"To beat off your enemy in a war," she claimed (referring to the IRA), "you have to suspend some of your civil liberties for a time."[53] Is it any wonder that contributions to terrorology – in general, little more than selective compilations of facts, pseudo-facts, and unfounded opinions – are enthusiastically welcomed as valuable additions to our understanding of the international order?

That the "ethic of authority" must be reimposed is a lesson constantly drawn in the scholarly literature, at learned conferences, and in the media. For example, at a recent conference in Washington on "counter-terrorism" (read: terrorism), Major Alastair Morrison, the former second-in-command of the SAS, insisted that "Society has to be educated to understand the price of freedom. It cannot afford the pampered luxury of mindless criticism of its own defenders while expecting terrorism to be wished away over a bottle of wine and a clever exchange of ideas."[54] The "price of freedom" can be very high, especially in contexts where hysteria is the norm and morality has gone on holiday.

In such a climate, it is hardly surprising to find reprinted in the international press William F. Buckley, Jr.'s suggestion that the West should be "gradually exterminating" terrorists in the fashion of the Argentinian military during the 1970s. That some of these neo-Nazi generals were subsequently brought to trial for gross violations of human rights is apparently an irrelevant consideration. Buckley urges the establishment of an international agency charged with "discovering and executing and directing offensive action against known terrorists and terrorist concentrations." This international Murder Inc. "would not traffic in live terrorists; only dead terrorists would serve its purposes, namely the extinction of a species."[55] That these remarks should pass without comment is an indication of the moral and intellectual depths to which mainstream debates about international affairs have sunk. One should also note that the metaphor of the terrorist as species – as if terrorism were in one's genes (and no doubt soon to be found related to the "Shi'ite gene") – completely denies any historical or social context to the acts of violence on which Buckley focuses. If terrorism, in Buckley's sense, is like rabies, then of course the terrorists will have to be put down. We cannot be allowed to think that terrorism might be a response (however inappropriate) to substantial injustices. For we would then have to consider what those injustices are and whether anything could be done about them, just the kind of constructive thoughts that cannot be permitted.[56]

Wilkinson's discussion contributes to all this, and his treatment of Northern Ireland is especially notable for its fear-mongering.[57] Consider, to cite just one example, his scholarly opinion about what would happen were British forces to be removed from the territory, again offered without any argument or allusion to facts. He writes that "civil war would ensue, and within the resulting terrorist enclaves, whether orange or green, foreign elements hostile to the interests of the United Kingdom, such as the Soviet KGB, would be tempted to interfere and establish alliances and bases with the belligerent movements" (p. 91). And just in case that does not scare the reader into acquiescing to current policy, he suggests later, apparently with a straight face, that "One could perhaps imagine certain difficulties arising for Britain in Northern Ireland if the Irish Republic were to become taken over by a Marxist-Leninist regime which proceeded to promote IRA terrorism as a form of surrogate war against Britain!" (p. 173). There are many things that one could imagine, but it is unclear why this particular fantasy should be one of them – unless the goal is insecurity rather than insight.

Wilkinson even adds an interesting twist to all this by suggesting that we have subversion not only from abroad to fear, but from within as well. After observing that "there are . . . large Palestinian communities in West Germany and the United States, Turks employed in France and West Germany, large Pakistani and Indian populations in Britain, and many different Indonesian minorities settled in Holland," Wilkinson goes on to warn us that "Clearly these are high-risk groups for terrorist infiltration" (p. 208). Those concerned with the survival of the West are therefore also advised to keep an eye on the minorities at home. (Note that apparently only non-white, non-Western minorities are of concern. Wilkinson does not seem worried that, for example, those of US, French, or Italian descent in Britain form "high-risk groups for terrorist infiltration" by the Ku Klux Klan, Action Directe, and the Red Brigade, respectively.) This should have the intended effects of whipping up even greater fear and distrust, thereby softening up the domestic population for its leader's "tough and unpleasant decisions," and of furthering the "marginality on the part of some groups . . . which has enabled democracy to function effectively."

I have focused at such length on Wilkinson's book because it is quite typical of the kind of work that now passes for a serious contribution to the study of violence in the international order.[58] It is patent, however, that there is no intellectual depth to it or to most of the terrorologist literature in which it finds a home. Terrorology is intellectually sterile, if not bankrupt, because the construct of "terrorism" employed by terrorologists was not developed in response to honest puzzlement about the real world, but rather in response to ideological pressures. Consequently, we should explain the gravity with which discussions of terrorism are received by reference to the centrality of the ideological needs, some of them discussed above, that are satisfied by terrorology's fundamental tenets. These tenets are never stated explicitly – at least not by its more sophisticated scholars. Rather, as we have seen, they are skillfully insinuated through many devices: for example, selective focus (e.g., "Arab terrorism"), omission (e.g., US terrorism), and biased description (e.g., "sheer bloody murder" (p. 213) versus "operational blunder" (p. 163)). In such ways, these assumptions become part of the framework within which questions get raised, answers are judged, and policies are formulated.

The strategy of framework-shifting has a number of advantages. For one thing, it requires a greater intellectual effort to question framework assumptions, as opposed to particular theses formulable within a given framework. For another, it is far easier to marginalize an individual who does manage to achieve this, who questions the dominant framework, than one who is content to quibble over details while abiding by the rules of the game. There are therefore intellectual as well as personal costs to be borne by those who wish to see their world aright. Often these can be considerable. But given the stakes, there is little choice.

Notes

1 *Terrorism and the Liberal State* (Macmillan/New York University Press, 2nd edn, 1986). Page references in parentheses are to this book.
2 Ian Gilmour, *London Review of Books* (October 23, 1986).
3 "[T]he war has moved from assassinations in the cities to indiscriminate bombing in the countryside," according to the Central American correspondent for the *Spectator* (a conservative UK periodical). Ambrose Evans-Prichard, *St Louis Post-Dispatch* (May 12, 1985); quoted in Alexander Cockburn, *Corruptions of Empire* (Verso, 1987), p. 396.
4 Chris Hedges, *The Christian Science Monitor* (April 6, 1985); also quoted in Cockburn, *Corruptions of Empire*, p. 396. According to Cockburn, the aerial bombardment of El Salvador is a "secret war" in the special sense of being "a military enterprise carried out by the United States and known to its victims, international observers, humanitarian organizations, foreign journalists and the domestic radical community but, for reasons of collective internal censorship, not reported in the mainstream media of the United States" (*Corruptions of Empire*, p. 394). This is an important example of the media dutifully operating according to "their own *voluntary* guidelines and *self*-restraint in terrorism coverage," as Wilkinson (p. 177) urges they do (employing, to be sure, a different conception of terrorism).
    The bombing continues to this day. For a recent eyewitness account by a US doctor of a bombing and strafing raid that killed five people (four of them children) and wounded sixteen others (eleven of them children), see Ann Mangamaro, "Villages Targeted in El Salvador Bombing," *Central Amenia Register* (July–August 1990).
5 Susan Ornstein, "El Salvador: A Mercenary's View," *Fort Myers' News Press*

(October 23, 1983); quoted in Michael McClintock, *The American Connection: Volume One* (Zed Books, 1985), p. 305.

6   From January 1987, Britain has provided training at Sandhurst for members of the El Salvadoran military. In its defense, the British government has urged that such training will have a "civilizing influence" – the exact nature of which can be appreciated by examining the murderous performance of the Atlacatl Battalion, trained from scratch by the US. See McClintock, *The American Connection*, pp. 307ff; also my "School for the Brutal," *The Guardian* (London) (December 19, 1986).

7   Quoted in McClintock, *The American Connection*, p. 288.

8   Jonathan Kwitney, "Tarnished Report? Apparent Errors Cloud US 'White Paper' on Reds in El Salvador," *Wall Street Journal* (June 8, 1981).

9   Quoted in McClintock, *The American Connection*, p. 289.

10 Quoted in McClintock, *The American Connection*, p. 290; originally quoted in *Time* (March 22, 1982).

11 There is indeed a terror link between the US and Cuba, but it runs in just the opposite direction from that assumed by Wilkinson. See Noam Chomsky, *Towards a New Cold War* (Pantheon, 1982), pp. 49ff and references given there. According to Chomsky, "The main target of terrorist attacks for the past twenty years has undoubtedly been Cuba;" he cites instances of Cuban boats and planes being attacked, embassies bombed, embassy personnel murdered and kidnapped, Cuban crops and livestock poisoned, attacks on Cuban oil refineries, bridges, and sugar mills, industrial sabotage and numerous assassination attempts on Castro, most of these acts of terrorism being organized or supported by the Kennedy administration. See also his "International Terrorism: Image and Reality" in this volume.

12 Understanding the term "terrorism" in its Orwellian sense is required in order to render intelligible many scholarly reflections on the topic. For example, we must do so when interpreting Philip Windsor of the London School of Economics, when he writes of the "American determination to stamp out terrorism." Taking "terrorism" literally, there plainly is no such determination: quite the contrary. (See his contribution to Lawrence Freedman, Christopher Hill, Adam Roberts, R.J. Vincent, Paul Wilkinson and Philip Windsor, *Terrorism and International Order* (The Royal Institute of International Affairs/Routledge Kegan Paul, 1986), p. 30.) Or consider the statement by Adam Roberts, Oxford University's professor of international relations: "Although state-sponsored terrorism is a major preoccupation of Western governments today," he writes, "there are dangers in excessive preoccupation with this aspect. It is an area in which facts are scarce and lurid theories abundant" (*Terrorism and International Order*, p. 11). These remarks are true only if we interpret "state-sponsored terrorism" to exclude Western-, in particular US-, sponsored terrorism, many significant instances of which are well documented (e.g., the Contras, UNITA).

13 Praeger, 1988.

14 Levitt, *Democracies against Terror*, pp. vii–viii. For a critical discussion of some of Laqueur's own work on terrorism, see Noam Chomsky, *Necessary Illusions: Thought Control in Democratic Societies* (South End, 1989), pp. 278ff.

15 Levitt, *Democracies against Terror*, pp. 4, 93.

16 Levitt, *Democracies against Terror*, p. 24.

17 Levitt, *Democracies against Terror*, p. 57. For more on Israeli hostage-taking, see Noam Chomsky, "Middle East Terrorism and the American Ideological System," in Edward Said and Christopher Hitchens (eds), *Blaming the Victims: Spurious Scholarship and the Palestinian Question* (Verso, 1988), pp. 126ff. The unstated rules governing choice of vocabulary in describing events in the Middle East are explored further below.

18 Levitt, *Democracies against Terror*, p. 1.

19 This work is typical of contributions to terrorology. For example, Jacob Zelinger, in a discussion of the "psychology of political terrorism," writes that "Terrorist ideology incorporates justifications for the use of violence against the state and the targets it deems to be representatives of the state" ("Characters of Assassination, *Times Higher Education Supplement* (April 28, 1989), p. 15). This formulation makes it senseless to consider whether states themselves can promote a "terrorist ideology" or engage in acts of terrorism – and indeed, consideration of state terrorism (*a fortiori* Western state terrorism) and the "psychology" of its functionaries is totally absent from Zelinger's discussion. Similar assumptions govern most "informed' commentary appearing in the large-circulation media. For example, Richard H. Ullman, professor of international affairs at Princeton, writes that "Like Western democracies, Israel will never be able to match its terrorist opponents tit-for-tat. In that deadly game of poker, the terrorists will always be able to up the ante. For, if the democracies try to match them, they will erode the principles that in the long run will enable them to prevail" ("What Did the Israelis Think Would Happen?," *New York Times* (August 2, 1989)). Here we have the usual line-up: the Western democracies (and Israel) versus the terrorists, the latter unconstrained by those principles of humanity that shackle the former.

20 See TAPOL *Bulletin* (UK), 69 (May 1985), pp. 12–14; TAPOL, 93 (June 1989), p. 1.

21 *East Timor: Violations of Human Rights* (Amnesty International, 1985). For an update, see *East Timor: Amnesty International Statement to the United Nations Special Committee on Decolonization* (Amnesty International, August 1989).

22 This cable was one of many published in a book which proved embarrassing enough to the Australian government to have been immediately banned by the Australian high court and ordered withdrawn from circulation. See G. J. Munster and J. R. Walsh, *Documents on Australian Foreign Policy, 1968–75* (Munster and Walsh, 1980). Some further excerpts are reprinted in *The War Against East Timor*, C. Budiardjo and Liem Soei Liong (Zed Books, 1984).

23 Neither will the reader of Britain's large-circulation newspapers or magazines. See my *East Timor and the Shaming of the West* (TAPOL Publications, 1985), esp. chapter 3, for more details.

Jane Robins, writing in the *Spectator* (September 27, 1986), inadvertently provides some insight into the British reluctance to defend the principles of self-determination and freedom beyond the case of the Falklanders. There

Alexander George

she advances the thesis that "Self-determination has its historical roots in Europe. Perhaps that is why it is hard to understand what it means when Africans use the term" – or when the East Timorese do. It seems to follow that those who support self-determination for non-Europeans (not to mince words, for non-whites) are simply confused or incoherent. Robins went on to claim that "There is no evidence that self-determination is the same as democracy, for some 'peoples' are quite happy to be ruled by other means." These views are perhaps untypical only in the openness of their racism and paternalism.

24 *Indonesia* (Amnesty International, 1977), p. 22. Other estimates range much higher. For an account of some of the events leading up to and following the bloodbath, see Julie Southwood and Patrick Flanagan, *Indonesia: Law, Propaganda and Terror*, Foreword by W. F. Wertheim (Zed Books, 1983). See also Carmel Budiardjo's contribution to this volume.

25 On February 8, 1986, UNITA forces attacked the village of Camabatela: "four hours later, 107 villagers lay dead, including the Methodist pastor, Diogo Pascoal Antonio, and four of his children, according to local authorities. Later, 13 of the 75 wounded who were taken to the hospital at Uige died from wounds inflicted by bullets, machetes and knives." One month later, the Reagan administration resumed arms shipments to UNITA (David B. Ottaway, "Rebel Massacre Haunts Angolan Village," *International Herald Tribune* (August 1, 1986)). More recently,

> Former supporters of UNITA . . . have asserted that the group's leader, Jonas Savimbi, has ordered the torture and killing of high-ranking dissenters in his ranks over many years. . . . Witnesses have told Amnesty International, the human rights organization, that Mr Savimbi has had opponents accused of being "witches" and then burned in bonfires at public rallies. One entire family, including three children aged 7 to 15, is said to have been killed this way in Jamba, Mr Savimbi's military headquarters in southern Angola, in September 1983. (Craig R. Whitney with Jill Jolliffe, "Ex-Allies Say Angola Rebels Torture and Slay Dissenters," *New York Times* (March 11, 1989); see also Christopher Hitchens, "Minority Report," *The Nation* (May 22, 1989), p. 690.)

> For further instances of UNITA terrorism, see Chomsky, "Middle East Terrorism and the American Ideological System," pp. 125–6. Predictably, Jeane Kirkpatrick hailed UNITA leader Jonas Savimbi as "one of the few authentic heroes of our times" (Colin Nickerson, *Boston Globe* (February 3, 1985); quoted in Chomsky, "Middle East Terrorism and the American Ideological System," p. 126).

26 Dianna Melrose, *Nicaragua: The Threat of a Good Example* (Oxfam Publication, 1985); Noam Chomsky, *Turning the Tide: US Intervention in Central America and the Quest for Peace* South End/Pluto Press, 1985); Reed Brody, *Contra Terror in Nicaragua* (South End, 1985); Peter Kornbluh, *Nicaragua: The Price of Intervention* (Institute for Policy Studies, 1987); Holly Sklar, *Washington's War On Nicaragua* (South End, 1989).

27 For further details, see Noam Chomsky, *The Culture of Terrorism* (South End/Pluto Press, 1988).

It bears noting that Wilkinson's own liberal state has done what it can to support the US in its war against Nicaragua. Out of a total of 15 judges at the World Court, only the British and Japanese representatives sided with the US position; when Nicaragua took the court's decision to the UN Security Council, calling on the US to obey the judgment, Britain abstained (the US defeated the motion by exercising its veto), and abstained again when the motion was brought before the General Assembly in October 1989 – an intriguing vote, given that Britain accepts the compulsory jurisdiction of the World Court. Britain was the only country in Europe not to send observers to the Nicaraguan elections in 1984 (although it did send them to the pseudo-elections held in El Salvador). Bilateral aid to Nicaragua hardly exists (it exists to other Central American nations), in spite of recommendations to the contrary by many aid organizations (e.g., Oxfam, War on Want, Christian Aid). Aid between Britain and Nicaragua reached a peak during the Somoza years and has declined steadily ever since the Sandinista revolution (Britain and the US are the only major aid donors who have given more in the last seven years of the Somoza regime than in the first seven after the revolution). Britain has constantly sought to oppose multilateral aid to Nicaragua: in 1985 leaked documents indicated that the UK Overseas Development Administration (ODA) had been instructed by the Foreign Office to "oppose proposals from Nicaragua by finding technical reasons for doing so" – with one ODA official appending the handwritten comment "If we can find them!". For documentation and further information, see *Nicaragua: Special Report* (Nicaragua Solidarity Campaign, 1987), and *The Thatcher Years: Britain and Latin America* (Latin America Bureau, 1988).

28 Elsewhere, Wilkinson claims that "West European reluctance to introduce economic sanctions against Libya following the Vienna and Rome airport outrages of December 1985, further fuelled American anger," thereby leaving the impression that Libya is known to be responsible, something in fact denied by both the Austrian and Italian governments (who believe the attacks were tied to Syria). See his contribution to Freedman et al., *Terrorism and International Order*, p. 53. The same technique of insinuation is used by Geoffrey Levitt in *Democracies against Terror*, when he quotes without comment Reagan's assertion that "there's irrefutable evidence of his [Gaddafi's] role in these attacks" (p. 72). For a good overview of the hysteria and the actual record as regards Libya, see chapter 3 of Noam Chomsky's *Pirates and Emperors: International Terrorism in the Real World* (Claremont Research & Publications, 1986).

29 *New York Times* (September 27, 1985). For further discussion of the hypocrisy of the reactions to this terrorist attack, see Cockburn, *Corruptions of Empire*, pp. 399–401.

30 See Philip Shenon, *New York Times* (May 14, 1985); Lou Cannon, Bob Woodward, et al., *Washington Post* (April 28, 1986). For some quotations and further references, see Chomsky, *Pirates and Emperors*, pp. 136ff. See

also Chomsky's "International Terrorism: Image and Reality," in this volume.

31 James LeMoyne, "In Human Rights Court, Honduras Is First to Face Death Squad Trial," *New York Times* (January 19, 1988). The article reports that "Killings by Government death squads in Honduras since 1980 are well known to the Reagan Administration and to the Central Intelligence Agency which trained Honduran soldiers who then worked in the death squads, according to several American officials and a former member of a Honduran death squad who said he was trained by the CIA." A few days later, the *New York Times* editors sought to rewrite the ugly historical record by claiming that "No one charges that Americans encouraged or took part in this official terrorism," thereby directly contradicting their own report of three days earlier (see quotations in text); *New York Times* (January 22, 1988).

32 The following comment by Wilkinson on the Middle East is perhaps the most offensive and astonishing in its dishonesty: "The September massacres of hundreds of Palestinian civilians in the camps of Sabra and Chatilla [sic] by Phalangist militiamen was tragic evidence of their vulnerability and the inability of the Israelis, the UN or any other body, to protect them" (p. 203). For a well-documented account of the Israeli role in the massacre, see sections 6.5 and 6.6 of Noam Chomsky's *The Fateful Triangle: The United States, Israel and the Palestinians* (South End/Pluto Press, 1983).

33 This convenient semantic twist is equally prevalent in "objective" reporting on the Middle East. Thus Robert Pear in a "news" piece asserts that "Israel is known for having a firm policy against terrorism and has often retaliated against those responsible for terrorist attacks." If this is literally true, then it follows that Israel does not engage in or sponsor terrorism and that when it does use force it does so only to defend itself against such attacks ("White House Reaffirms Anti-Terrorist Policy While Taking Steps to Work Around It," *New York Times* (August 4, 1989)). One corollary of the view that "No country takes a harder anti-terrorist line than Israel" ("Never Say 'Never Talk'," Op-Ed, *New York Times* (August 3, 1989)) is that Israel is capable not of terrorist kidnapping but only of retaliatory captures. Many instances of this were offered by mainstream reaction to Israel's illegal kidnapping of Sheik Abdul Karim Obeid and two others from Lebanon in July 1989 (with one person killed in the process, an irrelevant detail deemed unworthy of mention by most commentators). Thus, according to A. M. Rosenthal, "The Israelis did not kidnap the sheik. They captured him. The difference is not a matter of semantics but of the most profound political and moral importance. It is the difference between terrorism and antiterrorism" ("The Next Terrorist Crisis," *New York Times* (August 3, 1989)). William Safire obviously concurred, praising the kidnapping as "Israel's painful but gutsy decision to capture" the sheik ("No August Doldrums," *New York Times* (August 3, 1989)). A few days later, the kidnapping was downgraded even further to a "snatching [of] a suspected terrorist" ("The Moment to Free All Hostages," Op-Ed, *New York Times* (August 6, 1989)). Again, it is revealing that none of these commentators finds it worth mentioning that, according to Lebanese accounts, "as the commando squad was leaving the building, a

neighbor, Hussein Abu Zeid, opened his door, apparently to see what was happening. The Lebanese sources said the Israelis shot him in the head and he died instantly." Still, all in all a "daring arrest" (Jackson Diehl, "Israelis Seize Imam In Lebanon," *Washington Post* (July 29, 1989)). Unsurprisingly, when Jesse Jackson called this episode "an act of terror," he was met with immediate condemnation, e.g., by a representative of the American Jewish Congress who described Jackson's remarks as "incredible and unfortunate" ("Jackson Calls Moslem's Capture By Israelis an 'Act of Terror'," *Washington Post* (August 5, 1989)). See Chomsky's "International Terrorism: Image and Reality," in this volume, for further discussion of the "terror/retaliation" distinction; also Edward S. Herman and Gerry O'Sullivan's "'Terrorism' as Ideology and Cultural Industry," in this volume.

34 Philip Windsor, "The Middle East and Terrorism," in Freedman et al., *Terrorism and International Order*, pp. 30 (note there Windsor's use of the description "Israeli reprisals"), 26–7.

35 From "Terrorism: The Tribal Disregard for Human Life," *International Herald Tribune* (July 2, 1985) (reprinted from the *New York Times*).

36 *Psychological Operations in Guerrilla Warfare* (Vintage, 1985), p. 57.

37 *International Herald Tribune* (June 24, 1985). See also William Blum, *The CIA: A Forgotten History* (Zed Books, 1987); also Michael McClintock's "American Doctrine and Counterinsurgent Terror," in this volume.

38 Christopher Hill, "The Political Dilemmas of Western Governments," in Freedman et al., *Terrorism and International Order*, p. 95.

39 *Sunday Times* (October 17, 1971). Quoted also in Liz Curtis, *Ireland: The Propaganda War* (Pluto Press, 1984), pp. 31–2. These facts were known for some time, but deliberately suppressed outside Ireland, as Curtis fully documents.

40 I am referring, of course, to the British SAS's murder of three unarmed IRA members in Gibraltar on March 6, 1988. Shortly after, it was revealed that no bomb was found in their car (despite earlier official reports that one had been defused) and that, according to witnesses, bullets were fired into prostate bodies. When Amnesty International opened an investigation into the killings, Margaret Thatcher condemned their inquiry as "utterly disgraceful." (Colin Brown, "Amnesty Inquiry Enrages Thatcher," *The Independent* (April 1, 1988).)

41 This was not the last time the British government was held to have contravened the European Convention on Human Rights. In November 1988, the European Court held that Britain's Prevention of Terrorism Act (made law in 1973 to replace the Special Powers Act) was in violation of the Convention. And police behavior in the North is still far from a picture of "humanity and restraint:" Amnesty International continues to include Britain in its report on countries whose security personnel torture or harass suspects. Britain, incidentally, has been found in violation of the Convention more often than any other signatory; for the dismal statistics and references, see Bill Rolston's "Containment and Its Failure: The British State and The Control of Conflict in Northern Ireland," esp. n. 35, in this volume.

42 "Judgement at Strasbourg," *New Statesman* (September 10, 1976).

43   *Guardian* (November 17, 1971); *The Times* (September 3, 1976). Both comments (and many similar ones) are quoted in Curtis, *Ireland; The Propaganda War*, pp. 35, 37. Outright justifications for torture are not uncommon. *A propos* Israeli torture of Arabs, for example, it has been suggested that "One may have to use extreme measures – call them 'torture' – to deal with a terrorist movement whose steady tactic is the taking of human life" (Seth Kaplan, *The New Republic* (July 23, 1977); quoted in Chomsky, *The Fateful Triangle*, p. 127). For another example, see Michael Levin, "The Case for Torture," *Newsweek* (June 7, 1982).

44   "Judgement at Strasbourg."

45   For further examples and discussion of the convenient and oft-encountered distinction between "tragic error" (our violence) and "barbaric act" (their violence), see Edward S. Herman's "Civilized Repression," *Zeta Magazine* (June 1989).

46   Michael J. Crozier, Samuel P. Huntington and Joji Watanuki, *The Crisis of Democracy: Report on the Governability of Democracies to the Trilateral Commission* (New York University Press, 1975), p. 163.

47   Ibid., p. 106.

48   Quoted in Alan Wolfe, "Capitalism Shows its Face: Giving Up on Democracy," printed in Holly Sklar (ed.), *Trilateralism: The Trilateral Commission and Elite Planning for World Management* (Black Rose Books, 1980), p. 298.

49   Wilkinson's contempt for some of his fellow academics seems no less deep. He bitterly denounces the

> veritable zoo of conflicting sects and factions covering the whole spectrum of neo-Marxists and Third World revolutionism and anarchism [which] sprang up in the heart of Western Academia. And although these groups commonly identified with Third World revolutionary heroes such as Mao, Ho Chi-Minh and Guevara, their true intellectual mentors were figures such as Herbert Marcuse and Jean-Paul Sartre, embittered and ageing iconoclasts of the left who would never have been able to enjoy their freedom to spin fresh revolutionary doctrines and myths anywhere else but within the liberal societies they so profoundly despised. (p. 71)

This is the kind of venomous diatribe that passes for "scholarly analysis" when dealing with those who reject the official presuppositions about the homeland.

50   Crozier et al., *The Crisis of Democracy*, p. 185.

51   Quoted in G. A. Cohen's "No Habitat for a Shmoo," *The Listener* (London), (September 4, 1986), p. 6. For a challenging analysis of the function of education in the United States, see Samuel Bowles and Herbert Gintis, *Schooling in Capitalist America: Educational Reform and the Contradictions of Economic Life* (Routledge & Kegan Paul, 1976).

52   This fear is fanned to great effect from all quarters. The national press, for example, is all too happy to open its pages to representatives of the booming "security" industry who seek to alarm (and thereby drum up business) by

declaring, for example, that "there are now many millions of psychological victims of terrorism" (Michael Yardley, "What We Must Do to Curb the Terrorists," *The Times* (September 10, 1986)). Again, while the remark is false in its intended sense (employing terrorology's conception of "terrorism"), it is of course true when taken literally.

53 Quoted in Laura Flanders, "The 'Troubles' Turn Twenty," *Zeta Magazine* (June 1989), pp. 110, 111. For some instances of the ways in which many Britons have had to "sacrifice a little of the[ir] freedom," see Sheila Rowbotham's "Liberty at the Limits," *Zeta Magazine* (March 1989).

54 " 'Declare War' Plea to Beat Terrorists," *Guardian* (January 23, 1987).

55 "The Way to Fight Terror, As Learned in Argentina," *International Herald Tribune* (February 19, 1987).

56 Buckley is by no means the odd wild man. For example, recently a senior fellow at the Hoover Institution on War, Revolution and Peace argued in the national press that "it is time for a reassessment of the current prohibition on political assassination" (David Newman and Bruce Bueno de Mesquita, "Repeal Order 12333, Legalize 007," *New York Times* (January 26, 1989)). And the former director of special planning at the Pentagon bemoans that we "face a hurdle as infuriating as it is insurmountable: the President's people are proscribed by law from the singling out of specific individuals" for assassination, although we can still, thank God, "rain 500 pound bombs on a target, killing everything within reach, and do it within the law" (Noel Koch, "The US Can't Fight Terrorism Properly," *New York Times* (August 6, 1989)).

57 For some examples of media contribution to this endeavour, see Rolston's "Containment and its Failure: The British State and the Control of Conflict in Northern Ireland," in this volume.

58 For further discussion of Wilkinson and other official terrorologists, see Edward Herman and Gerry O'Sullivan, *The "Terrorism" Industry: The Experts and Institutions That Shape Our View of Terror* (Pautheon Books, 1990), part II, chapter 7.

5

The Terrorist Foundations of Recent US Foreign Policy

Richard Falk

1 Antecedents

The roots of indiscriminate political violence lie buried deep in human history. The Western experience is shaped by religion, geography, and a particular metaphysics of thought. Religion contributed the basic notion that a single God intervenes in history on behalf of a chosen, particular people, making enemies of that people candidates for indiscriminate slaughter, unto extermination. Sacred history as narrated in the Old Testament is replete with terroristic forms of combat, killing off hostile tribes down to the last woman and child. There are also "slaughters of the innocents" attributed to such evil rulers as the Egyptian pharaoh at the time of Moses or to King Herod at the time of Jesus's birth. Geography induced a sense of scarcity and wilderness that seemed to make survival of one's own group depend on the destruction of others, and to make inhabitants of the wilderness a species of lesser being that needed to be subjected for the sake of "civilization."[1] The age-old tension between sedentary and nomadic peoples resurfaced in the grotesque form of Hitler's genocidal mentality.[2] And the metaphysics of thought, given clarity by Hellenic philosophizing, emphasized both the autonomy of abstract reason and a dualistic conception of reality that privileged the "this" as compared to the "that," producing a series of devastating either/ or distinctions: mind/body, male/female, reason/emotion, citizen/ stranger, self/other, white/black.

More proximately, the practices and mind set of secular modernism gave a particularly destructive spin to this world picture. The West as the scene of modernist evolution claimed to be a vehicle for human progress. Science, technology, and industry created strong convictions that history and nature could be continuously shaped to serve the cause of human advancement. The West proved its "superiority" through long-distance navigation and on the battlefield, thereby extending its sway to most of the non-Western world, but also by its successful promotion of a materialist conception of betterment. By steps, the self sufficiency of reason and technology led to a kind of secularization of the imagination, leading Nietzsche to announce a hundred years ago that God was dead, and worse, that a kind of terminal nihilism would inevitably ensue.[3] Albrecht Wellmer expresses the resultant contemporary situation in a provocative manner that encompasses the whole climate of normative perception: "The degree of alienation, atomization, fragmentation, and uprooting that develops with the complexity of modern industrial systems, dramatically surpasses what Hegel analyzed as the 'loss of ethical life' in civil society."[4]

One aspect of this development, kept concealed by retaining the formal trappings of religion, was a tendency toward absolutizing the territorial state. The survival of the governing structure of the state (and its supportive elites) became widely accepted as the essential basis for order in the world, leading jurists and others to write about "a self-help system" in which war was the arbiter of last resort.[5] Liberal democratic political systems most arduously promoted the fiction of representative government serving to uphold the well-being of the general populace. Yet the latest embodiments of well-being seem geared to the primacy of the governing structure for even the most democratic of societies, disregarding the probable effects of virtual extinction of the citizenry. Nuclear war scenarios involve according priority to sustaining a capability for military retaliation and ensuring the physical survival of the top echelon of leaders and bureaucrats (and their logistical staffs) in wasteland settings. Such thinking can be rationalized as one more effort to make deterrence credible, but the shape of these plans also authoritatively conveys the prevailing understanding of what is most significant to the elite, and what emerges is this terminal resolve to rely on mass, indiscriminate destruction of civilian populations (and nature) even if the civilization has been destroyed.

Marx, and later Lenin, powerfully exposed those elements of modernism that entrapped and exploited the poor, including the pacifying role of religion and bourgeois democracy. Nevertheless, they were themselves unremitting modernists with their own exterminist mandate from heaven, and were even more extreme secularists than their capitalist counterparts, explicitly repudiating earlier traditions of spiritual accountability, while scoffing at constitutionalism as a bourgeois disguise for class oppression. In this regard, the capitalist/communist split served each side well, providing a sense of identity that necessitated and validated unconditional recourse to violence by each so as to destroy their adversary other.

103

Within this setting modern history has unfolded. The instruments of warfare have grown more and more devastating. The state has become the primary actor, and its interests in the world have been given unrestricted geopolitical, and even philosophical, blessing. From Machiavelli to Niebuhr, Morgenthau, and Kissinger there has been inculcated in public consciousness an ethos of violence that is regulated, if at all, only by perceptions of effectiveness. Machiavelli captured the modern, secular imagination by vividly advising the prince to use, as appropriate, even unscrupulous or deceitful forms of violence. A weapon or tactic is acceptable, and generally beyond scrutiny, if it works in the sense of bringing the goals of the state more closely toward realization. The only restraint is prudence, both in relation to capabilities and with respect to the agitation of resistance. Considerations of innocence, of human suffering, of limits on the pursuit of state policy are treated as irrelevant, being scorned by the leading practitioners of statecraft as ill-conceived "legalism" and "moralism."[6]

The wars of this century have carried this logic of modernism to an extreme (of near-fatal absurdity). World War I exhibited the enormous human costs of warfare as a method of conflict resolution carried on for the sake of geopolitical adjustment among societies of very similar kinds, and also the tendency of technological innovation (especially, the submarine and poison gas) to inflict greater and greater casualties upon the civilian sector, as well as to extend "the war zone" to encompass the whole of civil society. World War II carried this process much further, both by breakthrough weapons innovations and by conceiving of the industrial base of the enemy as part of its military capability, and hence making the civilian population integral to the war effort. By such an extension of belligerent thinking the whole society of the enemy became a military target, and more insidiously, winning the war justified demoralizing the civilian population by terror bombing or rocket attacks. Military reliance on terrorism became a routine of modern strategic warfare, comparable to earlier reliance on trench warfare or mobility, position, and surprise. Bombing Dresden or Tokyo was deliberately designed to devastate large cities and to inflict maximum damage on civilians, including women and children. A culmination of this type of behavior was undoubtedly the use of atomic bombs against Hiroshima and Nagasaki at the final stage of the war against Japan. The argument about motives continues, but even those who most explicitly defend the decision as "legitimate" claim only that lives were saved.[7]

Nothing better expresses the terrrorist logic of modernism than the juxtaposition of two opposite policies during World War II: regarding the tracks leading to Auschwitz as not worthy of being a military target and treating Hiroshima and Nagasaki as suitable experimental sites for demonstrating the barbaric potency of the new atomic weapons. Very possibly, the understanding of the passive and active faces of contemporary terrorism can be seen clearly in these distinct occurrences and their subsequent contradictory treatment. In the case of Auschwitz, there was a recurrent ritual of repudiation, including an official Geman acknowledgment of the criminality of such genocidal behavior, whereas in the case of Hiroshima and Nagasaki, a consistent official rationalization combined with historical evasion, backed up by the media and establishment scholarship, and more importantly, a continuation and deepening of the dependency on such tactics, hardening into a many-faceted acceptance of nuclearism as a way of life.[8] In reaction to a belated series of legal and moral repudiations of nuclearism,[9] a series of apologists have dutifully stepped forward to validate reliance on such expansive claims to destroy, not only civilians on a massive scale, but nature itself, including the human species.[10]

The cultural position supportive of terroristic policies, then, is overdetermined and blatant – for the sake of state interests, as perceived and defined by political leaders and their bureaucratic "supervisors," any scale or type of political violence that can be justified on instrumental grounds is acceptable. Considerations of law and morality are relevant to the extent that their selective invocation can help to present and justify a controversial policy. Furthermore, if policies involving the use of unrestricted or morally dubious forms of political violence are likely to arouse significant degrees of domestic opposition, there will be a tendency to keep the undertaking secret. The rise of "covert operations" is, in part, an effort to circumvent legal and moral objections to public policy, as well as to insulate the foreign policy process in democratic countries from dissent, international censure, and, more insistently, from the application of standards and procedures of accountability.

The circle is completed by the encroachment of the state upon the independent authority of civil society, even in a country that adheres to the rituals of political democracy and upholds the human rights of its citizenry. This encroachment is especially pronounced in the area of national security. The media is dominated by the state bureaucracy in this area, partly because there is a tendency to respect those with the fullest control over a subject-matter that is closely linked to the role of the state as custodian of the well-being of the citizenry, especially during periods of international hostility. If a country is "at war," as has been the case for the United States, psychologically and politically, if not behaviorally, ever since 1945, then the state is given a virtually unrestricted discretion that includes an array of emergency powers to enable it to carry out its prime role of offering protection against internal and external enemies.

This dynamic has been further accentuated by some closely related developments. Secrets about nuclear weaponry are especially guarded both from "enemies" and also from non-nuclear governments and from revolutionary political groups.[11] The technical nature of strategic doctrine and weapons procurement decisions makes ordinary citizens, including journalists, feel inadequate on their own; the expert with access to state secrets exerts a strong influence. And experts are not neutral specialists, but tend to be directly linked with special economic and bureaucratic interests in the perpetuation of militarism. Among other elements, "the revolving door" introduces crude economic and careerist incentives to sustain this militarist bias, which can only be resisted by bureaucrats and public officials of exceptional civic virtue. The penalties imposed on so-called whistle-blowers are heavy and notorious; in contrast, the rewards given to those who play the game are seductive and lucrative. It is almost impossible to object to policies and practices by invoking public interests; actions motivated by considerations of "law" and "morality" are typically treated as a species of "treason."[12] Even when respected operatives within the system exhibit concern about corrupt practices or safety procedures, harsh organizational pressures are brought to bear. For instance, workers in nuclear weapons facilities who questioned the impact of their activities upon environmental quality and safety were reportedly ordered by their superiors to see psychologists or psychiatrists.[13] Generally, in relation to military activities those who profess moral and legal concerns are treated as "unreliable" if not insubordinate. Bureaucratic reasoning on uses of force acknowledges no intrinsic roles for legal and moral inhibition.

Within this bureaucratic climate even elected leaders are reduced to positions of "passivity" and subordination. No president while in office has been able to challenge directly either principal source of indiscriminate violence: nuclearism or counterinsurgency warfare (renamed low-intensity conflict in the 1980s).[14] There exists some tradition of issuing warnings to the citizenry at the moment of departure from government, as Eisenhower did in his farewell address when he described the danger of "a military-industrial complex." But, in general, political democracy has come to exempt the national security choices of the state from any form of normative accountability, not just while the passions of war run high, but at all times. One of the big changes since 1945 has been the routinization of "emergency," the effective blurring of any boundary bewteen peacetime and wartime, along with an enormous expansion of the military and intelligence claim on the budget.[15] By now, "the state within the state," the invisible and essentially non-accountable part of the bureaucracy, has established great resilience, and a new condition of normalcy. To be sure, intelligence breakdowns and foreign policy failure have generated episodic calls for reform and explanation, but these calls are neutralized by pacifying TV docudramas in the form of hearings that treat contested Congressional–executive prerogatives as if they constitute the whole content of citizen concern. The Iran–contra hearings are exemplary in this regard, revealing the most profound and pervasive abuse of governmental authority, and yet concentrating almost exclusively on the allocations of responsibility between the bureaucracy – it is not that covert operations in defiance of international law and morality are repudiated, but rather that their performance must in the future be entrusted to the CIA, not farmed out on a freelance basis.[16]

The state also dominates media and academic discourse in these matters, even as it appears to be locked in combat. Leaders habitually complain of "leaks" and "a hostile media" that leans toward liberal views. But careful scrutiny of mainstream discussion, even heated controversy, reveals that it is restricted to a narrow band on the overall spectrum of policy discretion. It is acceptable for the media or academic experts to question the effectiveness of a given line of national security policy, or to reveal that specific governmental claims are exaggerated or based on deceit. But such questioning accepts as beyond discussion two major premises: that "evil" is concentrated in those who have at the time been stigmatized as "enemies" or adversaries of the United States; and that uprooting such evil at an acceptable cost is always a "legitimate" policy even if the violence relied upon is primarily directed at innocent civilians.

This framework of debate effectively validates reliance on terorrism as an acceptable instrument of US foreign policy and protects such behavior from any principled or fundamental line of criticism. The realist consensus, which is so widely accepted among political scientists as to be virtually unchallengeable in academic journals, regards law and morality as irrelevant to the identification of rational policy.[17] Indeed, the debate has become so skewed that the anti-interventionist position, to get a hearing at all, must be couched in purely pragmatic terms: so much so that the anti-interventionists are now labeled "hyper-realists," because their way of being heard is to contend that "the Third World doesn't matter."[18] Unless a political position satisfies realist conditions of argument, it will be ignored both by power-wielders and image-makers, and thus will be invisible on the big screens of societal communication.

2 The Appropriation of Language

In light of its repudiation of law and morality, it is astonishing that the modern state has been able to retain its *normative* supremacy over the dynamics of highly selective and prejudiced perception of political violence. What makes it astonishing is the successful, almost total, segregation of foreign policy debate from the discussion of the political behavior of enemies and adversaries. Foreign policy initiative are assessed almost exclusively by realist criteria, whereas adversary challenges are presented and filtered through a self-righteous, one-way moral/legal screen. Recourse to political violence by adversaries that threatens innocent life, or property for that matter, is condemned as "terrorism." Furthermore, positive images of Western values and innocence are portrayed as threatened by this new barbarism, validating a campaign of unrestricted political violence against those who are alleged to be "the terrorists."[19] The deeper Western tendency toward privileged dualism is invoked – the challenging political groups are presented as *wholly other* and as embodying *evil* and *menace*. The Third World, Marxism-Leninism, Islam, Arabs, and Palestinians are some of the political categories relied upon in the exercise of demonization.

Many incidents illustrate this phenomenon, but none more vividly than the international crisis occasioned in summer 1989 by the Israeli abduction of Hezbollah leader Sheik Obeid, which led to the retaliatory execution of Lieutenant Colonel William Higgins, an American Marine officer who had been serving with a UN peacekeeping force when taken hostage in Lebanon. There is no question that the abduction and execution of Col. Higgins, especially given his role as a participant in a UN peacekeeping operation, was a heinous crime. And arguably, Sheik Obeid, as a leader of an organization engaged in violence against innocent civilians, was a legitimate, belligerent target.[20] What is relevant to our argument, however, is the facile shift of levels of understanding, making the states of Israel and the United States the benevolent opponents of indiscriminate violence, and the Palestinian political movement and Iranian state wholly other, evil, and an appropriate target for unrestricted violence; that is, a shift that provides a legitimated mandate for terrorism (in the name of counterterrorism). Writing in the *New York Times*, Moshe Arad, Israel's ambassador to the United States, makes a characteristic claim: "America and Israel confronted terrorism this past week and held fast. For this, all who cherish freedom should be grateful." Ambassador Arad goes on to say "This confrontation between human concerns and the forces of darkness, presented these two democratic friends with a grave moral crisis and an acute political dilemma."[21]

What is so distorted and distorting in such an inflammatory interpretation is its central assumption that terrorist premises are not shared by all the protagonists in the relevant political struggle. From any objective standpoint, Israel and the United States more frequently rely on terrorism, and in forms that inflict far greater quantums of suffering on their innocent victims, than do their opponents. Even in the incident itself, the effects of political violence were not skewed in the manner the mainstream Western media suggested. Evidently, Sheik Obeid's abduction led to the killing of a neighbor who was "present" as a witness, an aspect of the incident barely noticed in press accounts, and never critically. Further, the US discussion of "retaliation" against targets in Lebanon made no serious claim that those who were charged with terrorism could be distinguished from the civilian population they were living among. Further, the claims of Israel and the United States to use violence within Lebanon, a sovereign state, at a time and place of their choosing possesses no basis in contemporary international law, although some sort of legal argument could be advanced given the special circumstances of anarchy prevailing in parts of Lebanon, grounding a kind of preemptive claim against incipient terrorism.[22]

But the main point remains the unchallenged use of political language to frame issues of choice in such a way as to associate an identification of "terrorist" practice exclusively with *the foreign other*, and correspondingly to endow the self (and allies) with the identity of a victim of terrorism. Such a deliberate confusion severely distorts the actualities of behavior – namely, the more pervasive embrace of terrorist attitudes and practices by "our side;" in this instance, by the United States and Israel. Such a demystification of discourse is not meant to excuse "terrorism" by the other side, or to shift the focus from the lesser to the greater source of terrorist behavior. A greater fit between activity and prohibition is essential to evolve a principled approach that repudiates all forms of political violence that do not respect civilian innocence.[23]

There is a further complicating issue that bears on both language and ideology. The political left has been charged in various ways with the encouragement of revolutionary violence, and hence accused of bringing "terrorism" into the world. Wellmer, in an otherwise seminally thoughtful essay, falls into the conceptual trap of associating terrorism exclusively with political violence from non-state sources of ferment.[24] Unless terrorism is conceptualized in a manner broad enough to emphasize the role of the state and the nature of total war in the nuclear age, the issue of responsibility and response is misrepresented by being restricted to the tactics and frustrations of the dispossessed.

In effect, an adequate approach to terrorism needs to stress the tendencies toward unrestricted political violence in the modern world. Even without any revolutionary challenges, recourse to terroristic forms of violence had become characteristic behavior in interstate behavior, being raised to apocalyptic heights by the prospect of a third world war fought with nuclear weapons. Thus "terrorism" as an objectionable form of political violence evolved quite independently of and prior to the spread of revolutionary movements. As such, the successful propaganda effort of recent years to associate "terrorism" with the revolutionary left, as

most vividly represented by Palestinian nationalism and Islamic fun-
damentalism, discloses the domination of *fact* by *image*: those that can
shape and shade the dissemination of images control the public perception of reality.[25] As suggested, even left critics generally start from the
prefabricated association of terrorism with the politics of the dispossessed, and try from that vantage point to explain and argue why such
patterns of violence have emerged so prominently in the late modern
phase of Western capitalist practice.[26]

3 Why Terrorism? The Complexities of US Foreign Policy since 1945

As argued, terrorism has become endemic to international relations in the
modern, period, especially in the course of international armed conflicts
or serious revolutionary challenges at home. The statist imperatives to
sustain "security" in the pursuit of perceived elite interests has been constructed on the basis of various versions of "realist" geopolitics; that is,
the use of force is assessed by instrumental means/ends criteria of cost
effectiveness, not by norms derived from law, morality, religion, and
cultural values.

The United States as an "ordinary" state assimilated this "terrorist"
ethos long before 1945. In the era of "discovery" and continental expansion, colonists in North America relied upon terrorist methods of indiscriminate violence and tactics of intimidation to disperse and decimate
the indigenous peoples of North America. Such a pattern, by now amply
documented, was combined with self-satisfying claims of a heroic civilizing mission that included pacifying the wilderness habitat of "savages."
This anticipates the contemporary discourse by which every adversary of
the US government is portrayed as wholly other and of inferior status,
and the main perpetrators of cruel violence are, by deliberate inversion,
portrayed and generally perceived as victims of barbaric resistance. The
encounter in historical circumstances is inverted, making the victim into
victimizer, and vice versa.

Similarly, in its first major overseas imperial venture – the Spanish
American War – the United States was confronted by a nationalist resistance movement in the Philippines. As with the wars against native
American peoples, the adversary was demonized (and victimized).[27] In
the struggle, US forces, with their wide margin of military superiority,
inflicted disproportionate casualties, almost always a sign of terrorist tactics, and usually associated with a refusal or inability to limit political
violence to a discernible military opponent. The dispossession of a people

from their land almost always is a product of terrorist forms of belligerency. In contrast, interventions in Central and South America in the area of so-called "Gunboat Diplomacy" were generally not terrorist in character, as little violence was required to influence political struggle for ascendency between competing factions of an indigenous elite.

The changed character of political resistance in Latin America (and elsewhere) contributed greatly to the increased use of terrorism as an instrument of colonial or imperial domination. Terrorism is likely to arise when an alien, hegemonic actor seeks to inpose its political will on an antagonistic and large popular movement – by its nature the military instrument is confronted by an opponent that is often virtually synonymous with "the people" of the nation, or a significant segment of it. Under these conditions, foreign military intervention can succeed only if the popular movement can be intimidated or utterly destroyed, not primarily the result of a battlefield encounter between opposing armed forces. Additionally, nationalist forces, if relying on force, are aware of their inferiority in battlefield technology. This circumstance favors tactics based on surprise and dispersion that are regarded by the foreign adversary as provocative and improper, thereby inducing and justifying retaliatory attacks against the civilian movement of opposition. Terrorism becomes the only viable military strategy in these circumstances, which exist especially in the interactions between the West and the Third World, but also in the relations between the Soviet Union and East Europe, and between Israel and the Palestinians of the occupied territories. But such tactics of resistance, although "unconventional," are not necessarily terrorism. It depends on the degree to which the targets of violence lack "innocence;" that is, are part of the intervening armed forces or bureaucracy.

Despite these dark forces, as well as the experience of slavery and acute racial discrimination, the United States managed to sustain a positive reputation and self-image as a country. Liberal constitutional order was established and maintained, creating an impression of citizen rights without the traumas and excesses that beset the French Revolution. The United States, as the first victor in an explicitly anti-colonial war, retained its emotional commitment to ideals of freedom and self-determination. Even the overseas enemies of the United States generally attributed its evil ways to a corrupt or imperial government that was manipulating the sentiments and distorting the traditions of the American people.

This relatively benign image of the United States, itself a misleading consequence of a favorably biased perception, has given way to a different, more dubious kind of identity that has evolved since 1945. Several factors help explain these changes.

US GLOBAL ASCENDANCY

The global ascendency of the United States after World War II originated in a setting that was viewed as susceptible to deterioration of position if action was not taken. With the former colonial powers losing their grip on Africa and Asia, a situation of geopolitical vacuum was feared. Furthermore, as the rivalry with the Soviet Union came to dominate the political imagination, in a setting where deliberate recourse to direct forms of anti-Soviet belligerency was unthinkable because of the expected costs of World War III, the stakes of conflict were perceived to center symbolically, and sometimes substantially, on control of contested Third World countries. Besides, some of these countries were the scene of strong revolutionary nationalist movements, making intervention on behalf of the status quo almost necessarily a war waged against the people indigenous to the country, a war possibly thinly disguised by a governing process that sought to be sustained with outside effort.

ISOLATIONISM

US leadership after World War II was concerned with a resumption of isolationist diplomacy, believing that it was necessary to *prevent* a new world war by staying involved in Europe during peacetime rather than waiting until the onset of such warfare, as was the case in World Wars I and II. Given the formidable military power of the Soviet Union, and the technology of destruction available to both sides, a preventive approach was seen as indispensable. In this regard, Europe was seen as the crucible for global conflict, yet incapable of self-management. To some degree, not yet historically documented, Moscow and Washington shared the assessment of dire consequences if Europe was left on its own. As a result, a divided Germany and a divided Europe emerged and became the front line for cold-war tensions and crises, yet also facilitating a *de facto* occupation of Europe through the formal medium of alliance arrangements and programs for economic recovery.

By itself such a geopolitical configuration would not induce reliance on terrorism. What induced terrorist practice in US security policy was a combination of a sense of "asymmetries" with a kind of technological addiction that induced an uncritical reliance on nuclear weaponry, and provided the major impetus for continuous innovation, the so-called qualitative arms race. The United States felt obliged to rely on its nuclear weapons option to sustain its commitment to European defense at an affordable level of expenditure. The Soviet Union was perceived as possessing shorter lines of communication, manpower superiority, and an inferiority in military technology, especially in relation to weapons of mass destruction. The United States lost its nuclear weapons monopoly more quickly than anticipated, but continued to aspire after nuclear weapons supremacy, or at least advantage.

Almost from the outset of the cold war, gaming scenarios indicated that the outbreak of war in Europe, given the weaponry concentrated within the region, would lead to hundreds of millions of deaths and virtually total European devastation. To make such an undertaking viable it was necessary to portray the adversary as a foreign other that was tainted by evil, in this instance in the form of communist ideology. The expansionist danger posed by the Soviet Union was probably always exaggerated, both to keep American public opinion supportive of a counter-traditional "entangling alliance" with European countries and to obtain the indefinite acceptance of American troops in Western European countries, as well as the abridgement of sovereign rights implicit in the acceptance of US leadership in NATO contexts, especially in relation to the permanent division and denuclearization of Germany.

The terrorist element here was disguised beneath the defensive language of "containment" and "deterrence," but the reality of US policy was a reliance on weaponry of mass destruction and on a policy, itself described as "a balance of terror," that came to characterize the relations between the two superpowers. Yet it was terroristic in essence, deploying nuclear weapons, drafting war plans, running maneuvers, and mounting nuclear threats in crises that portended the destruction on a massive scale of East European and Soviet civilian society and accepted the consequence of comparable devastation being visited upon the West. To some extent, the terrorism was confined to preparations and threats, but as E.P. Thompson and Mary Kaldor have argued, such conceptions are dress rehearsals, themselves a species of exterminist politics.[28]

THE NATIONAL SECURITY STATE

As suggested, the appropriation of political violence by the state has been guided primarily by "realist" criteria of effectiveness. This orientation is not especially recent, or particularly associated with the crusade against Communism and Soviet influence, but its terrorist character has been accentuated in this period since the end of World War II.

In a democratic society, where the attitudes of the citizenry are supposed to matter, recourse to terrorism can be constrained by an adverse public opinion. Such is particularly the case for the United States, a country whose self-image and myth are enveloped in mists of proclaimed innocence and decency, and where the government and its officials are subject to criticism and scrutiny by a nominally free media. How, then, can the practice of terrorism be legitimated within such a political culture?

Cold-war mind set
One important element in acquiring approval is to convince the public that their society is in jeopardy as a result of the designs of an unscrupulous, powerful, and evil enemy. The tactics of fear, if used successfully, tend to induce the citizenry to perceive the situation as an emergency in which all concerns must be subordinated to the requirements of the struggle. The acceptance of a cold-war view of US national security assured the government abundant resources and a wide ambit of discretion to do whatever seemed effective. It was no time to be squeamish. Political survival was allegedly at stake.

Several consequences flowed from this outlook. From 1947 onward, the country was mobilized for war despite the absence of combat. It became a permanent condition in which an enormous military establishment became a normal ingredient of government, and tied in a pervasive way to a network of powerful corporations and to the grass roots via the labor market. Under such circumstances, the military option was essentially available to the political leadership in all circumstances, provided it did not persist too long or fail to produce victory. Criticism and opposition were confined to marginal voices, which were often portrayed as of dubious loyalty. Efforts were made in academic life and the entertainment industry to purge those who would not subscribe to the cold-war worldview. McCarthyism helped discipline dissent, and although itself finally rejected, left a legacy of intimidation behind.

The only democratic constraint that existed was associated with ineffectuality, as during the latter stages of the Korean War, and even more formidably in reaction to the continuation of the Vietnam War after the Tet Offensive.

Secrecy, deceit
To avoid criticism and controversy, there was a temptation by the government to rely on secrecy and public manipulation. The emergence of the CIA as a major player in national security policy-making was an important development. The CIA's role subtly expanded from that of an intelligence agency (that is, informational) to that of a paramilitary arm of government entrusted with a non-accountable budget and a mandate to conduct "covert operations." These undertakings often involved terrorism of the most primitive sort – assassination plots against foreign leaders or support for violent takeovers of constitutional governments.

Even with the cold-war mind set a significant portion of the public was not prepared to endorse such activities. Also, the reputation of the United States in international circles depended on suppressing such conduct, which went against the grain of claims to be a country guided by religious tradition, moral principle, and legal rule.

A similar process was used to remove, as much as possible, issues of nuclear weapons policy from the democratic process. Ever since the development of the atomic bomb in the Manhattan Project, great secrecy has surrounded the subject, endowing the technology with an added mystique. After the existence of the weaponry was established, even Congressional participation was restricted to appropriations discussions about budgetary priorities, of relevance only to the pace of development and the size of the arsenal. No debate over the propriety of such weaponry has ever seriously entered US political life. It has been left to the peace movement, especially Physicians for Social Responsibility and the Lawyers' Committee on Nuclear Policy, to raise questions about survival, medical capability, and legal status. Religious institutions also have challenged nuclearism on moral and spiritual grounds. Even these challenges did not arise until the cold war had started to subside in the mid-1970s, and they have been neutralized by detente diplomacy and arms control palliatives.[29] A new era of public acquiescence in nuclearism is underway, which includes entrusting the leadership with discretion to threaten and use nuclear weapons without advance guidelines or even consultation. As well, billions are being appropriated for new nuclear weapons systems, including several with first-strike potentialities.

Invisible government

The momentum of this national security process is guided and sustained by a permanent corps of career bureaucrats who are neither elected for appointed, but who impose severe constraints on the political leadership. These bureaucrats are linked to the media, to private industry – even to its criminal underground – and to the ultra-right. Whether the Kennedy brothers were actually assassinated by direct or indirect conspiracies emanating from these sources is almost inconsequential. The intimidating influence of these sources on public policy is evident, revealed in a crude form by the Iran–Contra disclosures.

Normally, this invisible government functions behind the scenes, but its definite influence is in the direction of sustaining a posture of permanent, no-holds-barred war against the declared enemies of the US Government.

Racism

Part of the process of accepting terrorism is to dehumanize its targets. This process was carried very far by the way the Asian land wars were

115

fought, and facilitated by the remoteness and abstractions of bureaucratic settings. In general, the non-Western, non-white world was seen as susceptible to Marxist influence and as posing a threat to American values and the American way of life. These Third World enemies were also portrayed as fanatical monsters, as subhuman beings whose lives were of no account. Such a primal terrorist orientation pervaded the practice of counterrevolutionary warfare, particularly in Vietnam, climaxing in such undertakings as "crop destruction" programs, denying food to the countryside, and the Phoenix program of mass assassination of the civilian infrastructure in places where the National Liberation Front was suspected of influence. The same sorts of practices were being financed and encouraged by the United States in Central America in the 1980s, and the broader posture toward political violence was being rebaptized as "low-intensity warfare."

4 A Concluding Comment

These various elements of the national security state help explain the embrace of terroristic practices as a regular instrument of foreign policy. A national security ideology linked to the realist world picture of its operational ideology is generally unrestrained by law and morality when dealing with "enemies." Considerations of prudence are relevant, although often minimized, by macho imperatives to achieve "victory," to be "a winner."

The pursuit of national security objectives at other historical junctures would have been less terroristic, but the dual preoccupation with deterrence by reliance on indiscriminate nuclear weaponry and with the defeat of revolutionary nationalist movements with deep popular roots has placed a premium on terroristic methods; that is, on intimidating threats and modes of political violence designed to frighten civilian populations overseas into unwanted submission to various forms of oppressive and exploitative rule. On reflection, if these are the main elements of US foreign policy, it is evident that terrorism and "national security" are virtually interchangeable orientations toward political violence, with the latter terminology serving a sanitizing role useful in sustaining a measure of "legitimacy" in the eyes of the public, and, to the extent that language socializes, in sustaining a high degree of self-esteem among policy-makers and their advisers. This process is aided by locating "terrorism" in the foreign other, a process that can build on the racist convenience of non-Western challenges.

Several developments offer some modest encouragement. First of all, the continuing dynamic of popular criticism of deterrence as morally and legally deficient erodes claims of governmental legitimacy, and encourages defection by members of the managerial elite. This criticism is reinforced by a process of condemnation in church and professional (lawyers, doctors) circles.

Secondly, the Gorbachev approach to global policy has undermined the US picture of the world as caught up in an inevitable arms race and of itself as challenged by an expansionist, totalitarian adversary. Gorbachev's forthcoming approach to nuclear disarmament – replete with unilateral initiatives and broad concessions on negotiating posture – makes it increasingly clear that alternatives to nuclearism and deterrence are available, offering a variety of incentives. Furthermore, the Soviet withdrawal from the maelstrom of interventionary rivalry in Third World settings, given tangible form in its retreat from Afghanistan, removes whatever shred of plausibility existed for the extension of the containment doctrine from its Euro-Pacific origins to revolutionary battlegrounds in the Third World.

Thirdly, a retreat from terroristic practices to some extent is being mandated by domestic developments. The Vietnam defeat – after a massive terrorist enterprise, widely exposed – generated "the Vietnam syndrome;" that is, public inhibitions on repeating direct and massive American military involvement in Third World struggles. Although the Vietnam syndrome has not led to an abandonment of terrorist approaches – far from it[30] – it has altered and moderated their character to some extent. Despite an obsessive preoccupation with the Sandinista government in Nicaragua, a popular president was unable to mobilize support in Congress or the public for direct and large-scale US intervention. As a consequence, terrorism by proxy, while inflicting terroristic costs on the Nicaraguan population, proved unable to mount a real military challenge, despite the smallness of Nicaragua and its proximity to the United States.

Fourthly, pressure on public resources is helping to dim the ambitions of Pentagon planners. The military budget is directed more at maintenance of the bureaucracy than at expanding its operation into contested zones. The challenge from Japan cannot be translated so easily into a justification for the protection of a hegemonic position in the Third World. The failure to address trade and budgetary deficits is increasingly seen as a greater threat to the US world position that are revolutionary nationalists in the Third World.

Finally, the nature of national security is itself being redefined to bring to bear a series of non-military factors connected with environmental, energy, and demographic trends.[31] To the extent that "national security" is reoriented, the practice of terrorism loses its grip on the political imagination of leaders and citizens alike.

At the same time, one should not be too pollyannaish about the future.

Richard Falk

The American national security establishment has reaffirmed its *faith* in deterrence in depressingly conformist terms; the deterrence consensus holds firm. Additionally, the media and policy-makers have successfully transferred the imagery of "enemy" and the stigma of "terrorism" to Third World revolutionary groups. Striking "terroristically" at such groups is in some sense even less restrained than it was within earlier cold-war contexts, as there exists now almost no fear of escalation. There has also been a shift from the containment approach of the East–West rivalry to a more avowedly imperial need to safeguard trade routes, markets, and sea-lanes as essential to the maintenance of American security.

In the end, we are as enmeshed in the embrace of a terrorist foreign policy as at any point in our history as a country. To attempt to loosen this embrace will depend on popular challenges of a drastic sort, which embody stronger visions of peace and justice, and accept law and morality as indispensable ingredients of US foreign policy.[32] The prospects for repudiating terrorism, then, can be associated more generally with the hopes of a progressive politics in this country and elsewhere.

Notes

1   Imaginatively, persuasively argued in Frederick Turner, *Beyond Geography* (Viking, 1980).
2   An interpretation along these lines can be found in Michel Tournier's brilliant, neglected novel *The Ogre* (Doubleday, 1972).
3   Set forth clearly in Nietzsche's preface to *Will to Power* (Random House, 1967), pp. 3–4. Nietzsche did not anticipate a further rotation in the wheel of Western consciousness that produced "the death of secularism," and a possible second chance for religion. Cf. Richard Falk, "Religion and Politics: Verging on the Postmodern," *Alternatives*, XIII (1988), pp. 379–94.
4   Albrecht Wellmer, "Terrorism and the Critique of Society," in J. Habermas (ed.), *Observations on "The Spiritual Situation of the Age,"* (MIT Press, 1985), pp. 283–308, at p. 298.
5   This conception of international "order" as a form of anarchy is most powerfully depicted in Hobbes, *Leviathan* (Blackwell, 1946) and, in juridical terms, in Emmerich de Vattel's treatise, *The Law of Nations* (Carnegie Classics, Fenwick trans. of 1758 edn, 1916). The most influential contemporary formulation is Hedley Bull, *The Anarchical Society* (Columbia University Press, 1977).
6   Even a statesman and thinker as concerned with humane values as George F. Kennan issued a call for "realism" in his famous series of lectures, *US American Diplomacy, 1900–1950* (Mentor, 1952). Kennan was arguing at the time primarily against an American tendency toward "idealism" that had exerted an allegedly distorting influence on the formation of a foreign policy based on vital interests.

7 Cf., for example, the careful and comprehensive assessment in McGeorge Bundy, *Danger and Survival: Choices About the Bomb in the First Fifty Years* (Random House, 1988), pp. 52–97.

8 See Robert Jay Lifton and Richard Falk, *Indefensible Weapons: The Political and Psychological Case Against Nuclearism* (Basic Books, 1983).

9 The legal literature is surveyed in Arthur Selwyn Miller and Martin Feinrider (eds), *Nuclear Weapons and International Law* (Greenwood Press, 1984). The most forceful and influential moral critique is Jonathan Schell's *The Fate of the Earth* (Knopf, 1982).

10 Such is the implication of endorsing deterrence as a posture for the indefinite future, as is done by Harvard Nuclear Study Group, *Living with Nuclear Weapons* (Harvard University Press, 1983); Joseph Nye, *Nuclear Ethics* (Free Press, 1986); and McGeorge Bundy, *Danger and Survival*, esp. pp. 584–617.

11 Cf. Amory Lovins's discussion of the dangers of nuclear proliferation and terrorist acquisition of nuclear weapons. See Amory B. Lovins and L. Hunter Lovins, *Energy/War: Breaking the Nuclear Link* (Harper & Row, 1980).

12 The most spectacular recent instance involves the Israeli prosecution of Mordecai Vanunu for diclosing to the public information about Israel's stockpile of nuclear weapons. Cf. *Israel's Bomb: The First Victim. The Case of Mordecai Vanunu* (Spokesman, 1988).

13 Cf. reports to this effect discussed in the press. See *New York Times* (August 6, 1989), pp. 1, 24.

14 Also, the 1960s conception of counterinsurgency agenda extended in the 1980s to include selective concerns about international drug traffic and illegal immigration.

15 Cf. Richard Falk, "Nuclear Weapons and the End of Democracy," in Falk, *The Promise of World Order* (Temple University Press, 1987), pp. 77–92.

16 On the background see Jonathan Marshall, Peter Dale Scott, and Jane Hunter, *The Iran–Contra Connection* (South End, 1987). See also Noam Chomsky, *The Culture of Terrorism* (South End, 1988).

17 To some extent, conservative writers are exceptions to this generalization, grounding their foreign policy claim on some normative conception of the values at stake.

18 Cf. critical discussions of "hyper-realist" anti-interventionism in the series of articles in the section "Defining and Defending American Interests," *International Security*, 14 (1989), pp. 5–160.

19 E.g. Uri Ra'anan, Robert L. Pfaltzgraff, Jr., Richard H. Shultz, Ernst Halperin, and Igor Lukes (eds), *Hydra of Carnage: The International Linkages of Terrorism and other Low-Intensity Operations* (Lexington Books, 1986).

20 Cf. Richard Falk, *Revolutionaries and Functionaries* (Dutton, 1988), pp. 162–91, where such distinctions are drawn to clarify the core character of terrorism as violence against those who are innocent.

21 *New York Times* (August 7, 1989), p. A15.

22 Also, it is arguable that Lebanon forfeited some of its normal rights as a state because it lacked a government capable of exerting territorial authority.

23   This is the central argument of Falk, *Revolutionaries and Functionaries* cf. also Wellmer, "Terrorism and the Critique of Society," criticizing both tendencies on the left toward what he calls "false distancing" from and "false solidarity" with revolutionary groups that practice terrorism.

24   Such a misleading conceptualization is also present in an otherwise excellent book by Richard E. Rubenstein, *Alchemists of Revolution: Terrorism in the Modern World* (Basic Books, 1987).

25   Undoubtedly, the most influential effort along these lines was Claire Sterling's *The Terror Network* (Holt, Rinehart and Winston, 1981).

26   Among the most notable and honorable exceptions here are Noam Chomsky, *Pirates and Emperors: International Terrorism in the Real World* (Claremont Research, 1986); Edward S. Herman, *The Real Terror Network: Terrorism in Fact and Propaganda* (South End, 1982).

27   One of the best accounts is that by David Howard Bain, *Sitting in Darkness: Americans in the Philippines* (Houghton Mifflin, 1984).

28   E.g., E.P. Thompson, "Notes on Exterminism: The Last Stage of Civilisation," *New Left Review*, 121 (May–June 1980), pp. 3–31; Mary Kaldor, *The Imaginary War* (Blackwell, 1990).

29   There has been a tendency since 1945 for there to be an ebb and flow in public concern about nuclear war. Cf. Robert W. Tucker, *The Nuclear Debate* (Holmes & Meier, 1985).

30   For continued endorsement see the influential Pentagon study *Discriminate Deterrence*, Report of the Commission on Integrated Long-Term Strategy (Department of Defense, January 1988), pp. 13–22.

31   For helpful depictions see Michael Renner, "National Security: The Economic and Environmental Dimensions," Worldwatch Paper 89, Washington Worldwatch Institute (May 1989), pp. 1–78; Jessica Tachman Mathews, "Redefining Security," *Foreign Affairs* 68 (1989), pp. 162–77.

32   Such a position is argued in Richard Falk, "The Extension of Law to Foreign Policy: The Next Constitutional Challenge," in Alan S. Rosenbaum (ed.), *Constitutionalism: The Philosophical Dimension* (Greenwood Press, 1988), pp. 205–21.

6

American Doctrine and
Counterinsurgent State Terror

Michael McClintock

1 Introduction

A military doctrine of counterinsurgency has played a dominant role
in the foreign policy of the United States in many world regions since
the early 1960s. Counterinsurgency provided a new cutting edge for a
developing concept of political warfare.[1] The doctrine's unique contribution was the legitimation of state terrorism as a means to confront
dissent, subversion, and insurgency. The characteristic organizational
forms of the counterinsurgency state were vast formations of paramilitary
irregulars, elite Special Forces-style units, and powerful centralized
intelligence agencies under military control. The situations of mass state
terrorism that are the norm today or existed in the recent past in many
United States-backed counterinsurgency states are the outstanding
heritage of counterinsurgency doctrine.

An aggressive doctrine of counterinsurgency first gained ascendance
with United States policy-makers in 1961, with the inauguration of President John F. Kennedy. In the less than three years of his presidency,
Kennedy succeeded in inducing the armed forces to develop a counterinsurgency doctrine for export and to see doctrine converted into action
in numerous theatres overseas. A reoriented foreign assistance infrastructure – of military and civilian agencies – provided an effective delivery
system for this new weapon of the cold war. At the time of the assassination in Dallas in November 1963, American counterinsurgents were active
in dozens of countries in Africa, Asia, and Latin America.

Counterinsurgency and its offensive counterpart unconventional warfare (UW) were on the agenda from the start in 1961. UW initiatives
inherited by the incoming administration included the ousting (and murder) of Patrice Lumumba in the Congo and the far-advanced plans for

the invasion of Cuba. The counterinsurgency side of political warfare, however, had been largely ignored by the Truman and Eisenhower administrations. The new president moved promptly to fill what he and his advisers saw as a gap in the American arsenal, and an imbalance with Soviet UW capabilities. The first steps to redress the situation followed just ten days after the inauguration, when the National Security Council considered proposals for an "expanded guerrilla program;" a four-fold expansion of the army's Special Forces (to some 4,000 men); and an immediate budget allocation of $19 million to make it all possible.[2]

The new emphasis on counter-guerrilla (and guerrilla/unconventional) warfare was ratified on February 3 in Kennedy's second National Security Action Memorandum (NSAM 2), "Development of Counter-Guerrilla Forces." Perhaps most importantly, the Special Forces, the army's UW guerrilla warfare specialists, were for the first time instructed to turn their unconventional skills toward *counter*-guerrilla operations. Special Forces "expansion . . . would be directed toward the development of a counter guerrilla capability for use in situations short of limited war, such as sub-belligerency and overt insurgency as well as in limited war situations."[3] The poachers were to become gamekeepers.

The military establishment, reluctant to turn its mainstream regulars into either guerrillas or counter-guerrillas, was content to see the Special Forces take on the new counterinsurgency brief. (They resisted, unsuccessfully, Kennedy's efforts to confirm the special elite status of the expanded Special Forces by permitting their wearing of non-regulation green berets.) Special Forces were already isolated from the military mainstream, a consequence perhaps less of their special skills and elite status than of their role as a covert action force associated with the paramilitary operations of the CIA. Military unease over the propriety of some "guerrilla" tactics already established in Special Forces doctrine had emerged in the 1950s and remained as the new administration began.[4] In a sense the military abdicated its responsibility to take on a direct role in implementing the new policy. Rather than reviving or adapting the conventional tactics of peace-keeping and military occupation developed before and in the course of World War II, the army passed the buck for counterinsurgency – with full responsibility and authority – to its covert action specialists. The Special Forces formula of UW was to be applied to the new field of counterinsurgency. The option suggested both a shortcut – unconventional tactics were hoped to be quicker and more cost effective – and a cop out: no major adjustment in the United States' order of battle would be required to meet the new president's requirements.

The public side of the new policy was set out in a series of presidential statements to congress and the nation that defined a newly potent threat to the United States and proposed a remedy. The president's message to congress on defense policy and the budget on March 28, 1961, was perhaps the most eloquent of his statements on counterinsurgency, and proved successful in catching the imagination of the public and the Congress (and ensuring the funding required).[5] The nation's defense against the nuclear menace having been secured, a new line of defense was to be thrown up to defeat the indirect aggression of subversion and "wars of liberation:" "The free world's security can be endangered not only by a nuclear attack, but also by being nibbled away at the periphery . . . by forces of subversion, infiltration, intimidation, indirect or nonovert aggression, internal revolution, diplomatic blackmail, guerrilla warfare or a series of limited wars."[6]

The military's own rhetoric was more muted, its enthusiasm for the new task rather less than the president's own. But by the end of 1961 each of the armed services was making an effort to develop its own counterinsurgency resources – and so to claim a part of the budgetary pie available for the task.[7] An 18-month progress report from Joint Chiefs of Staff Chairman Lyman L. Lemnitzer in July 1962 summarized developments in doctrine, training, and the organization of specialized counterinsurgency forces and facilities within the combined forces.[8] The introduction to the paper gave an up-beat characterization of the military response, and an oblique reference to the personal efforts of the president and the president's men to push the military and foreign policy establishment into terrain on which they felt uncomfortable:

In January 1961, when the President announced his determination to add "still another dimension" to our national arsenal, in the form of a counterinsurgency program, few understood that he contemplated anything more than a short-term tactic for fighting guerrillas. Subsequently, it became plain that what the President had in mind was nothing less than a dynamic national strategy; an action program designed to defeat the Communist without recourse to the hazard or the terror of nuclear war; one designed to defeat subversion where it had already erupted, and, even more important, to prevent its taking initial root.[9]

The doctrine of counterinsurgency by mid-1962 was both a statement of presidential policy, a broad view of the world and the United States' foreign policy aims and objectives, and a basket of military tactics.[10] The big picture of counterinsurgency was seen to require "a blend of civil and military capabilities and actions to which each US agency . . . must contribute."[11] "The safeguarding of the developmental process" required "the training of adequate and balanced military and police forces . . . as well as bilateral and multilateral developmental assistance, advice, and information programs."[12] The development side, of course, was not

123

altogether neglected; it was, however, generally subordinated to the military dimension of counterinsurgency.

The military side of the new dimension to the national arsenal, despite the larger doctrine's prescription of an innovative political side to counterinsurgency, was, in fact, largely oriented to what the joint chiefs had disparagingly called "short-term tactics for fighting guerrillas." The military's part in the non-military aspects of what the Lemnitzer report called "a strategy of both therapy and prophylaxis" was operationally confined largely to the encouragement of military civic action in target countries.[13] Civic action projects could include anything from road building to digging wells and holding periodic health clinics, but their *raison d'être* was to support military objectives. Civic action projects were designed in part for their psychological impact on the local people (it was the main "hearts and mind" component of counterinsurgency), while often including projects of direct military utility such as road building to provide access to trouble spots. To the armed forces, civic action served a tactical purpose; larger initiatives intended to nip subversion in the bud through reform or development were seen as matters for other agencies; the military task was to provide the security without which development could not proceed.

Not surprisingly, the military (and to a remarkable extent the civilian foreign policy establishment) saw their foreign military counterparts as the prime medium of the social, economic, and political dimension of counterinsurgency, the "nation building" that would make them safe from subversion.[14] A view then common in American foreign policy – and academic – circles was that a requisite for development was a certain standard of political order; that the military in developing nations constituted the primary institution with the capabilities to establish or preserve order; and that military managers provided a means to achieve political order and development in one go. Counterinsurgency doctrine's emphasis on order and economic growth encouraged the theorists of authoritarianism and provided levers through which military institutions were reinforced as political actors. The joint chiefs' 1962 paper on "counterinsurgency accomplishments" saw this as the principal means for "Killing the roots of insurgency. A non-shooting military undertaking:"

> Of all the changes which our military forces have undergone in reorienting themselves to pursue the counter-insurgency battle, probably the greatest of all has been a peaceful area – helping allied military forces to strengthen the social and economic base of their countries and, in so doing, to create a better image of themselves. . . . the military nation-building role is not foreign to the US – it having been a major task of our military forces in the latter half of the nineteenth century.[15]

The non-military aspects of counterinsurgency, from the tactical concept of targeted civic action projects to the vast economic development schemes of the Alliance for Progress, provided much of the public face of the new doctrine. The hard end of counterinsurgency, however, its dimensions of violence and systems of military organization, played the decisive roles on the ground in the counterinsurgency states. A civic action project to build a schoolhouse in a peasant community which had been the object of counterinsurgent violence – its men taken off by "death squads" or flattened by bombing – might reasonably fail to impress the survivors. More telling were the tactics of counterinsurgency, and organizational models through which distinct sectors of target populations were turned one against the other. Counterinsurgency doctrine's most striking characteristic was that it prescribed fighting guerrilla insurgencies with a mirror image of guerrilla dynamics; an image, at least, of how American unconventional warriors saw the guerrilla's organization, tactics, and general secrets of success. The guerrilla *modus operandi* was to be adopted uncritically as an instrument for the use of governments at home.

2 The Cold War Crucible

A doctrine and apparatus for subversion and covert paramilitary operations (UW) preceded counterinsurgency doctrine from the first years of the cold war. In the Joint Chiefs of Staff *Dictionary* in the 1960s, UW was defined as encompassing the related fields of guerrilla warfare, evasion and escape, and subversion, "conducted within enemy or enemy-controlled territory by predominantly indigenous personnel, usually supported and directed in varying degrees by an external source."[16] The United States specialists in unconventional warfare then included both covert-action paramilitary specialists attached to the CIA, and the US Army's Special Forces, based at the Special Warfare Center at Fort Bragg, North Carolina.[17]

The trend that led ultimately to the pegging of American counterinsurgency doctrine to the resources and doctrine for offensive *guerrilla* warfare dates to the immediate aftermath of World War II. As the first conflict of the cold war blossomed in Greece, and American wartime expertise was called upon to crush a resistance movement got out of hand in the Philippines, policy-makers in Washington pondered whether the United States could afford to be bound by the limits of the law (and the conventions of armed conflict) in the newly dangerous world of the cold war. A proposal put forward to the joint chiefs of staff in September 1947 by State Department analyst George Kennan responded to the new insecurity of the post-war world, and complemented his better-known concept of containment. The proposal, drafted by ex-OSS officers Charles Thayer and Franklin Lindsay, was to set up a "guerrilla warfare school and a guerrilla warfare corps" under the Defense Department so that Soviet unconventional warfare could be met in kind:

> I think we have to face the fact that Russian successes have been gained in many areas by irregular and underground methods. I do not think the American people would ever approve of policies which rely fundamentally on similar methods for their effectiveness. I do feel, however, that there are cases where it might be essential to our security to fight fire with fire. [18]

The stated rationale for the departure from the norms of conventional warfare was that in the new world of the cold war the enemy respected no rules, and that the United States must have the moral fibre to respond in kind. The September 1947 proposal prompted a series of studies of guerrilla warfare for the joint chiefs, and a JCS position paper for the Secretary of Defense (August 17, 1948) concluding that the United States should have the means to support foreign resistance movements in guerrilla warfare; but that the peacetime responsibility in this area should be the CIA's. [19] The professional military then, and later, were uneasy about involving the regular armed forces in activities at or beyond the margins of the acceptable under the rules and usages of war.

The Korean War experience with the adversary's use of guerrilla and psychological warfare catalyzed the military's renewed interest in the field, whatever its qualms. The result was the opening in May 1952 of the Psychological Warfare Center at Fort Bragg, North Carolina, and the founding in June that year of the first of the army's Special Forces groups, attached to the center. The center had a two-fold function: the rebuilding of a psychological warfare (psywar) capability along World War II lines and the development of army UW resources. [20] For the latter role a Special Operations Division was created and staffed with veterans of US guerrilla warfare ventures – like army officers Colonel Wendell Fertig, who had commanded guerrillas in the Philippines, and Colonel Aaron Bank, who with the OSS had worked behind the lines with the French Resistance. The Special Forces provided its action arm.

In the immediate post-war period the object was to develop a capability for *unconventional* warfare to match that of the Soviet Union. Post-war US Army studies of Soviet partisan tactics convinced analysts that a whole new area of previously untapped power was available for Soviet aggression, and that the United States could play the same game. The intent was not to counter insurgencies, but to encourage and support partisan-style resistance movements to combat Soviet occupation forces in Eastern Europe. The first post-war "special" forces within the military were established in order to establish and assist guerrilla forces, not to fight them. It was considerably later, in the 1960s, that the two roles were combined in the same forces.

The origins of counterinsurgency doctrine in the army's secret programs of psywar and UW contributed to place the doctrine and its programs within the same penumbra of secrecy that surrounded the intelligence world. The triple role of its military specialists – as nominal specialists, at the same time, in psywar and UW and in the far broader (and ostensibly less martial) field of counterinsurgency – further encouraged policies of secrecy, including a tendency toward compartmentalization both within the military establishment and, later, when counterinsurgency programs proliferated all over the world, within the foreign assistance bureaucracy. Although the task at hand was nominally like that of the Marines before World War II, ostensibly to aid in the establishment of law and order overseas, in practice it was more akin to the covert operations of the intelligence world, and equally resistant to oversight.

The counterinsurgency specialists of the Special Forces by and large remained insulated from the conventional forces of the American military – and far away from the American public. American and allied special warfare specialists overseas, in contrast, were generally integrated into the heart of allied armed forces – and in the closest of contact with the public on an everyday basis. The special warfare forces, and, more importantly, the special doctrines of the armed forces, were more pervasive within the target countries, if only because of the relative influence of the foreign military establishments to which they were introduced. And as counterinsurgency doctrine was eminently action-oriented and organizationally explicit, its military promotion – supported of course by the CIA and other civilian agencies as well – was to have enormous influence.

3   The Special Forces: UW and Counterinsurgency

It was perhaps logical that training and the development of operational doctrine was in large part delegated to the army's Special Warfare Center and Special Forces: the peremptory demand for counterinsurgency training in 1961 found only the CIA and the Special Forces prepared with a rudimentary doctrine and a gung-ho readiness to take on the task. The American counterinsurgents at Fort Bragg were not policemen or administrators, however, but specialists in UW, warfare at or beyond the margin of the permissible under the rules of war. Those responsible for formulating doctrine at Bragg included veterans of American-led or assisted partisan forces in Burma, China, and the Philippines during the

Japanese occupation; and in occupied Europe (some were embittered European émigrés). The Special Forces, in turn, were cold warriors trained to penetrate behind the lines in the lead-up to World War III to raise guerrilla forces in Eastern Europe, and to provide a manpower pool for the covert operations of the CIA. The Kennedy administration brought the shadow warriors into the daylight, putting them up as models on which to build security services for internal security overseas; a role in which they would have been unimaginable at home. America's unconventional warriors would subsequently specialize and train foreign personnel in the skills of both the "guerrilla" and the "counter-guerrilla," skills that in practice were presented as interchangeable.

The Special Warfare Center at Fort Bragg became a principal counterinsurgency training establishment from the fall of 1961, adapting its guerrilla (UW) curriculum to apply to counter-guerrilla warfare. Fort Bragg then held, and holds to the present, primary responsibility for the formulation of counterinsurgency doctrine. In their UW mode the Special Forces' mission was necessarily covert, and under the constraints implicit in operations within "enemy-held" territory; this general mission remains unchanged in the 1990s ("to develop, organize, equip, train and direct indigenous military and paramilitary forces . . . with particular attention to subversion, other underground/auxiliary activities and guerrilla tactics").[21] The Special Forces in counterinsurgency, in turn, would employ much the same range of tactics and organizational concepts with the full collaboration of host governments, the only constraints being those offered by domestic opposition groups.

A January 1962 report from the chairman of the joint chiefs of staff described the new counterinsurgency courses introduced at Fort Bragg, and praised the increase of its student capacity from 527 in mid-1961 (when it had yet to take up the counterinsurgency training function) to, 1,212 for 1962.[22] But the Special Warfare Staff Officer Course summarized in the joint chiefs' report was in large part concerned with the organization and tactics of offensive guerrilla warfare: "provides orientation on the basic organization for Special Forces operations and the tactics and techniques of guerrilla force organization, development, utilization, operations, and demobilization; psychological operations; guerrilla and counterguerrilla practical exercise."[23]

The Special Forces training role was in large part performed on the spot overseas. The principal medium of instruction was the Mobile Training Team (MTT), generally comprised of ten enlisted men and two officers: the Special Forces combat/training "A" team that remains the standard operational unit of the force. The counterinsurgent role of Special Forces "A" teams, too, was generally described in the context of their original speciality, organizing behind-the-lines "guerrillas:" wearing their new hat,

Special Forces would raise "guerrillas" to fight guerrillas. In this regard, the Secretary of the Army described the "A" team in 1963: "a detachment . . . consisting of ten enlisted personnel and two officers can effectively organize, control, and assist in the operations of a foreign guerrilla force of more than one thousand men."[24]

The new counterinsurgents remained concerned primarily with what they did best: the *organization* of tame guerrillas for UW. There was little dissent over the proposition that such forces would suffice to combat revolutionary insurgencies as well as to combat standing governments and conventional armed forces. The merging of the two marginal strains of military endeavor, UW and counterinsurgency, followed. To borrow the terms of the late Marshall McLuhan, the medium – the Special Forces and Special Warfare Center – became the message – an unconventional doctrine of counterinsurgency. The tactics of special, covert operations provided a base line in counterinsurgency, and indeed the tactics tended to overwhelm the larger strategy outlined by the policy-makers. And for the counterinsurgency states, unconventional tactics devised for overseas operations in exceptional circumstances became the conventional means of the everyday program of government.

The juxtaposition of doctrines of offensive "guerrilla" warfare and counterinsurgency was first apparent in the training materials of the Special Forces on the eve of the Kennedy administration,[25] and in 1961 received a seal of approval from the military establishment. Special Forces training schedules, in particular, stressed the interchangeability of the skills required, with consecutive practical exercises alternating between guerrilla and counter-guerrilla scenarios. The training arrangements at Fort Bragg for non-Special Forces Americans and for foreign officers followed a similar approach to what was seen as a single military discipline. Brigadier General William P. Yarborough, commander of the Center and school during the Kennedy administration, described the training offered in 1963:

> The Unconventional Warfare Course and the Counterinsurgency Course are two sides of the same coin. The UW Course emphasizes the problems of creating an effective guerrilla force in enemy territory during a hot war situation; the CI Course deals with the reasons behind dissident movements and the techniques used in combatting guerrilla forces and revolutionary movements. Thus the UW Course teaches how to help defeat an enemy by developing guerrilla forces, and the CI Course teaches how to prevent Communist inspired dissident movements and guerrilla forces from succeeding.[26]

Counterinsurgency, however, was something more and something less than the flipside of unconventional warfare. It incorporated new features and its scope for application was far more extensive; it was far easier to wage cold war inside friendly countries than in the harsh world behind the lines of the real cold war. And counterinsurgency was less than wholly distinct from UW; where areas in friendly countries were considered dominated by the adversary, the counterinsurgents retained the option to revert to unabashed UW tactics.[27] The legitimation of the use of terror was a common denominator – an area in which the merging of the two doctrines and their respective practice was most apparent, and most distinct from conventional military doctrine.

The development of counterinsurgency doctrine as an offshoot of the UW establishment responded to both political and institutional demands. The new president had demanded an immediate, off-the-shelf response to the threat of insurgency on a global scale. He was known to be an admirer of American UW capabilities, and in particular of the romantic aspect of the army's Special Forces. He was impatient for action and had been a harsh critic of French long-view colonial counterinsurgency during a visit to Indochina as a young congressman in 1951. JFK wanted a military tool – men and doctrine – that could be converted into action almost immediately, with a promise of at least a modicum of success in the short term that would provide the steel behind long-term plans of development and reform.

The armed forces, in turn, were not particularly enamored of the prospect of taking on long-term commitments to help their allies police their own countries. The military had had considerable pre-World War II experience in "pacification" and post-war experience in the politics of military occupation; the gendarmerie function had lost its glamor. The new scenarios of "wars of liberation," moreover, were defined by consensus as part of a global military offensive by the Soviet Union, a new dimension of a cold war in which the old rules of armed conflict had been cast aside. A response rather more dramatic than the traditional training of military police could thus be justified. The counterinsurgency dimension of the cold war, then, would be presented in cold-war colours.

The conception of the new counterinsurgency as a "special" discipline provided a means through which the armed forces could avoid a radical reappraisal and adjustment of the United States' conventional military establishment, mission, and doctrine while still meeting the president's demands for counterinsurgency capabilities. As a "special" field of warfare, counterinsurgency was seen to be best practiced by the same elite forces assigned responsibility for unconventional warfare. Both were seen as areas outside the normal sphere of military tasks, to be assigned special units within each of the military services, and segregated from mainstream, conventional forces. And, vice versa, by insulating the mainstream from the counterinsurgents, the armed forces were more comfortable with the incorporation of unconventional tactics into the counterinsurgent repertoir. The armed forces, with the president's blessing, redeployed the special warfare establishment to work its special magic on the new battlefields of internal war. Perhaps, the thinking went, the Special Forces and an adaptation of UW doctrine would permit the quick fix of overseas troubles that had already been shown possible in UW operations in Guatemala, Iran, and elsewhere in the 1950s.

4 The Doctrine: A Kind of Political Warfare

Although it required an energetic and imaginative president to bring counterinsurgency out into the open, the basis of the operational doctrine had already appeared in the military journals in the 1950s, in articles calling for a new, unconventional approach to the cold war, an American form of political warfare. Already in the 1950s American unconventional warriors with experience in wartime, behind-the-lines guerrilla units, and in the post-war conflicts in Greece, Korea, and the Philippines published extensively in journals like the Army Command and General Staff College's *Military Review*. They were advocates of both an American guerrilla – UW – capability and a reappraisal of the threat offered by enemy guerrilla forces. Reprints in American journals of British writing on counter-guerrilla operations and, more importantly, French military writing on the 1950s French concept *guerre révolutionnaire* prepared the ground for an American doctrine adapted to revolutionary guerrilla movements.

The American military journals after Kennedy's inauguration were replete with arguments for a "special" response to the new threat of insurgency. A March 1961 *Military Review* article, "A Proposal for Political Warfare," was representative of the enthusiasm with which no-holds-barred responses to "revolutionary warfare" were received in some quarters of the foreign policy establishment. The article recommended an American turn to "political warfare" as the panacea with which to "conclusively deter all-out aggression, parry limited war gambits, cope with guerrilla activity, and . . . to mount counterrevolutionary offensives in countries subverted to communism:"[28]

> Political warfare is a sustained effort . . . to seize, preserve, or extend power, against a defined ideological enemy, through all acts short of a shooting war by regular military forces, but not excluding the threat of such a war. Political warfare, in short, is warfare – not public relations. . . . It embraces diverse forms of coercion and violence including strikes and riots, economic sanctions, subsidies for guerrilla or proxy warfare and, when necessary, kidnapping or assassination of enemy elites.[29]

Political warfare was, of course, already a part of the American arsenal, although its application had hitherto been oriented primarily toward offensive operations – covert or clandestine – against governments that were undesirable in the context of the cold war. The United States already had a doctrine and an apparatus for the clandestine waging of the cold war, the discipline the armed forces – and the CIA – called UW. It provided a conceptual basis for the unconventional aspects of counterinsurgency doctrine.

A body of doctrine applicable to counterinsurgency existed as the product of the United States' considerable experience in wielding a big stick since the turn of the century, collated notably in the Marines' *Small Wars Manual* of 1940. The makers of the new doctrine jumped the track and started from a radically different tradition. Rather than being an elaboration of proven small wars tactics (and occupation policies), the doctrine emerged from the development after World War II of a UW capability intended for the waging of covert offensive operations within territories occupied by "the enemy." The emphasis immediately after the war was not on how to *fight* guerrillas, but how to field one's own guerrillas.

The doctrine that emerged applied the no-holds-barred orientation of UW and adapted its range of tactics to domestic affairs. Counterinsurgency's conceptual framework was itself unconventional. Insurgency was seen to be most vulnerable not to conventional police work or military tactics but to a mirror image of guerrilla tactics and organization. Insurgencies were to be countered using the same tactics a partisan force might employ to harry and defeat a foreign invader. Guerrilla organization would be broken down and defeated by the creation of a counterorganization of paramilitary irregulars. These would include both a counterpart to elite guerrilla cadres – to be modelled on the army's elite Special Forces – and to the common or garden variety of guerrilla militia, to be provided by civilian irregulars recruited in accord with political, economic, ethnic, religious, or other criteria. And the advantages of no-holds-barred guerrilla tactics would be cancelled out when the same tactics were employed by the counterinsurgent. Dirty warfare would be countered with dirty tricks, deception, and deceit. Terror would find response in counterterror.

The counterinsurgent rationale for terror combined a conviction that terror was expedient with a premise that terror was the prime tool – and prime advantage – of subversive guerrillas. The latter consideration provided a kind of moral incentive to opt for expedience: the counterinsurgent could use terror to rapidly and efficiently overcome the greater terror of the adversary. A classified US Army Special Forces manual dated December 1960, *Counter-Insurgency Operations*, is one of the first to refer explicitly to the use of counterinsurgent *terror* as a legitimate tactic.[30] The manual specifies that among "Principals of Operation" (sic) were the routine use of "guerrilla/terrorist tactics" in field operations and "punitive" actions. An outline of prescribed "government operations" includes as distinct categories " 'Q' Operations and Provocative actions" and "Terror Operations."[31]

The terror rationale in December 1960 appears to have been a straightforward conviction that guerrilla terrorism – and punitive violence – was effective. The references to terror in manuals and training materials after 1960 generally occur in the context of doctrinal writing on guerrilla methodology. Terror was held to be the most powerful weapon of the guerrilla, the freedom to resort to terror the guerrillas' principal advantage over the counterinsurgent. Counterinsurgent terror was characterized as a drastic but effective means by which subversive terror could rapidly be brought to a halt. Subversive terror would be met with remedial counterinsurgent terror, justified as tit for tat and by prospects for a quick fix. The introduction of new terminology in 1961 further fixed the ethical gloss to the concept: the terror of the counterinsurgent would henceforth be distinguished as "counterterror." The role of "Counterterror Teams" in Vietnam after 1961, the introduction of counterterror concepts to Colombia in 1962, and the proliferation of "counterterrorism" in Central America after 1966 are discussed briefly below.

The references to counterterrorism in written doctrine after 1960 refer both to hypothetical insurgency situations, and to the particular experiences of the Philippines and Vietnam. A book-length 1966 pamphlet from the US Department of the Army, for example, outlines a prototype "counterterror campaign" in South Vietnam called Operation Black Eye: "Selected Vietnamese troops were organized into terror squads . . . Within a short time Viet Cong leaders – key members of the clandestine infrastructure – began to die mysteriously and violently in their beds. On each of the bodies was a piece of paper printed with a grotesque human eye."[32] The operation was cited in the Army manual as an example of the use of "uncertain threat" in a terror campaign: the "eyes" – thoughtfully printed by the US Information Service – turned up not just on corpses but on the doors of suspects.[33] The imprint of a "White Hand" on the door of potential "death-squad" victims in El Salvador or Guatemala performs much the same function. Central American officers today are perhaps familiar with this Vietnam "death-squad" antecedent through access to the same unclassified manual, through more detailed classified instructional material, or through personal contact with American training personnel.

Similar tactics used in the Philippines during the Huk Rebellion (roughly 1946–54) continue to be cited in US Army psywar training materials. The Department of the Army's 1976 psywar publication, DA

Pamphlet 525-7-1, refers to some of the classic counterterror techniques and accounts of the practical application of terror. These include the capture and murder of suspected guerrillas in a manner suggesting the deed was done by legendary vampires (the "asuang"); and a prototypical "Eye of God" technique in which a stylized eye would be painted opposite the house of a suspect.[34]

The formal elaboration of the counterterror concept in the 1960s – and in the context of "international terrorism" today – has stressed as a key to its justification that it be selective in application and limited in scope. Discussion of the concept in US Army manuals and publications distinguished between "selective counterterror" – which was a legitimate tactic – and "mass counterterror" – which was not. Selective counterterror is discussed, for example, in the 320-page *US Army Handbook of Counterinsurgency Guidelines* (1966).[35] A single admonition against the overuse of "counterterror" appears in the manual; counterinsurgent planners are warned not to cross the line between tactical terrorism and total extermination: "You may not employ mass counter-terror (as opposed to selective counter-terror) against the civilian population, i.e. genocide is not an alternative."[36]

The concept of counterterror, the legitimate use of extralegal, state terror to combat insurgency, was in application difficult to limit once introduced. It was a legitimating idea that broke down the behavioral standards of both constitutional law and the mainstream doctrine the US military had taught its own and foreign forces since before World War II. It made a nonsense of the pontificating of the United States' political leaders about the rule of law, and the West Pointer's approach to military science "by the book." The new approach held that the rules of war and peace could be set aside without particular qualms on the uneasy presumption that they would not be jettisoned altogether but would be held temporarily in abeyance.

The doctrine was not, moreover, designed primarily for American or other forces with particular aptitudes for self-control. Nor was its dissemination limited to security systems facing last-ditch emergencies. The doctrine was deliberately promoted as a multi-situational *system* to which any security system could be adapted and within which counterterror was just one small aspect. Packaged for export, counterinsurgency doctrine was handled as a kind of off-the-shelf antisubversive software for use anywhere and anytime. Its counterterror component, in essence a matter of attitude, was welcomed particularly in political systems in which the armed forces already had a disposition to deal harshly with dissidents. It was perhaps the exception rather than the rule that giving a green light to state terror resulted in the short, sharp surgical intervention – and the return to a rule of law – that its advocates may have envisioned.

A 1966 *Military Review* article that outlined the theoretical frame-work of "counterterror"/"counterorganization" was reprinted in the Guatemalan army's own *Revista Militar* in October that year, just as a state of siege was declared and the army launched the first of its since ceaseless waves of political killings.[37] The counterterror concept was first introduced in its crudest form: "if a bridge is blown up, detain all of the villagers of the area and execute a few hostages."[38] This, the reader was admonished, was inadvisable. The counterinsurgent required more sophistication; "combatting guerrilla terrorism with counter-terrorism" was best pursued selectively through the organization of "guerrilla-type irregulars" who know the local terrain and the local people as well as the guerrillas, and so would target only the guerrillas for counterterror.[39] The prescription of local irregular forces was made in accord with the concept of counterorganization. The premise was that a mirror image of guerrilla organization would provide the counter-insurgent with a local infrastructure with skills, local knowledge, high motivation, and organizational virtues which would more than match the subversive guerrilla.

The 1966 article suggested the counter-guerrilla would permit the counterinsurgent to apply terror selectively and effectively. It stressed that the need for selective action "makes it essential that the counter-guerrilla be trained and equipped so that he has even more mobility, commitment and idealism than the guerrilla himself."[40] But the counter-terror campaign just then getting under way in Guatemala was a whole-sale clearance, by extermination, of the suspect population in a large rural area. Military commentators called the 1966–7 Guatemala campaign *"el Contra-Terror:"* some 8,000 people were slaughtered in two provinces alone in the six months from October 1966.[41] As antiterrorism experts Brian Jenkins and Cesar Seresers later wrote, "the objective of the 'counterterror' was to frighten anyone from collaborating with the guer-rilla movement."[42]

The distinction between selective and mass (or discriminate and indis-criminate) counterterror, in Guatemala as elsewhere, was more apparent than real. And in numerous counterinsurgency states the very composi-tion of the counterorganizations – comprised of local elites, religious or ethnic minorities, or the paladins of privileged political parties – militated toward counterterror becoming rather more genocidal than less.

The concept of counterorganization, like that of counterterror, osten-sibly mimicked an insurgent model.[43] Civilian irregular forces were to be raised by the regular armed forces to operate as counterinsurgency auxiliaries; elite Special Forces' style commandos were to be organized to match elite guerrilla forces for covert operations; and, where feasible, mass organizations with both political and paramilitary aspects would be set up to provide a framework for regimentation and control of the population (membership could be made obligatory). The system provided for the mibilization of amenable social sectors on the counterinsurgent's behalf and for an organizational basis on which the neutral – or suspect – population could be regimented and controlled.

The counterorganization formula often foundered on its narrow recruitment base. The doctrine could not compensate across the board for the real-world factors which, with ideology, provided the motivation for insurgency. Recruitment of an offensive counterorganization, as a consequence, relied largely on a turn to social sectors already sympathetic to the counterinsurgent cause. Those sectors feeling threatened by the insurgency (or by the social, racial, or religious groups predominating in the insurgency) often needed little encouragement to exercise violence against their social adversaries. The counterorganization cocktail often ensured that the assigned military task would become supercharged by questions of class, race, religion, or ideology. To achieve a short-term objective the counterinsurgent would revive ancestral intercommunal hatreds and passions best undisturbed. The combination of counterterror with counterorganization in practice tended to mean there was neither selectivity or restraint in the use of violence.

The counterorganization aspect of the doctrine is often clearly visible through the changing structures of the security systems – a "before" and "after" – of counterinsurgency states. The doctrine's influence to this end can be measured through doctrinal writing on counterorganization in many of the counterinsurgency states. Articles on counterorganization in the military journals of El Salvador and Guatemala in the 1960s and 1970s are a case in point.[44] The changing attitudes of military establishments toward elite Special Forces-style formations and toward civilian para-military organizations, too, can often be observed in military journals and the public statements of military spokesman. The actual introduction of innovative military and paramilitary structures, however, most visibly puts flesh to doctrinal shifts.

The premise that revolutionary insurgents win support through terror and intimidation not illogically encouraged a "self-defense" dimension to counterinsurgency. A stated rationale of counterorganization is that local people, if armed and organized, would play a major part in defending themselves from guerrilla depredations. As noted in a 1966 study, "An important part – possibly the most important part – of counter-organization of the population is the organization of its self-defence against revolutionary intimidation and exactions."[45] The premise was restated more recently in the 1984 report of the Kissinger Commission on Central America. United States doctrine was said to require:

two forms of military action, to be carried out by two distinct types of forces. First, local popular militias must be formed throughout the country (with whatever minimal training is feasible and with only the simplest weapons) to prevent the insurgents from using terror to extract obedience . . . Since this localized protective militia cannot be expected to resist any sustained guerrilla attack, US counterinsurgency methods also require the availability of well-trained and well-equipped regular forces in adequate numbers.[46]

The "self-defense" rationale was all very well, of course, in cases in which an adversary did in fact prey on the populace at large, unconcerned with local support. That this was rarely the case meant that self-defense forces would not be raised simply by handing out arms. A situation would hardly merit the term "insurgency" if a government was enough in tune with the bulk of the people to risk arming them. For public consumption and at a theoretical level, however, the "self-defense" ideal was a dominant element in counterorganization. But in practical terms, American doctrine (like that of the French and British) stressed that special care should be taken in selecting particular locals known to be loyal to the government, preferably military veterans and reservists, or others that stood out readily from the suspect mass:

> Needless to say, the most critical problem . . . will be that of screening recruits for loyalty . . . The best risks probably will be those who have previously served the government . . . militia units should be hand-picked . . . staffed with local reservists, and, if possible, commanded by small cadres of regulars . . . It would be desirable that the militiamen be drawn from former members of the armed forces.[47]

The "self-defense" principle has been cited in many counterinsurgency states as the rationale for paramilitary networks. The popular, community-wide systems of the doctrinal ideal, however, were the exception rather than the rule in the American sphere of influence. The *armed and motivated* paramilitary forces were generally composed of social sectors quite distinct from the mass of the population. The self-defense principle, moreover, has long served as a prime rationale for army public relations campaigns seeking to justify clandestine "death squads" of so-called "vigilantes" (notably in Brazil, Guatemala, El Salvador, Argentina, and most recently in Chile, Colombia, and the Philippines). The organization of "the people" as a militia, the arming of "the people," was inconceivable to armies whose reason for existence had become that of arbiter between the people and the state and defender of the status quo.

The counter-guerrilla, the friendly guerrilla to combat subversive guerrillas, was often distinguished in doctrine and practice from organizations set up on a home-guard or political-militia basis. They were to provide the grass-roots irregular counterparts of elite Special Forces-style formations. The May 1961 field manual *Operations against Irregular Forces* (FM 31–15), for example, distinguished between local civil self-defense units – with a strictly defensive function – and "Friendly guerrilla units," through which to fight fire with fire.[48] Later manuals made a distinction between *paramilitary* forces, which included locally based but nationally or regionally organized self-defense forces, and *irregular* forces, distinguished by a more select recruitment base, higher motivation, and offensive deployment.[49] The paramilitary–irregular distinction continues to be drawn in 1980s manuals; the 1981 manual on *Command, Control, and Support of Special Forces Operations* (FM 31–22) discusses advisory assistance for "host country" regular forces, paramilitary, and irregular forces.[50]

American-led counter-guerrilla irregulars were among the principal executors of "counterterror" in Vietnam, its best-known scenario. Most commentators, however, have discussed this only in the context of Operation Phoenix, revealed in 1971 to be a program of political murder carried out by some 30,000 counterterrorists. But American-led counterterror teams (CTs) of 6–12 men – "death squads" in all but name – had operated under CIA and army Special Forces auspices years before (most Special Forces in Indochina served under CIA control until July 1963).[51] The formal mission of the Special Forces at least as late as mid-1965, two years after these forces were removed from CIA control, continued to center on the organization and deployment of counter-guerrilla irregulars with a "counterterror" function.[52] The principal Special Forces-run counter-guerrilla structure from 1961 to 1970, the Civilian Irregular Defense Group (CIDG) system, was organized primarily among Montagnard tribesmen in the Vietnamese highlands. CIDG forces operated on a mercenary basis, and by 1968 totalled some 52,000 members: 42,000 serving as strike forces attached to Special Forces camps, and a 10,000-member mobile strike force operating throughout the country.[53]

Standing orders issued to Special Forces in January 1965 (LOI [Letter of Instructions] 1), and described by an army evaluation team as their "most important mission statement," exemplified the crossover between unconventional, guerrilla warfare tactics and counterinsurgency. Special Forces and CIDG were to establish operations zones in the border areas; "to establish rapport with local population;" to "Initiate guerrilla type operations within operational zone against VC controlled areas;" to "Assist in establishing population control;" and, among other things, to "Conduct operations to dislodge VC-controlled officials, to include assassination."[54] The same LOI set out actions to interdict "interior infiltration routes" in counterterror terms:

> CIDG will conduct clear and hold, patrol and ambush type operations to seal off, interdict and pacify areas . . . Concurrently with the above, small and highly trained units, utilizing counterguerrilla techniques will be operating out of the camps . . . *ambushing, raiding, sabotaging and committing acts of terrorism against known VC personnel.*[55] (italics added)

The permissible targets of these early American-run "death squads" were ambiguously defined: and in any case distinguishing Viet Cong "supporters" or members of the guerrilla infrastructure called for skills for which assassins are not particularly well known. Similar language was used in a secret 1962 report to the joint chiefs of staff following a visit to Colombia by a team headed by the commander of the Special Warfare Center.[56] In the "Secret Annex" to the report, General William P. Yarborough recommended immediate action against Colombia's then quiescent insurgency, using the "guerrilla" tactics of UW. Civilian and military personnel were to be selected for "clandestine training" for integration into a "civil and military structure" that would turn the tables on the subversives. The personnel were to be both counterterror adepts and "reformists:" "This structure should be used to press toward reforms known to be needed, perform counter-agent and counter-propaganda functions and *as necessary execute paramilitary, sabotage and/or terrorist activities against known communist proponents* (italics added)."[57]

The counterorganization concept was often defined explicitly in doctrine as appealing naturally to local elites – or those who like to enjoy elite privileges. Even in those cases, like that of Vietnam, in which rural elites showed little disposition to put their own lives on the line, American planners saw the ideal counterorganization as elite based, and performing "counterterrorism" as an intrinsic function. A secret June 1964 directive on combined US/government of South Vietnam pacification efforts laid down the counterorganization objective for eight critical provinces. The first priority after an area had been "cleared" by the military was to be the creation of "a basically civilian counter-terrorist organization on the precinct level . . . *It will be created from among the young elite which exists everywhere; those who have a stake in the community because they have a family, own a house or a piece of land, are ambitious to get ahead in business, profession or politics*" (italics added).[58] In practice, the counterterrorist organizations of Vietnam were more typically composed of members of ethnic and religious minorities, and even members of Saigon's criminal underworld.[59]

In their elite, commando-style aspects, counterinsurgency forces established on the US model included the Vietnamese and Chinese Nationalist Special Forces and the Special Forces established in many Latin American armies in the 1960s and to date. Some of the latter were distinguished by names in pre-Hispanic languages alluding to a warrior past. The Guatemalan Special Forces are the *Kaibiles*, Quiché for "warrior;" the Peruvian Civil Guard has its *Sinchis*, Quechua for "warrior;" the first of El Salvador's crack 1980s counterinsurgent battalions was the Nahuatl *Atlacatl*.[60]

Some counterinsurgency systems did distinguish clearly between irregular counter-guerrilla strike forces and mass paramilitary organizations combining local political and security functions. Mass organizations could be in concept modelled on the so-called "self-defense," "civil defense" or "home guard" forces established by French and British colonial administrations (notably in Indochina and Malaya respectively). These locally based paramilitary forces provided a framework for the natural allies of the colonial administrations (including the European planters and mine-operators themselves and their own security personnel) to be armed and integrated into a security structure. They could also serve the dual purpose of harnessing local manpower to perform static security duties and providing a framework for the control of the participants themselves. The suspect population could be induced or required to take responsibility for certain basic security tasks – particularly in communities that were relocated and concentrated on security grounds (into strategic hamlets, "new villages" or any number of variations). In Vietnam, variations on the mass counterorganization model emerged as extensions of earlier French colonial systems of Civil Guard and Self-Defense (*autodéfense*) forces (after 1963 known as the Regional and Popular Forces, RF/PF or "Ruff Puff" to the American advisers).[61] From a combined force of around 100,000 in 1961 they grew to 180,000 by the end of 1963, and in 1972, when the regular army stood at 570,000 troops, there were 520,000 "Ruff Puff" forces.[62]

Counterorganization could also take the form of paramilitary militias recruited on an ideological basis. A prototype was the system of part-time, live-at-home Greek National Guard Defense Battalions. Set up during the Greek Civil War, the system provided a vehicle for the mobilization of right-thinking civilians to provide local security.[63] It subsequently became a system for political indoctrination, a manpower pool for political thuggery, and a model for similar organizations elsewhere.[64] Later variations on the theme included the Philippines' 1950s civilian guards, which under the long Marcos administration became first the Barrio Self-Defense Forces and then in the 1970s, the still existing (under another name) Civilian Home Defense Forces (CHDF).[65] The

Guatemalan variation was set up during a three-year military government, 1963–6. It was based on the army's military commissioners' system (*comisionados militares*), and provided for tens of thousands of local landowners, plantation guards, and militants of far-right parties to be armed and deputized as army auxiliaries (the regular army then numbered some 8,000). The Guatemalan system followed the prescribed counterorganization formula, drawing upon a ready-made recruitment base, coopting – by deputizing – virtually the entire rural membership of the extreme-right-wing Movement of National Liberation party (known then for its slogan "the party of organized violence"). But military commissioners and their auxiliaries were technically part of the army's active reserve.

Among the best-known organizations set up in the 1960s that combined the paramilitary with the partisan political was El Salvador's paramilitary organization ORDEN (Spanish for "order"). ORDEN, administered by the armed forces but ostensibly a civic organization, provided a grassroots intelligence network, and a counterinsurgency manpower pool of tens of thousands that has played a major role in El Salvador's long-running "counterterror." When El Salvador's President Fidel Sánchez lauded ORDEN in a 1967 speech, he observed that "organizations like ORDEN" had been established in South Vietnam, the Philippines, Guatemala, and elsewhere, and "Our free world allies . . . are willing to assist also in the concrete case of ORDEN."[66] ORDEN could mobilize some 100,000 members (not all of them armed) under army and national guard direction by the mid-1970s. Although nominally outlawed in October 1979, its structure and many of its members subsequently reemerged in the 1980s civil defense patrol system.[67]

In the 1980s several manifestation of mass counterorganization have emerged which are aimed at the control both of the counterorganized and of the active insurgent. Examples include the *de facto* obligatory civil defense organization set up in Guatemala's Indian highlands in 1981–2, civil defense organizations set up in Peru's Ayacucho, Huancavelica, and Apurimac departments since 1982, and a civil defense militia system supported actively by the United States – with rather less success – in El Salvador. In the Philippines, the metamorphosis of the CHDF system since the fall of Marcos has included the reinforcement of an elaborate military command and control structure, and the mobilization and deployment of vast new forces as so-called "vigilantes." The Philippines system has recently moved toward the model of *de facto* obligatory participation, where refusal to join military-controlled paramilitary organizations may result in reprisals on the "with us or against us" principle.

5 Paved with Good Intentions?

Nearly twenty years ago congressional hearings questioned whether the United States' security assistance programs were aiding the people of the countries assisted or abetting their torture, imprisonment, or murder. When Senator Fulbright concluded that US programs in Latin America appeared to have "brought change and progress toward democratic processes to a standstill," an expert witness responded wryly: "I don't know that we have done this deliberately."[68]

Good intentions or bad, torture, "disappearance," mass killings, and political imprisonment became the norm in many of the nations most heavily assisted by the United States in Latin America, and elsewhere. Repression in itself was not new. But from the mid-1960s new patterns of repression, and new organizational forms for its implementation, emerged in close association with US security assistance programs. And perhaps surprisingly, in many areas repression prompted resistance in new forms and of new potency. Assistance and advice to combat insurgency sometimes fuelled insurgency. Dissent and discontent blossomed into revolt and revolution.

Most critics in the United States saw the terror tactics of its Third World allies as a somehow natural feature of traditional military despotism, if the terror registered at all. The United States was blamed for what it did *not* do to stop atavistic practices, and for supporting military regimes which seemed to rely on terror because they did not know better. There was a presumption that there had always been paramilitary groups, "death squads," and "disappearances;" that torture was a traditional practice too deeply entrenched in national cultures for United States advisers to combat; and indeed that Third World armies had always seen the maintenance of *internal*, not external, security as their own primary mission.

In the mid-1970s, disquiet peaked in the media and the Congress over the nature of the United States' relationship with the agents of torture and murder in allied states. Detailed testimony during William Colby's confirmation hearings as CIA director brought details of the "practical," bloody side of the United States' Operation Phoenix in Vietnam. The examination of the police and military assistance programs found the United States was too closely tied to agencies of torture and political murder for comfort. In both cases, the CIA was a natural lightning rod for criticism and blame. The CIA had administered Phoenix. The CIA had used other counterinsurgency programs, like the Agency for International Development (AID)'s police training program, as vehicles through which to place its personnel in positions of influence. The CIA was more easily cast as the bad guy than the US Army or the government itself. In any case, the net effect was to create concern not primarily that United States personnel were themselves purveyors of torture or administrators of assassinations, but that their *public identification as such* and their intimate association with the primitives wielding the pistols and the cattle prods were damaging to the image of the United States.

The traditional security systems of many United States allies began to change in the early 1960s, toward a greater involvement of military institutions in the dirty work of internal security, with the military taking on the roles previously played by the political police. Institutional changes proceeded, sometimes coinciding with the take-over of government by military regimes. In the same period, the substance of American military assistance and police assistance programs changed qualitatively. Traditional military training and equipment programs were supplanted by programs geared explicitly toward counter-insurgency. And counter-insurgency doctrine brought in its train elite Special Forces, paramilitary "counterguerrilla" irregulars, and a concept of "counterterror."

The new military regimes in many of the nations that had benefited from American assistance, and the armies that would dominate weak civilian frontmen, were qualitatively different from their predecessors. In Latin America the tyrannical men on horseback of the past had largely been supplanted by military bureaucrats and institutional rules of succession. Perhaps more important with respect to the human rights catastrophes that ensued were changes in the way the military institutions responsible saw the threat of dissent and subversion, and the roles appropriate to the armed forces in overcoming them. In many cases, the emergence of death squads and "disappearances," mass killings, and the routinization of torture accompanied changes in written military doctrine – as observed through the publications and proclamations of the respective institutions – and visible changes in the organizational structure of the security systems at issue. The military concept of doctrine, like the religious ("that which is taught, what is put forth as true", to quote Webster's) provided a starting point from which to distinguish policy from happenstance.

The combination of organizational and tactical innovations, and their stated rationale – that subversives should be fought with their own methods – had a common denominator. Each of the military institutions experiencing radical changes in organization and methods had been the beneficiary of extensive civilian and military security assistance from the United States since the 1940s (and some from considerably earlier). Until the 1960s, however, internal security had largely been delegated to civil, political police organizations – including the classic secret police.

143

American military assistance concentrated on training Latin American armies in traditional military skills and inculcating conventional military doctrine.

The covert, extraordinary, and illegal aspects of counterinsurgency comprise only a small part of the written doctrine and require little in the way of direct hands-on involvement by United States personnel. It is these extraordinary aspects of counterinsurgency doctrine that have tended to overwhelm, and make either meaningless or absurd, parallel pressures for "reforms known to be needed." The elaborate programs of civic action or "nation building" promoted as an integral aspect of counterinsurgency were, even when pursued in good faith, sabotaged by the ethos of "anything goes" that dominated its strictly military side. And since the 1960s, whether defined as the doctrine of "Internal Defense and Development" – counterinsurgency's late-1970s incarnation – or as "low intensity warfare," the non-military and the conventional military side of counterinsurgency continue to be subordinated to the precept that counterinsurgency is a "special" kind of war in which "special" operations and tactics unacceptable in other theatres take precedence. The maxim that the rule of law – the law of peace and indeed even the law of war – can legitimately be set aside to achieve counterinsurgency objectives remains in place.

Counterinsurgency from its inception as a doctrine was defined as a "special" discipline, and its adepts as elite, "special" forces which required unconventional tactics, secrecy, and extraordinary license to perform their tasks – just as the operatives of the post-war intelligence agencies were defined. Although the counterinsurgency specialists comprised a small part of the United States' military establishment, insulated from its regular forces and the public, it would be the special warfare adepts, from the Army's Special Forces, and the equivalent air-force, navy, and CIA personnel, that would provide the main interface with allied military establishments: the bulk of security assistance programs advisers, trainers, and planners on the ground overseas.

Although themselves an elite, the special warfare personnel of the United States were not limited to organizing or training a proportionally small and "special" force overseas. As a consequence, armies such as that of El Salvador in the 1980s were virtually remade in Special Forces image. On the one hand, elite units trained in counterinsurgency by the Special Forces, like the Atonal or Atlacatl battalions, proliferated; on the other, virtually every officer now in service there has benefited from Special Forces training and advice, and some of the dark side of the Special Forces "guerrilla/counter-guerrilla" tactics can be presumed to have been absorbed. Certainly it is astonishing to imagine the "guerrilla" specialists of the US army (any more than the British SAS commandos) being wasted teaching a conventional curriculum on military logistics – or as convincing professors of humanitarian law.

The blueprint (or "software") for paramilitary organization as an instrument of "anything goes" counterinsurgency was similarly fraught with danger, proposing as it did that the new irregulars be recruited in a manner reinforcing existing deep divisions in the target society. The "friendly" (counter-) guerrilla was for safety's sake to be recruited from social sectors set apart from the suspect mass: groups already known to share a counterinsurgent motivation or trusted and prepared to serve as mercenaries. The make-up itself of the new counter-guerrilla forces, from Vietnam and the Philippines to Central America and Colombia, tended to exacerbate existing conflict situations: recruits were drawn from elites and their employees, ethnic or religious minorities, or extremist political parties. The net result was to create, or further set apart, an armed elite aloof from the majority of the population. Provided with modern weaponry and sharing the regular armed services' discretionary powers of life and death, the new paramilitaries could act out ancestral conflicts and pursue group interests in the course of counterinsurgency. Where paramilitary organization built upon divisions of race, class, and ideology, counterinsurgency assumed new dimensions of violence quite above and beyond the textbook prescriptions even of "counterterror."

But in the final analysis, the "anything goes" orientation of the new doctrine itself may have played the primary role in catalyzing the mass state terror of the counterinsurgency states. The concept of "counterterror" in itself legitimated the scrapping of the rule of law in a manner which no other aspect of American military doctrine, or foreign policy, has even approximated. Seemingly a little thing, just a small part of a larger doctrine, "counterterror" represented the United States' green light for state terrorism; a light that has been difficult to extinguish.

6 The Doctrine Today

Where does the doctrine stand today? Clearly the concept of counter-organization remains in place. At the time of writing, paramilitary systems of civilian irregulars – of varying kinds – remain at the heart of counterinsurgency systems in El Salvador, Guatemala, Colombia, Peru, and the Philippines in perfect accord with longstanding United States military doctrine. A 1980s effort to establish a paramilitary civil defense militia in Honduras appears to have collapsed – not through want of trying by American advisers, but through Honduran indifference to the scheme. And the 1984 Kissinger Commission report confirmed that the civilian irregular was still expected to play a major role in counterinsurgency.

Is "counterterror" still part of the counterinsurgency formula? Counterterror*ism* as a term of art for *international* operations did enter the foreign policy vocabulary in the early 1980s. The Reagon administration for a time made frequent references to the legitimacy of reactive and preemptive "counterterrorism," but did so in the context of taking unilateral action in the international arena against "international" terrorists and states aiding them. The principle of "fighting fire with fire" in the teeth of international law is certainly of a kind with counterinsurgent terror, however, and suggests the latter, too, remains within the bounds of legitimacy. The "counterterrorism" declarations by the administration have certainly served as a signal to allied "counterterrorists" that anything still goes in the unconventional wars of terrorism and insurgency, whether international or domestic.

Although it is unlikely that prescriptions of the use of terror will surface in the army field manuals of the era after President Carter and his human rights policies, less formal documents continue to emerge that do so. The US government manual prepared for UW against Nicaragua (*Psychological Operations in Guerrilla Warfare*) is perhaps as close as we will get to documentary confirmation that the 1960s concept remains basically unmodified.[69] The manual details methods for the legitimate use of terror (although referring to the correct actions of US-backed "guerrillas," not "counter-guerrillas") and repeats the same arguments and uses the same terminology as US Army training materials from the 1960s (indeed, including verbatim passages from one 1967 US Army field manual).

Similarly, the categorization of counterinsurgency as a "special" discipline, an offshoot and an aspect of UW, remains fixed in American doctrine.[70] The US Army's Special Forces continue to exercise primary responsibility as specialists and trainers in both UW and counterinsurgency; and indeed, Special Forces today provide most of the American trainers overseas for foreign military personnel. They and other American "special operations" forces also retain the *skills* for counterterrorism/terrorism in, respectively, counterinsurgency and UW. A recent study on Special Operations Forces (US and Soviet) by the US Congressional Research Service outlines the tasks required of such forces, and describes their "Military Assistance, Advice and Training" role as covering "Unconventional warfare and internal defense/foreign internal defense, terrorism, and counter-terrorism."[71] A chart with a breakdown of the basic tasks required by Special Operations Forces includes such classics as Assassination and abduction ("A & A"), hostage taking, random killing and maiming, sabotage, capture, and termination.[72] Definitions are equally enlightening:

Assassination and abduction are illegal special operations employed offensively for sociopolitical purposes. Official actions to capture or kill key insurgents and transnational terrorists ("Termination") are legal and defensive. Assassination and abduction (A & A) are direct, discriminating, essentially decisive, economical, and occasionally unique ways to achieve required results.[73]

Termination is defined variously as referring to " 'surgical' antipersonnel operations against transnational terrorists and key insurgents,"[74] "Legal steps to kill individuals or groups"[75] and "A euphemism for killings by authorities of individuals or groups engaged in illegal and/or warlike activities."[76]

A footnote to a chart outlining the US command structure as it relates to distinct Special Operations tasks notes that it excludes from its scope "political assassination, which is illegal; also political abduction and terrorist acts listed on Figure 2 [hostage taking, random killing and maiming] because of official and public disapproval."[77] Another footnote adds, however, that both the United States and the Soviet Union "back associates that sometimes employ tactics shown, but the United States disapproves in principle."[78]

Who, then, are the associates still engaged in programs of state terrorism? Prime candidates are the armies and paramilitary forces of the counterinsurgency states, where political assassination and abduction and random killing and maiming remain the order of the day. Who are the advisers and trainers assigned to the forces of the counterinsurgency states? They are the United States military's unconventional warfare specialists, the US Army Special Forces, the poachers turned gamekeepers. And the doctrine still dominating the internal affairs of the counterinsurgency states is much the same as the doctrine of counterinsurgency that crystallized from its roots in unconventional warfare in the first years of the 1960s.

Notes

1   There is, of course, another side to political warfare. The immediate post-war period saw the development of a doctrine and a capability for "unconventional warfare," defined as covert, offensive "guerrilla"-style operations in enemy-held territory. The army's Special Forces establishment was founded in 1952 to provide the United States an offensive capability for behind-the-lines guerrilla warfare; their *counter*-guerrilla role awaited the 1960s. The role of terror and paramilitary organization in unconventional warfare, counterinsurgency's parent doctrine, can also be shown in written doctrine and in historical experience, but is beyond the scope of this paper.

2 A comment on proposals made in the Defense Paper, which is part of the Defense Limited War Task Force Report by Defense Secretary Robert S. MacNamara, is made in a memorandum, (February 1, 1961), filed with National Security Action Memorandum (NSAM 2) "Development of Counter Guerrilla Forces," (February 3, 1961), Kennedy Library, National Security Council, Box 328. Most of the NSAM 2 file remains classified.

3 Ibid.

4 The records of the Department of the Army, Office of the Chief of Psychological Warfare (1951–4), in Record Group 319, National Archive, Washington, DC, provide considerable insight into differences of opinion over what was considered militarily proper even in the field of UW.

5 John F. Kennedy, "Defense Policy and the Budget: Message of President Kennedy to the Congress, March 28, 1961," in Richard P. Stebbins, *Documents on American Foreign Relations, 1961* (Council on Foreign Relations/Harper & Row, 1962), pp. 51–63.

6 Ibid., p. 60. Other versions of the speech refer to "lunatic blackmail" rather than "diplomatic;" see Willard F. Barber and C. Neale Ronning, *Internal Security and Military Power; Counterinsurgency and Civic Action in Latin America* (Ohio State University Press, 1966), p. 31, citing the *Congressional Record*.

7 The emphasis on the part of the Navy and Air Force was to develop their own elite special operations forces and facilities – from the Navy SEALs (Sea, Air and Land Commando-type troops) to Special Air Commandos based at a new Special Air Warfare center at Eglin Air Force Base in Florida. The air-force approach combined the army focus on what were in essence commando-style forces trained and equipped for raiding and behind-the-lines operations with the specialized aircraft already loaned by the air force to the CIA for behind-the-lines operations during the Korean War.

8 L.L. Lemnitzer, "Memorandum for the Special Assistant to the President for National Security Affairs" (July 21, 1962), Subject: Summary Report, "A Summary of US Military Counterinsurgency Accomplishments since January 1, 1961" (Carrollton Press Declassified Documents Series (R:242C)). For a summary of details on training accomplishments and institutional adjustment to counterinsurgency requirements outlined in the Lemnitzer paper and others, see Michael McClintock, *The American Connection, vol. 1* (Zed Books, 1985), chapter 2.

9 Ibid. The records of the Kennedy administration, and the numerous books on the period, detail the personal involvement of the president, his brother Robert Kennedy, and dedicated counterinsurgents like Walt Rostow and Roger Hilsman in pushing through counterinsurgency programs. The bureaucratic linchpin of the effort was the top-level policy and operations group set up in January 1962 (NSAM 124), the Special Group (Counter-insurgency), "To assure the use of US resources with maximum effectiveness in preventing and resisting subversive insurgency in friendly countries."

10 A document setting out "US Counterinsurgency Doctrine" was approved by the Special Group (Counterinsurgency) and the president for dissemination to US agencies and overseas posts as National Security Action Memorandum

182. The 30-page paper, entitled "Overseas Internal Defense Policy," was a first effort at a comprehensive statement of "a doctrine for countering subversive insurgency where it exists and to prevent its outbreak in those countries not yet threatened, yet having weak and vulnerable societies" (Maxwell D. Taylor, "Memorandum for Mr Bundy, Subject: Counter-insurgency Doctrine" (August 13, 1962); transmittal memorandum for the doctrine paper promulgated as NSAM 182, "US Overseas Internal Defense Policy," Kennedy Library, NSF, NSAM 182, Box 338). The operational side of the doctrine is elaborated in the field manuals and training materials of the armed forces.

11 NSAM 182, p. 13.

12 Ibid.

13 During the Kennedy period the term was defined as "the use of preponderantly indigenous military forces on projects useful to the local populations at all levels in such fields as education, training, public works, agriculture, transportation, communications, health, sanitation, and others contributing to economic and social development, which would also serve to improve the standing of their military forces with the population. (United States forces may at times advise or engage in military civic actions in overseas areas)" (see Barber and Ronning, *Internal Security and Military Power*, p. 6). The definition in 1986 – still valid – of military civic action does not differ in kind: "The use of mainly indigenous armed forces to implement economic and social programs, that benefit local populations, partly to improve the popular image of those forces" (see John M. Collins, *US and Soviet Special Operations*, Draft Committee Print for Special Operations Panel, House Armed Services Committee (Congressional Research Service, December 23, 1986), p. 108.

14 "Nation building," too, remains a military concept in the eighties, defined in the glossary in Collins, *US and Soviet Special Operations*, p. 108, as "Activities by a developing country, unilaterally or with outside assistance, to create or strengthen popular acceptance of political, economic, legal, social, and other programs, thereby enhancing internal security."

15 Lemnitzer, "Memorandum for the Special Assistant," p. 7.

16 US Joint Chiefs of Staff, *JCS Publication 1, Dictionary of United States Military Terms for Joint Usage* (GPO, August 1, 1968). The same definition appears in the 1974 edition of *JCS Publication 1*.

17 The Center and school were initially founded in 1952 as the Psychological Warfare Center; were renamed the Special Warfare Center in 1956; and in 1969 became the John F. Kennedy Center for Military Assistance. Fort Bragg continues to be the headquarters of the US Army Special Forces, with the commander of the Center serving as the Special Force top commander.

18 "Establishment of a Guerrilla Warfare School and a Guerrilla Warfare Corps," Franklin Lindsay and Charles Thayer, in Joint Chiefs of Staff discussion papers, JCS 1807 (November 19, 1947): Record Group 165, ABC files, 352.1 Guerrilla (September 15, 1947), National Archives. The document is introduced by a letter of September 29, 1947, from George F. Kennan, then director, Policy and Planning Staff of the Department of State.

Michael McClintock

19 JCS 1807/1 of August 17, 1948, is cited in Alfred H. Paddock, *US Army Special Warfare: Its Origins* (National Defense University Press, 1982), pp. 72–3. Principal peacetime responsibility for unconventional warfare was assigned to the CIA in May 1948.

20 Paddock, *US Army Special Warfare*, p. 83.

21 Collins, *US and Soviet-Special Operations*, p. 24.

22 L. L. Lemnitzer, "Memorandum for the Special Group (CI), Subject: Military Training Related To Counter-Insurgency Matters (U)," (January 30, 1962): NSF, Special Group, Military Training Report, Box 319, Kennedy Library.

23 Ibid.

24 Cited in Major John S. Pustay, USAF, *Counterinsurgency Warfare* (Collier–MacMillan, 1965), p. 169.

25 See, for example, Special Warfare Center, *Counter-Insurgency Operations* (December 1, 1960), an unnumbered, classified manual that represents a first tentative effort to incorporate UW tactics into a *counter*-guerrilla doctrine. The manual is on file at the Kennedy Library: Presidential Office Files (POF); Justice ("US Army Report"); "Counter-Insurgency Operations" (December 1, 1960).

26 Brig. Gen. William P. Yarborough, "US Special Warfare Center," in US Department of the Army, Office of the Chief of Information, *Special Warfare US Army: An Army Speciality* (US Department of the Army, 1963), p. 61. A psychological operations course was also offered at Fort Bragg, covering all aspects of psychological warfare, in consonance with the Center's psywar origins. After 1961, however, Psywar's 1950s poor relation, special warfare, had taken over as the Center's star attraction, catching up with its December 1956 name change to Special Warfare Center.

27 The evidence of this shifting between the norms of counterinsurgency and UW and back, in a single theatre over time, is most apparent in declassified documentation from the Vietnam War, and is discussed further in Michael McClintock, *With the Best of Intentions: Special Warfare and Low Intensity Conflict* (Pantheon Books, forthcoming).

28 Frank R. Barnett, "A Proposal for Political Warfare," *Military Review* (March 1961).

29 Ibid.

30 Special Warfare Center, *Counter-Insurgency Operations*.

31 Ibid., pp. 69, 86–7. The "Q" operation takes its name from the "Q" ships of wartime – converted freighters designed to offer enticing targets to enemy warships, while concealing heavy armament behind workaday tarpaulins.

32 Department of the Army, *Human Factors Considerations of Undergrounds in Insurgencies*, DA Pam 550-104 (US Government Printing Office, September, 1966), p. 184.

33 Ibid.

34 See in particular, Edward G. Lansdale, "Practical Jokes," in US Department of the Army *Psychological Operations*, DA Pamphlet (US Department of the Army, 525-7-1 (April 1976) p. 770.

35 Headquarters, Department of the Army, *US Army Handbook of Counter-*

150

insurgency Guidelines for Area Commanders, An Analysis of Criteria, Department of the Army Pamphlet no. 550-100 (US Department of the Army, January 1966). Cited in McClintock, (*The American Connection*, vol. I, p. 42.

36   US Department of the Army, *US Army Handbook of Counterinsurgency Guidelines for Area Commanders*, p. 225.

37   Brig. Gen. Michael Calvert (UK), "El Patron de la Guerra de Guerrillas," *Revista Militar de Guatemala* (October–November 1966), pp. 50-8; reprinted from *Military Review* (July 1966). Calvert wrote from his own experience in the British army; his argument was that the German approach to counter-terror was too clumsy. Insurgency required a more refined, selective approach. His Guatemalan readers may have missed some of the subtlety. US Army doctrinal materials applied by the Guatemalan army at the time included a mimeographed, Spanish-language translation of the School of Special Warfare's *Guide for Counterinsurgency Planning*, Special Text (ST) 31/176 (US Department of the Army, 1963). A facsimile, reportedly obtained from Guatemalan army sources in the 1960s, is included in Alejandro de Corro, *Guatemala, La Violencia*, **CIDOC** Dossier 19 (CIDOC, 1968).

38   Calvert, "El Patron de la Guerra de Guerrilas," p. 50.

39   Ibid.

40   Ibid., p. 58.

41   McClintock, *The American Connection*, vol. II, pp. 84-5.

42   Brian Jenkins, Cesar D. Sereseres, "US Military Assistance and the Guatemalan Armed Forces: the Limits of Military Involvement in Latin America" (June 1976, typescript). The authors also noted the broad brush with which terror was applied: "Blacklists were compiled which included not only those suspected of working with the guerrillas but also those suspected of Communist leanings."

43   For a summary of the concept see McClintock, *The American Connection*, vol. 1, pp. 33-8. An American counterinsurgent's-eye view is provided in Lt. Col. (US Army) John J. McCuen, *The Art of Counter-Revolutionary War: The Strategy of Counter-Insurgency* (Stackpole Books, 1966), particularly in chapters V ("Counter-organization") and VI ("Counter-terrorism").

44   The change over time in the structure and tactics of the security systems of Guatemala and El Salvador, in practice and in written doctrine, is discussed in McClintock, *The American Connection*, vols I and II, *passim*.

45   McCuen, *The Art of Counter-Revolutionary War*, p. 107.

46   White House, *Report of the National Bipartisan Commission on Central America* (US Government Printing Office, January 1984), pp. 95-6, cited in McClintock, *The American Connection*, vol. II, p. 282.

47   McCuen, *The Art of Counter-Revolutionary War*, p. 107.

48   US Department of the Army, *Operations against Irregular Forces* (FM 31-15) (US Department of the Army, May 1961), pp. 32-5.

49   US Department of the Army, *US Army Counterinsurgency Forces* (FM 31-22) (US Department of the Army, November 1963), pp. 82-4, distinguished between "Self Defense Units," "normally . . . the primary paramilitary force" charged with local security, and "Civic Defense Groups,"

which differ in their "origin, status, and method of management and support." The latter play the counter-guerrilla role, and are recruited from "primitive tribes in distant and remote areas, people in rural areas, minority ethnic groups, and miscellaneous groups such as workmen's militia, youth organizations and female auxiliaries." Special attention is given to the utility of "primitive tribal groups" as resources for "hunter-killer teams." The paramilitary–irregular distinction is made after 1966.

50 US Department of the Army, *Command, Control, and Support of Special Forces Operations*, FM 31-22 (US Department of the Army, December 23, 1981), section 2, p. 7, section 9, p. 3. The manual supersedes TC 31-20-1 of October 22, 1976, and is a "new style," large format, easy-reading edition interpersed with large *Boys Own Paper*-style drawings of chaps in Special Forces uniform.

51 For a summary of sources on Phoenix and the CT Teams – renamed Provincial Reconnaissance Units (PRUs) in 1966 – see McClintock, *The American Connection*, vol. I, p. 45-9. See also Thomas Powers, *The Man Who Kept the Secrets: Richard Helms and the CIA* (Pocket Books, 1979), p. 228; Victor Marchetti and John D. Marks, *The CIA and the Cult of Intelligence* (Dell, 1974) pp. 122-5, 236-7. Shelby L. Stanton, *Green Berets at War: US Army Special Forces in Southeast Asia 1956-1975* (Arms and Armour Press, 1985) provides the details of the phasing out of CIA control, code name Operation Switchback.

52 Department of the Army, Army Concept Team, Vietnam, "Employment of a Special Forces Group" (April 20, 1966) (Carrollton Press Declassified Documents Series (R:204B)).

53 For detailed and meticulously documented accounts of the Special Forces in Vietnam and the CIDG, see Stanton, *Green Berets at War*, and the Department of the Army's Vietnam Studies volume, Col. Francis J. Kelly, *US Army Special Forces 1961-1971* (US Department of the Army, 1973). For force levels see Stanton, pp. 176, and *passim*. The CIDG program was shut down in December 1970, with the Special Forces contingent itself withdrawing from Vietnam in March 1971.

54 Army Concept Team, Vietnam "Employment of a Special Forces Group," pp. F-12, F-13, Annex F, "Counterguerrilla Operations in Border Surveillance", to LOI 1 (January 1, 1965).

55 Ibid., Annex F, p. F-14, "Counterguerrilla Operations Against Interior Infiltration Routes," to LOI 1.

56 William P. Yarborough, "Memorandum to the Joint Chiefs of Staff, Subject: Visit to Colombia, South America by a Team from Special Warfare Center, Fort Bragg, North Carolina, Secret Annex" (February 26, 1962): J. F. Kennedy Presidential Library, Box 319, National Security Files; Special Group; Fort Bragg Team; Visit to Colombia.

57 Ibid., "Secret Supplement, Colombian Survey Report." The brief of the Special Warfare survey team was to prepare the way for the first of a series of Special Warfare Mobile Training Teams due to arrive in Colombia in early March 1962.

58 Joint chiefs of staff, "Combined GVN-US Effort to Intensify Pacification

Efforts in Critical Provinces" (June 19, 1964) (Carrollton Press Declassified Documents Series (1979:90A)).

59 Former Special Forces officer Shelby L. Stanton notes the role of Saigon gangsters plugged into the CIDG program. See his *Green Berets at War: US Army Special Forces in Southeast Asia 1956-1975*, pp. 47, 66.

60 See McClintock, *The American Connection*, vol. II, p. 57n; the first unit of Kaibiles was the Guatemalan 1st Special Forces Company, modelled on the US Army Special Forces and set up under the US Military Assistance Program 1963-6. According to the 1966 Department of State report *US Internal Security Programs in Latin America*, vol. II, pp. 11-13 (Internal Security Programs Evaluation Group, November 30, 1985), the program trained the Kaibiles and "a CT Detachment."

61 South Vietnam's security system in the 1950s included a paramilitary civil guard and a self-defense militia; the guard in 1957 had some 54,000 members, the militia some 50,000. The guard in the 1950s was made up primarily of Catholic former members of pro-French militias from the north. See Ronald H. Spector, *Advice and Support: the Early Years of the US Army in Vietnam 1941-1960* (Free Press, 1985), pp. 320-5.

62 McClintock, *The American Connection*, vol. I, pp. 25-6; and Robert W. Komer, *The Malayan Emergency in Retrospect: Organization of a Successful Counterinsurgency Effort*, R-957-ARPA (RAND, February, 1972), pp. 82-3.

63 These were the *Tagmata Ethnofylackha Amyns* or TEA battalions (McClintock, *The American Connection*, vol. I, pp. 37-8).

64 The TEA battalion system is cited as a model counterorganization in McCuen, *The Art of Counter-Revolutionary War*, pp. 111-12; their role as political thugs and the call for their disbandment prior to the 1961 elections is noted in Andreas Papandreou, *Democracy at Gunpoint: The Greek Front* (André Deutsch, 1971), p. 77.

65 The Philippines' civilian guards system, through which semi-private guards served large landholders and local government officials, had already played a significant role during World War II, assisting the Japanese occupation forces to maintain local security – and agricultural production. The guards became an integral part of the counterinsurgency structure in the course of the Huk Rebellion. The Barrio Self Defense Forces and the 1970s CHDF were far more sophisticated organizationally, tieing local detachments into the armed forces command structure through local constabulary posts.

66 Cited in McClintock, *The American Connection*, vol. I, p. 207. Like the Philippines CHDF, which built upon the constabulary's administrative net, El Salvador's ORDEN was administered through rural National Guard posts. (The Philippines' constabulary and the Salvadorean National Guard are both integral parts of their respective armed forces.)

67 McClintock, *The American Connection*, vol. I, pp. 204-22, 325, 340-3.

68 From US Congress, Senate, *Survey of the Alliance for Progress: Compilation of Studies and Hearings* (US Government Printing Office, 1968), p. 304. The response was from Edwin Lieuwen, a harsh critic of US military assistance programs.

Michael McClintock

69 "Tayacán" (CIA), *Operaciones Psicológicas en Guerra de Guerrillas* (CIA, 1983). An English-language edition, with an introduction by Aryeh Neier and Joanne Omang, was published as *Psychological Operations in Guerrilla Warfare* (Vintage, 1985).

70 See, for example, US Department of the Army, *Command, Control, and Support of Special Forces Operations*, FM 31-22 (US Department of the Army, December 23, 1981). In 1981 terminology, counterinsurgency became "Foreign Internal Defense."

71 John M. Collins, Draft Committee Print for Special Operations Panel House Armed Services Committee, *US and Soviet Special Operations* (Congressional Research Service, The Library of Congress, December 23, 1986), p. 83, figure 16, "Tasks connected to skills."

72 Ibid.

73 Ibid., p. 84. The 1981 Special Forces manual cited above (FM 31-22), pp. 2-7, refers to missions to "Abduct selected personnel" as a task in UW.

74 Ibid., p. 76, figure 15, "Special tasks across the conflict spectrum."

75 Ibid., p. 7, figure 2, "US and Soviet Special Operations related to tasks."

76 Ibid., p. 114.

77 Ibid., p. 15, figure 6, "US High Command related to Special Operations tasks."

78 Ibid., p. 7, figure 2.

7

Containment and its Failure: The British State and the Control of Conflict in Northern Ireland

Bill Rolston

1 Introduction

It may be of interest to recall that when the regular army was first raised in the 17th century, "suppression of the Irish" was coupled with "defence of the Protestant religion" as one of the two main reasons for its existence.[1]

In the past seven years there have been approximately 300 terrorist incidents in Great Britain . . . which have resulted in the deaths of 75 people and over ten times as many injured. The overwhelming majority of these incidents have been connected with the situation in Northern Ireland.[2]

That a former British Secretary of State for Northern Ireland could note that "the Irish problem" had led to a majority of deaths from "terrorism" in Britain in the 1970s is overwhelming proof that the army formed 300 years previously for "the suppression of the Irish" had singularly failed in its task. In fact, throughout those three centuries "the Irish problem" had frequently burst out of the confines of Irish society to leave its mark on the international scene. In 1691, 11,000 Irish soldiers who fought on the Jacobite side against William III's accession to the British throne were shipped on British ships to France where, as a specific Irish Brigade in the French army, they confinued to fight against Britain. One hundred years later it was French soldiers, who had landed in Mayo and declared a Republic in support of the United Irishmen's rebellion in the north, who were shipped back to continental Europe. In the nineteenth century the Fenians, formed simultaneously in New York and Ireland, invaded Canada (then a British colony), led an uprising in Ireland, and carried out a bombing campaign in Britain.[3]

During all this time Britain was far from inactive. Pacifying Ireland involved Britain in military activities and an endless array of emergency laws. Farrell notes that between 1800 and 1921 there were 105 separate Coercion Acts initiated by Britain in Ireland.[4] And Mulloy states: "in the first half century after the Act of Union [1800] Ireland was ruled by the ordinary law of the land for only five years."[5]

Despite the legal, military, and other weapons used, Ireland was not pacified – as the instances of international ripples of "the Irish problem" cited above prove. Given that, it would seem that Britain has been involved not so much in "suppressing the Irish" as in seeking to contain the violence and uncertainty which derive from British involvement in Ireland within Ireland itself.

2 Containing "the Troubles"

Despite the British government's stated intentions of obtaining political consensus in Northern Ireland, the only policy that is implemented in practice is one of crisis management, that is, the effort to contain violence through emergency measures.[6]

The overarching act of containment in the twentieth century was the partition of Ireland in 1921. Partition was no solution to "the Irish problem" as far as Ireland was concerned. In relation to the South, Farrell notes: "For all but four years or so of its 64-year existence, the independent Irish state has lived under some form of emergency legislation."[7] As for the North, emergency legislation has been an unbroken tradition. Yet in another sense partition *was* a solution – for Britain. It quarantined Ireland, leaving the problems of policing an unsatisfactory arrangement to the Irish themselves. With the exception of the late 1930s, "the Irish problem" had few military effects in Britain itself, and even fewer political effects.

Since the emergence of "the troubles" in the North in the late 1960s, British policy, as before, has been to attempt to contain the problem, to ensure, in the words of then British Home Secretary Reginald Maudling, that violence is "reduced to an acceptable level."[8] That has required massive military commitment and financial support.[9]

As a result, Northern Ireland has ended up as "one of the most policed societies in the free world."[10] According to Baldy (p. 113), West Germany has 0.6 internal security personnel for every 1,000 of its population, France 1.6, Italy 3.5, and Northern Ireland 8.4.

These broad figures disguise a major shift in Northern Ireland in the 1970s from the primacy of the British army to a reliance on the local Royal

Ulster Constabulary (RUC) and Ulster Defence Regiment (UDR) as the first line of counterinsurgency (the policy known as "Ulsterization"). One measure of this is the extent to which indigenous forces suffered an increasing proportion of the casualties.[11] Moreover, the shift meant that the RUC in particular was at the forefront of enacting another major strategy in the 1970s, that of "criminalization". Prior to the mid-1970s, internment had been in operation. When this was phased out, sentenced prisoners had "political status." The removal of that status meant that political offenders were to be reclassified as criminals, a shift that republican prisoners fought all the way up to the hunger strikes of 1980 and 1981.[12] In the pursuit of criminal status the RUC were helped by the absence of juries (as a result of changes proposed in the Diplock Report, 1972)[13] and the latitude allowed in definitions of acceptable evidence (as a result of the Gardiner Report, 1975).[14] Confessions were beaten out of suspects.[15]

The collapse of such heavy-handed methods led to changes in tactics in the early to mid-1980s. Initially suspects were convicted on the uncorrobborated evidence of alleged accomplices (the "supergrass" system),[16] despite such convictions being impossible under British law as it operated in Britain itself. Following the collapse of this strategy there was a brief but bloody switch to one of shooting suspected republican activists on sight (the "shoot-to-kill") policy).[17] Finally, in 1988, one more sacred element of the rule of law, the right to silence, was dispensed with; the silence of a suspect under police interrogation can now be taken by the (juryless) court as corroborative proof of guilt. The tradition whereby the court cannot deduce any guilt from silence still operates in Britain. All of these changes in Northern Ireland pulled the indigenous RUC to the forefront of counterinsurgency.

3   Exporting the Problem

One bomb in Oxford Street [London] is worth ten in Belfast.[18]

One death in London is worth twenty in Belfast.[19]

Containment as a strategy seeks ideally to confine the political violence to Northern Ireland, and to specific ghettos within Northern Ireland. But ideals are elusive; thus in reality it is accepted that counter-state violence necessarily breaks out of the ghettos.

The last decade has seen an increasing convergence between the British and Southern Irish states in relation to the ideal of containment. Although the IRA has a policy of not opening up a second front in the

South, there are a number of ways in which "the troubles" have "overflowed" into the South. Bank robberies and kidnappings have been a vital source of funding for republican groups. In addition, the IRA has killed prestige British targets in the South.[20] Furthermore, other groups have not ruled the South out of bounds for military actions; Irish National Liberation Army (INLA) operations, as well as "maverick" activities,[21] have taken place. Moreover, loyalist groups, arguing that the IRA is a "foreign" group launching its attacks from the "safety" of the South, have from time to time conducted military operations there.[22]

Britain has experienced more direct military consequences of the Northern "troubles." Following on the logic of the Fenians in the 1880s and the IRA in the 1930s, republicans have periodically carried the war to Britain.[23] The levels of violence experienced in Britain as a result of the Irish conflict are relatively small. Yet they have been used as the excuse to employ the most remarkable measures in Britain itself. Of these the most draconian is the Prevention of Terrorism Act (PTA), which allows for the banning of political organizations, the exclusion of individuals from Britain, and the holding of suspects for interrogation for up to seven days.

The PTA was enacted in the immediate aftermath of and in response to two bombs in Birmingham in November 1974 which left 21 dead. The Act's purpose has been to screen the Irish population in Britain rather than to pursue people in regard to specific offences. Scorer and Hewitt, reviewing the Act's operation during the 1970s, revealed that 93.3 percent of those detained in Britain under the PTA were not subsequently charged with any offence.[24] The 1980s showed no change in this respect, with the Colville Report confirming that 92 percent of those detained in Britain between 1978 and 1988 were released without charge.[25]

The PTA has been remarkably cost ineffective in terms of identifying and apprehending people for specific offences. It has therefore been a blunt instrument directed at the whole Irish population in Ireland and Britain. Its message to them has not merely been to behave themselves, for a number of Irish people in Britain have clearly not misbehaved and yet found themselves in jail for long periods of time.[26] The import of the Act, especially since it has been made permanent in 1989, is a simpler one: confine your misbehaving to Ireland. Nowhere is this more obvious than in the practice of "exclusion orders." Under the PTA, Irish people have been excluded from Britain. The Colville Report gives a total of 283 such exclusions between 1978 and 1988, 242 of which were to the North of Ireland and 41 to the South.[27]

The irony is that while Britain is prepared to send to Ireland rather than to prison people who have not been proven to be guilty of any offence in Britain, it will not repatriate those who have in fact been found guilty under its legal system – namely, Irish republican prisoners. In recent years about 60 such prisoners have applied for transfer to the North of Ireland,[28] but to date only one application has been successful, that of a prisoner who had a religious conversion and completely disowned his past activities. British policy in this regard – as in relation to the punitive sentences handed out to republican prisoners in Britain[29] – fits the general strategy of containment. Irish prisoners are treated in an exemplary manner, the message being once again: confine your activities to Ireland.

4   International Repercussions of the Irish Conflict

Overseas attacks have a prestige value and internationalise the war in Ireland. The British government has been successful in suppressing news about the struggle, but we have kept Ireland in the world headlines.[30]

Irish republicans have even managed to extend their military activities to mainland Europe.[31] But such ripples of the Irish conflict have been relatively few, and their effect on Western Europe as a whole has been negligible, given that the attacks have been confined in the main to British military targets. Yet the prestige value of such operations from the IRA's point of view is beyond doubt. Moreover, the infrequent arrests of activitists on such operations, of people accused of arms acquisition, and of people wanted by the British for alleged offences in Northern Ireland, have led to a further element in the internationalization of the Irish conflict – the presence of Irish republican prisoners abroad.[32]

Because of such prisoners, extradition requests are forwarded by Britain. Extradition provides a useful study in the politics of containment. Farrell stresses the way in which extradition has been reinterpreted in recent times.[33] Extradition arrangements have always contained political exception clauses; that is, the political nature of the act was a valid defence against extradition. "Political" came to be seen as a quality of the motivation of the political offender. However, more recently Western European nations and the United States have attempted to claw back this liberal definition, switching to defining "politics" as inherent in the act itself. In short, violent acts against established nation states are not to be defined as "political" but as "terrorist." In the European context, Britain has been at the forefront of establishing this new definition, especially in relation to Irish political activists, but with varying degrees of success.

The constitution of the Republic of Ireland lays claim to the whole of the island of Ireland as the national territory. Despite the fact that most governments have been reluctant to pursue this claim relentlessly, it has had an effect on extradition practices. It was unthinkable to extradite to a part of the territory where foreign laws prevailed an Irish citizen seeking to overthrow such laws. The political exception clause was thus religiously accepted. However, the Anglo-Irish process which began with meetings between prime ministers Thatcher and Haughey in 1980 led to a break with tradition. In 1984 Dominic McGlinchey became the first republican to be extradited from the South to the North, and others have followed in the years since.

The softening of Anglo-Irish relations in respect to security has not, however, ensured Britain an easy ride. A number of fiascos, most notably the failure to extradite Evelyn Glenholmes in 1987[34] and the Ryan affair (see below) in 1988, revealed that the Southern government could not break totally with tradition. Moreover, there was obvious public disquiet in the South about the number of innocent Irish people in prison in Britain on "terrorism" charges, and misgivings about the system of justice in the North, especially with shoot-to-kill operations occurring.

Equally problematic from the British point of view has been the behaviour of certain European Community partners. Holland extradited two IRA prison escapers to Northern Ireland in 1987, but rejected a number of the offences specified on the warrants, including a murder charge. France has rejected three extradition applications for IRA and INLA members on the grounds that they were political offenders. And in 1988 Belgium refused to extradite Father Patrick Ryan to Britain on suspicion of arms acquisition offences, and instead flew him to the South of Ireland, which in turn declined to extradite him. Thatcher's fury at this turn of events revealed that in this, as in other conflicts she has had with European Community partners, she expects everyone else to toe the British line, despite their own laws and customs, and their genuine concern over the state of justice for republican defendants.[35]

However, Thatcher's "special relationship" with President Reagan bore fruit in the form of more systematic attempts by the US authorities to extradite republicans. Most notable has been the case of Joe Doherty, another prison escaper. He has been held in prison in the US for six years on the strength of Britain's desire to have him returned to Northern Ireland. Courts have consistently upheld his claim that his offences were political, despite high-level attempts by the US authorities to have the decision overturned. The authorities have switched to trying to deport Doherty as an illegal alien, while Doherty is seeking political asylum.[36] The British have not won; Doherty has not been extradited. Yet the lengths to which the US authorities have gone to return Doherty shows both the successful redefinition of the political exception clause and the willingness of the US to accept British definitions of justice.

The extradition cases at least have been out in the open, in the spotlight of media attention. Less obvious has been the extent of cooperation between various security forces to prevent Irish republicans operating outside Ireland. For example, Bishop and Mallie note that British, Irish, American, and Canadian cooperation led to the arrest of two republicans in Canada in 1982 on suspicion of arms acquisition.[37] And in 1988 the British newspaper the *Independent* exposed the involvement of TREVI, a group comprising the justice and interior ministers of all European Community states, in the operation which led to the assassination of three IRA members in Gibraltar.[38]

The slotting of "the Irish problem" into such international anti-terrorism mechanisms is very useful from the British point of view. The international repercussions of the conflict in Ireland, as has been said, have not been major. Yet they have been enough to require Britain to justify its actions abroad. There is no doubt that international opinion was a major element in the phasing out of internment in 1976 and its replacement by "criminalization." Now Britain can point to the fact that "the rule of law" prevails in Northern Ireland. The fact that the legal system has been distorted beyond recognition is easily forgotten in the blaze of rhetoric. "Criminalization" has been a success in propaganda terms. Less successful was the management of an inevitable consequence of "criminalization," the republican hunger strike of 1981. Republicans won the international propaganda battle, but the experience of fending off international criticism over this, as well as over the Falklands/ Malvinas crisis the following year, enabled the British to perfect their propaganda machine. The British spare no expense in presenting Northern Ireland as a normal democratic society under seige. How exactly those laying seige are presented depends to an extent on the audience. Thus, while no one in Britain or Ireland genuinely believes that the IRA is a Marxist terrorist organization, that spectre is raised by government ministers for American consumption, where it is hoped to have maximum effect in scuttling support for the IRA.[39]

In the European context the more useful spectre is that of international terrorism. Once this discourse is invoked, British ministers are on comfortable ground. Northern Ireland, after all, is top of the league, as Minister of State Nicholas Scott told an audience in Munich in 1986: "the province has endured the most sustained and vicious terrorist campaign in Western Europe since the end of the Second World War."[40] There is no arguing with such credentials. Within the discourse of the fight against international terrorism, claims that Northern Ireland is a colony of Britain or that the war is an anti-imperialist one are quickly dismissed. Northern Ireland is an instance of international terrorism and Britain is merely the democratic state reacting to save democracy.

5 Analyzing Northern Ireland: Counterinsurgency Theories

The IRA are by no means typical of present-day terrorist movements, most of which have international support and strong transnational links.[41]

They are peddling it to the broader public as a war of national, ethnic and religious liberation . . . The war they are really fighting, though, is hardly distinguishable from the one waged by Armed Parties everywhere – by the Red Brigades in Italy, say.[42]

Despite organizations such as TREVI, it is the *lack* of international cooperation against "terrorism" that is at the forefront of the concerns of a number of "terrorism" experts. Lodge, for example, identifies the main problem in European Community cooperation as being to balance the need to take Community-wide action with the need to preserve the individual sovereignties of each member state.[43] Wilkinson is less constrained in his criticism.[44] Although praising the efforts that have been made at the European Community level – regular meetings of ministers of the interior since 1976, and the inauguration of the European Convention on the Suppression of Terrorism in 1977 – he condemns the continued existence of the political exception clause in extradition arrangements and berates the "disgraceful slowness" of member states in ratifying the above-mentioned Convention. European tardiness is, in Wilkinson's view, one example of a wider international malaise in relation to "terrorism."

The "enemy," on the other hand, is said to be in much better shape. Wilkinson charts the growth of the supposed "terrorist international" from the conference of the Afro-Asian-Latin American People's Solidarity Organization in Havana in 1966 through meetings in the early 1970s in Lebanon, Algeria, Japan, and Dublin, to the final international division of terrorist labour whereby arms and intelligence are shared and joint and proxy operations are carried out.[45] As an example of the last of these Wilkinson says that the IRA blew up the West German embassy in Dublin in 1972, an operation which was then claimed by the Red Army Faction (RAF).

Unsubstantiated claims such as those of Wilkinson are at the core of Sterling's hysterical consideration of Ireland.[46] Thus we have the IRA training in Jordan in 1969, in Cuba in 1972, in the Lebanon in 1972, and in Libya in 1976, acquiring Dutch assistance to assassinate Ambassador Sir Richard Sykes in 1979, and splitting a huge Palestinian arms consignment with the Basque separatist-movement ETA in 1980. For good measure, Hewitt adds another: the IRA supplied the explosives to the Basques to kill Spanish prime minister Carrero Blanco.[47]

The neatness of such claims is that they are basically beyond refutation. In the shady underworld portrayed by people like Sterling these things *could* be true, and that is all the evidence that is needed. In fact, the absence of harder evidence is proof of the "terrorists" ability to cover their tracks. Better to believe that what could be probably is. Nowhere is this more obvious than in the pages of the popular British press. In the early years of "the troubles" such papers "sighted" Russian instructors and Chinese and North Korean sharpshooters on the streets of Belfast. More recently, the fascination is with the weaponry the IRA is supposed to have. Although Sterling claims that the IRA has had helicopters and SAMs (surface-to-air missiles) since 1972,[48] it was the late 1980s before SAM-hysteria caught on. In 1987 a British popular newspaper, the *Daily Star* (December 30, 1987), predicted that the IRA was about to use SAMs to shoot down civilian passenger planes. A few weeks later the same paper (January 11, 1988) revealed that the IRA was planning to smuggle SAMs into England in gypsy caravans to shoot down helicopters.

Such fantasies might be dismissed if they were confined to this one newspaper. However, the *Irish News* (November 21, 1988) reported that the IRA could be using SAMs already, as a British army helicopter pilot had reported hearing an unexplained "whoosh" as he flew over County Fermanagh. The *Independent* (August 7, 1988) could assure its readers that "a notorious West German terrorist" had been spotted at the British army's headquarters on the Rhine the day after a soldier was killed by an IRA bomb in London. And the *Sunday Times* (February 1, 1987) carried details of a proposed joint Libyan–IRA operation to free their respective prisoners from British jails.

The quality papers, unlike the populars, at least usually acknowledge that the source of their information is the security arm of the state. But the space given to the stories lends them a credibility that masks the essential role they play in the propaganda war. Apart from the security forces, another source of media representations is the involvement of government ministers in propaganda. Ministers have virtually unquestioned access to the media, so that the ogres they conjure up become quickly part of the popular assessment of "reality." Chief among these ogres is Colonel Gaddafi. Secretary of State Tom King frequently echoed Sterling's presentation of Gaddafi as "the Daddy Warbucks of terrorism:" "We take seriously the fact that Northern Ireland could be the object of an international drive supported by the Libyan government."[49]

There is no denying that Gaddafi pledged support for the IRA as far back as 1972 and as recently as 1988,[50] nor that that support has materialized on a number of occasions.[51] But such is the value of the ogre to the British that it is also clear that if Gaddafi did not exist, he would have had to have been invented. He allows the British to represent Ireland as a war between good and evil, democracy and terror. Conversely, British (and Western) paranoia is highly useful to Gaddafi, allowing him to parade his revolutionary zeal and credentials.

In the midst of this propaganda war, what is certain is that British and Libyan claims about Libyan support for the IRA must be viewed with great caution. When the layers of propaganda are stripped away, the reality may be less than the rhetoric. Thus, a British briefing from 1984 – written prior to the November 1987 capture of the *Eksund*, bound from Libya to Ireland with an extensive armoury on board – concluded that "much Libyan comment on Irish terrorism may be dismissed as rhetoric provoked by strained Anglo-Libyan relations. Evidence of specific aid, with the exception of the *Claudia* incident, has so far been circumstantial."[52]

In similar vein, those with less of an axe to grind than British ministers and security personnel tend to dismiss the wilder claims of the IRA's incorporation into the terrorist international. For example, a spokesperson for the Federal Prosecutions Office in Karlsruhe, West Germany, dismissed claims of links between the IRA and the RAF in the bombing of a British army base in Dusseldorf in 1988: "Our indications are that the IRA considers itself a group of freedom fighters and does not consider RAF's goals genuine."[53] Baldy concludes more generally: "Assertions abound that the IRA is linked with foreign terrorist organisations. At best, these links are tenuous."[54]

Guelke's conclusion is the most sober of all.[55] He stresses that while Sinn Fein has cultivated links with other separatist groups in Western Europe, and finds ideological affinity with the struggles of the Palestine Liberation Organisation (PLO)[56] and African National Congress (ANC), the IRA's concern has been with arms acquisition. In this light, many of the political contacts have not been particularly helpful, requiring the IRA, like the INLA, to buy weapons from "very diverse contacts, some of which are essentially commercial and criminal rather than political."[57]

Such sober assessments are a breath of fresh air in a literature of which the worst is not noted for its ability to distance itself from state propaganda. For Sterling the IRA is fighting a proxy war for Libya and ultimately the Soviet Union.[58] Clutterbuck prefers to concentrate on the evil ingenuity of the IRA, who timed shooting incidents in such a way that "the IRA's pre-drafted story, amended as necessary, could be issued to the press in time for news bulletins or newspaper deadlines – but carefully calculated to ensure that police or army accounts would be too late."[59]

O'Ballance's obsession is with the extent to which the IRA survives through internal terror; its foothold in the ghettos "was obtained, and retained, by intimidation alone."[60]

It would be all too easy to dismiss this section of the counter insurgency fraternity as the lunatic fringe and to concentrate on more "objective" theorists. But sophistication is not the same as objectivity. Sophisticates and lunatics have much in common. Firstly, all counterinsurgency theorists agree on at least *some* of the methods for defeating "terrorism." Tugwell and Clutterbuck put a lot of faith in media controls,[61] while for Wilkinson the game plan is much more complex,[62] involving 14 rules, only one of which involves the "countering of terrorist propaganda and defamation." Similarly, while some army officers may stress the military solution, the more sophisticated counterinsurgency experts would argue that their view of military tactics as only *one* element in the overall strategy does not lessen their commitment to military means. Reid, for example, stresses the military option: "Military success against terrorists could have been possible if armed force had been deployed against the terrorist organisations while they were still weak. In 1969–71 this option was not acceptable to the British government."[63] Similarly, Kitson is so determined to separate the terrorist fish from the water of the community that he concludes: "conceivably it might be necessary to kill the fish by polluting the water."[64]

Wilkinson, on the other hand, argues not only that there must be "no resort to indiscriminate repression," but that terrorist activities must not be allowed to deflect the government from furthering social and economic welfare in the areas where "terrorists" are based.[65] As someone who served as a colonel in Northern Ireland, Evelegh cannot be judged to be soft on security, yet he urges the government to become much more involved in ameliorating social and environmental problems in nationalist areas in order to remove the grievances on which "terrorism" thrives.[66]

Secondly, despite the differences between them, all counterinsurgency experts agree that the priority is to defeat "terrorism." O'Brien, the Republic of Ireland's only member of the fraterntiy, may not have much time for the sorts of social and economic reform urged by Wilkinson and Evelegh, but his toughness on "terrorism" is unquestionable. One of his five rules for defeating "terrorism" is: "Convincing the terrorist that he is not going to get his own way (that involves refusal to talk with him since . . . he is not accessible to rational argument . . .)."[67] But this is identical with another of Wilkinson's rules: "no dialogue or negotiation with terrorists"[68] – the same Wilkinson who in other ways appears a dove when compared with O'Brien.

In a similar vein, Hewitt, comparing Northern Ireland, Cyprus, Italy, the Basque country, and Uruguay, argues that "negotiating a truce with the terrorists is a short-sighted policy. Negotiations will not lead to resolution of the conflict . . . The most desirable policy is one which results in the capture of terrorists without the general population being subjected to constant harassment by the military."[69]

Thirdly, the ultimate measure of the relative uselessness of distinctions between hawks and doves, lunatics and sophisticates, is the extent to which all are agreed on the identification of the "terrorist" as the source of the problem. Defining "terrorism' takes up vast amounts of space in the literature of counterinsurgency: for example, Schmid lists over 100 definitions of the word and spends 100 pages deriving his own definition.[70] Yet, in the specific case of "terrorism" in Ireland, it would seem that for the most part the debate is settled. "Terrorism" is instigated by the "terrorists" themselves against the democratic state. The only matter for debate, then, is the question of what motivates the "terrorist." Here agreement is not so total, with some experts following the "evil genius" theory, and others the "pathetic weakling" approach. One can even find these polar opposites within one theorist's writings. Thus Wilkinson can assure us that "the typical terrorist tends to be above average intelligence and education", and yet further on that "very often the actual bomb planter is a pathetic and politically illiterate individual."[71]

Where is the evidence for either personality portrait? The truth is that there is remarkably little. Sluka thus identifies two of the major weaknesses of counterinsurgency theorists as being, first, "a near total failure to arrive at empirical conclusions derived from microanalytic, first-hand research in the communities that support guerrillas," and, second, a reliance on "information and interpretations provided by the governments and security forces fighting guerrillas."[72]

The counterinsurgency experts thus become apologists for the state in its propaganda war against opposition.[73] Even those who criticize the state do so in order to perfect its efficiency in countering "terrorism."[74] Nowhere, however, do they attack the fundamental definitions and goals of the state in relation to "terrorism."

6 The British State and Northern Ireland

The British government's role in Northern Ireland is not as "honest broker" or "peacemaker," but as a crutch for the loyalist majority.[75]

[The Anglo-Irish Agreement] is a declaration by the British that there is no British interest, strategic or otherwise, in being in Ireland.[76]

The notion that "terrorism" begins with groups opposed to the democratic state by definition excludes the possibility of the state being defined as "terrorist." When the question of 'state terrorism' is broached at all, it is usually in relation to the state's proxy involvement in "terror." Rarely is the role of the state in creating and perpetuating "terrorism" examined thoroughly, especially in the case of Ireland. This is a grave oversight. The British state cannot be said to be "terrorist" in its dealings with Northern Ireland in the same way that the Israeli state is in Lebanon or the state of El Salvador internally. In fact, part of the political problem is in agreeing whether the British state's relation to Northern Ireland is internal or external. But whichever political conclusion is reached in that regard, there is no denying that the role of the British state needs more careful analysis than it has had to date in the literature of counter-insurgency.

Such a shift of focus would attempt to see how the state is neither the innocent victim of irrational violence nor the neutral arbiter between warring factions, but is itself party to the political system wherein "terrorism" emerges as a politically rational act. This is not merely to say that the state's zeal in repression can lead to an increase in "terrorism" rather than its eradication. Admonitions along such lines are often little more than messages to the state to be more careful, more targeted, nicer about repression. It is to say rather that repression has such a long and respectable history in Ireland that it is the first instrument which the state reaches for when faced with political problems.

Frequently British reforms in Ireland do not amount to much more than a feeble substitute for repression. Where the priority is the containment of political violence, political initiatives perform much the same task as military ones. In various epochs Britain has had few qualms about being open and determined in its military suppression of Ireland. However, in this most recent round of "troubles," international opinion has acted as a partial brake on open militarism. The British state does not become engaged in systematic retaliation exercises in the same way as it did during the War of Independence in Ireland in 1919, nor in the manner of the Israeli state today. The preservation of image has become all important because of a number of factors – the growth of the mass media, the "special relationship" between Britain and the US, Britain's membership of the European Community, the relative power of the civil liberties lobby, etc. But image creation is not the same as problem solution, as the case of the Anglo-Irish Agreement shows.

As was suggested earlier, the states in Britain and the South of Ireland have a common interest in containing the Irish problem to Northern Ireland. Policing partition costs the South four times per capita what it costs Britain.[77] But the relationship betwen the two states has had an increasingly political element as well. In 1980, Charles Haughey and Margaret Thatcher agreed to give greater consideration to "the totality of relationships in these islands." For Northern SDLP leader John Hume this was a cue to take the Northern Ireland problem to a higher plane. His advances to the Southern government led to the creation of the New Ireland Forum, where the SDLP and three major parties in the South examined possible political solutions. Fine Gael preferred the notion of joint authority for Northern Ireland, and Fianna Fail the unitary state solution. But these, and a third option of federalism, were rejected out of hand by Thatcher.

Yet the pressure was building up. Irish academics such as Boyle and Hadden were urging some system of joint authority.[78] A right-wing think tank in Britain was arguing that it was strategically important for the Irish and British governments to cooperate more systematically "in the interests of mobilising the greatest possible resistance to republican terrorism."[79] Under concerted and sophisticated lobbying from the Irish government, influential US politicians produced a carrot and a stick, criticizing Britain for various aspects of its treatment of Northern Ireland and promising money if some movement towards a political solution was inaugurated.[80] Finally, the European Community jumped on the bandwagon with its first and to date only official political assessment of British rule in Northern Ireland, which criticised Britain slightly and urged "the establishment of joint British-Irish responsibility" for Northern Ireland.[81]

The Anglo-Irish Agreement emerged in November 1985. It was hailed by both signatories as significant progress in the healing of the Northern rift. The fact that the Agreement promised little and delivered less is not the point of focus here.[82] The Anglo-Irish Agreement's main importance is in relation to its international consumption, especially in the US. Britain had suffered a number of major defeats on the propaganda front in the US, beginning in 1978 with the criticism by four major politicians of treatment of suspects interrogated by the police in Northern Ireland. Even President Carter's seemingly benign promise of money for economic development,[83] in the event of political progress in Northern Ireland, was in effect criticism of the British for the failure of progress. In addition, a major campaign against the main republican support group in the US, Irish Northern Aid (also known as Noraid), had only partially succeeded. The US authorities had brought charges of illegal arms acquisition against some Noraid personnel, and the group had been forced reluctantly to register as an agent of the IRA under the Foreign Agents Registration Act. But these advances, as well as the obsession with discovering the exact amounts of money collected by Noraid and where it had ended up,[84] did not negate the fact that Britain had not won the real battle against Noraid, the propaganda one. After all, even if the IRA does acquire funds for arms via Noraid, the curtailment of that source cannot be expected to halt the IRA's campaign. Moreover, registration under the Foreign Agents Registration Act is a harmless formality, required also of the groups set up in 1984 to raise funds for Fianna Fail, the government party in the South of Ireland. The real battle against Noraid has not been about guns, but about ideas and influence,[85] and it is a battle that has not been won by the British.

Similarly, the campaign on the MacBride Principles has left the British as losers. Fashioned on the Sullivan Principles in relation to South Africa, the MacBride Principles are based on the idea that US investment in Northern Ireland can be used as a lever to encourage the breakdown of job discrimination practices. The British government's retort has been that the MacBride campaign seeks to curtail badly needed investment in Northern Ireland. In fact, it has not done so, but it has put pressure on the British government to introduce in January 1990 much tougher (although still inadequate) legislation on job discrimination than it would have done otherwise. Ten states have endorsed the Principles and 14 others are on course to do so. The British response has been to spend large sums of money in countering the campaign; Kearney estimates that the cost over three years has been five times the cost of running the Fair Employment Agency in Northern Ireland for 12 years ($27.5 million versus $5 million).[86] Yet the campaign has, in the insulting analogy of US Consul in Belfast Myers, continued to "spread like AIDS."[87]

In the face of such defeats, the Anglo-Irish Agreement has become an excellent propaganda weapon. It is a statement of intent. But such is the vagueness of its proposals that what is intended is open to interpretation. In the US it is, in Guelke's words, seen as "a transitional step to a united Ireland."[88] No matter that it is presented to unionists in the North as a bulwark *against* a united Ireland.[89] The fact that it can be seen as both is proof that it is about neither. Through the Anglo-Irish Agreement, containment has reached dizzy international heights.

7 Conclusion: Beyond Containment

In no way can or will the Provisional IRA ever be defeated militarily.[90]

Attempting to defeat the IRA is not a viable or sensible option. It can only deepen the suffering and prolong the agony.[91]

After twenty years of the most recent round of "troubles" in Ireland, it would seem that few if any lessons have been learned by the British state. Political initiatives have come and gone. Their failure has consistently been blamed on politicians in the North of Ireland, but this is only part of the explanation. Many such British initiatives have been poorly conceived or reluctantly undertaken, an exercise more in saving face than in genuine progress.

The fragility of British commitment to political initiatives is most clearly shown in their reaction to major IRA actions. In 1974 the Birmingham bombs led to the Prevention of Terrorism Act being rushed through Parliament. A decade and a half later the repressive reaction is still the most immediate. After an IRA bomb killed 11 people at a Remembrance Day service in Enniskillen in November 1987, former Lord Chancellor Lord Hailsham, in language worthy of Ayatollah Khomeini, stated that the bombers were "servants of the devil" who had "taken evil into their souls", and that they should hang.[92] Former Northern Ireland Office Minister Sir Philip Goodhart suggested that the IRA should hand over the bombers to the security forces or assassinate them personally.[93] By contrast, official responses were more muted. Yet the IRA operation in Enniskillen, and further operations the following summer which led to the deaths of six soldiers by one bomb in Lisburn, County Antrim, and eight soldiers by another bomb in Ballygawley, County Tyrone, proved incentives to introduce even more repressive legislation. In 1988 the Criminal Justice Order removed the right of silence of "terrorist" suspects in courts in Northern Ireland, and a broadcasting ban was introduced to prevent Sinn Fein elected representatives having access to radio or television. Despite talk from time to time of the need for political solutions, the mask slips occasionally. Government actions speak loudly. So too do government words. After the IRA killed three people in Coagh, County Tyrone (one of whom they accused of being a leading loyalist), Home Secretary Douglas Hurd stated: "I believe that, with the Provisional IRA and some of the Middle-Eastern groups, it is nothing really to do with a political cause any more. They are professional killers. That is their occupation and their pleasure and they will go on doing that. No political solution will cope with that. They just have to be extirpated."[94]

The tragedy is that chances for progress have been missed. British politicians have endlessly bewailed the supposed mindlessness of republicanism. Yet they have not seized the opportunity from the politicization of republican struggle which occurred in the 1980s, after the hunger strike. Sinn Fein in elections has been able at maximum to command 40 percent of the nationalist vote in the North. This is hardly the case of a few mindless psychopaths intimidating people to obey them.

Nor is the action of the British mindless. There is a logic evident. Each IRA "atrocity" becomes the trigger for the next act of repression. The effect is to push republicanism back to being what it was in a previous era, a more or less solely armed force movement. It has survived as that for most of the last century. It can do so for at least a century more.

The crucial question of course is why the British should constantly choose the repressive over the political option. One answer is that their imperialist and colonialist past has led them to reach for repressive tools in insurgency situations as an automatic reaction. The habit has been so long established that it is not easily broken. The confrontationist style of politics adopted for the last decade by the current British government does not create an atmosphere for the breaking of such old habits, although it must be added that the Thatcher regime does not have a monopoly of repression in relation to Ireland. Thirdly, the current government in particular genuinely believes that repression can work. Specifically, they are convinced that all that is needed is time and even better interstate cooperation for "terrorism" in all its European guises to be obliterated. There are few in the upper reaches of power who subscribe to the notion that Irish "terrorism" is symptom rather than cause, and that therefore political solutions must be sought. Finally, for the more thoughtful Tory there must be the realization that ultimately there is only one political solution possible. Northern Ireland as a state has not been able to survive without "emergency" laws, strong-arm tactics, and greater or lesser levels of repression. The logic of this historical lesson is that the choice is to continue repression or to disengage. The latter option is not one that can be publicly countenanced in a government obsessed with jingoism and adamantly opposed to executing U-turns, no matter how great a drain Northern Ireland is on finances or morale. Repression is the bedrock of the continued existence of the state. Reforms can be pursued in as far as they may woo people in Northern Ireland away from supporting "terrorists" or deflect international criticism. But the British no longer view them as steps on the road to a political solution. Direct rule and continued repression are not the basis of a political solution, but they have become for the British all that is possible in a situation where the ultimate political solution is unacceptable.

In short, "the Northern Ireland problem" cannot be contained. Given that, there is a way forward which at least logically is staggeringly simple. The British must sit down and talk with the republicans *as equals*. They would do so in the realization that the republicans would lay one basic demand on the table – the manner and timing of British withdrawal. Such a move would be a recognition that repression and containment have not worked and that even the most radical and distasteful conclusions, from the British point of view, must be drawn from that failure.

The British, locked in their tradition of repressive responses to insurgency, are unlikely to embrace such a strategy easily. No matter that the British have met the republicans as equals in the recent past, albeit furtively and without developments; Prime Minister Harold Wilson and Secretary of State William Whitelaw met the IRA in the early 1970s, and Secretary of State Douglas Hurd met leading members of Sinn Fein in

171

1979. No matter either that opinion polls in Britain reveal that the British public wants withdrawal,[95] albeit lacking the sophistication of republican analysis of the reasons for such withdrawal. No matter, finally, that the rest of the world, including Britain's closest allies, seems to believe that a united Ireland is an inevitability. Speaking from his vantage point of proximity to the American defence forces, Baldy sums up what probably represents a widespread international conclusion in words scarcely distinguishable from republican argument: "I believe the harsh reality of Northern Ireland is that the province will ultimately revert to its larger whole, subsumed by the land from which it was carved. The province is an artificial contrivance – a stillborn infant given life by Britain and sustained by British resources. The infant struggles, but knows the outcome."[96]

The British state is unlikely to listen to its own citizens on this matter or to international opinion, even if it comes from sources close to the Pentagon. Instead it has the camouflage of the Anglo-Irish Agreement and the comforting words of reassurance of its home-grown counter-insurgency experts that republican demands are not a part of the political agenda. For the British state there is nothing beyond the latest unsuccessful attempt at containment other than the next attempt at containment.

Notes

1   F. Kitson, *Low Intensity Operations* (Faber and Faber, 1971), p. 24.
2   M. Rees, "Terror in Ireland – and Britain's Response, " in P. Wilkinson (ed.), *British Perspectives on Terrorism* (Allen and Unwin, 1981), p. 85.
3   Despite their anti-British activities, the Fenians commanded substantial support within Britain. Marx notes that "a couple of hundred thousand" people demonstrated in London in support of an amnesty for Fenian prisoners on October 24, 1869 (K. Marx and F. Engels, *Ireland and the Irish Question* (Lawrence and Wishart, 1978), p. 388).
4   M. Farrell, *The Apparatus of Repression*, Derry, Field Day Pamphlet 11, 1986, p. 5.
5   E. Mulloy, *Dynasties of Coercion*, Derry, Field Day pamphlet 10, 1986, p. 8.
6   New Ireland Forum, *Report* (Dublin Stationery Office, 1984), p. 14.
7   Farrell, *Apparatus of Repression*, p. 25.
8   Quoted in Sunday Times Insight Team, *Ulster* (Penguin, 1972), p. 309.
9   It is estimated that between 1969 and 1982 the additional expenditure incurred by the British in law, order, protective services, and the courts in Northern Ireland was £2,642 million (at 1982 prices). Add to this the estimated cost of keeping the British army in the North (£1,550 million), and the total cost of "security" has been £4,192 million. The RUC alone cost £1,444 million between 1971 and 1985, and the UDR £234 million between 1971 and 1984 (figures from Irish Information Partnership).

10 T. Baldy, *Battle for Ulster: A Study in Internal Security* (National Defense University Press, 1987), p. 12.

11 For example, in 1972 there were 103 British soldiers killed and 43 indigenous security personnel (17 RUC and 26 UDR). Between 1983 and 1987 inclusive there were 44 British soldiers and 137 indigenous personnel (90 RUC and 47 UDR) killed. There is evidence recently of a partial swing back to the previous situation, with 22 British soldiers and 13 indigenous personnel (3 RUC and 10 UDR) killed in 1988. In August 1988, Sinn Fein President Gerry Adams stated: "Callous as it may sound, when British soldiers die it removes the worst of the agony from Ireland" (quoted in the *Observer* (August 7, 1988).

12 See D. Beresford, *Ten Men Dead* (Grafton, 1987).

13 Diplock Report, *Report of the Commission to Consider Legal Procedures to Deal with the Terrorist Activities in Northern Ireland*, Cmnd 5185 (HMSO, 1972).

14 Gardiner Report, *Report of a Committee to Consider Measures to Deal with Terrorism in Northern Ireland*, Cmnd 5847 (HMSO, 1975).

15 The extent of these beatings was confirmed by police doctors, an Amnesty International report, and a report commissioned by the British government and written by Judge Bennett. For a comprehensive review of these reports and other evidence, see P. Taylor, *Beating the Terrorists?* (Penguin, 1980).

16 See Belfast Bulletin 11, *Supergrasses*, 1984; T. Gifford, *Supergrasses: The Use of Accomplice Evidence in Northern Ireland* (Cobden Trust, 1984).

17 See K. Asmal, *Shoot to Kill: International Lawyers' Inquiry into the Lethal Use of Firearms by the Security Forces in Northern Ireland* (Mercier, 1983).

18 Irish Republican Army (IRA) source, *New York Times* (February 26, 1975), cited in M. Moodie, "The Patriot Game: The Politics of Violence in Northern Ireland," in M. Livingstone (ed.), *International Terrorism in the Contemporary World* (Greenwood Press, 1978), pp. 94–110.

19 Scotland Yard detective, quoted in Baldy, *Battle for Ulster*, p. 58.

20 Most notably Ambassador Christopher Ewart-Biggs in July 1976 and Earl Mountbatten in July 1979.

21 Such as the kidnapping of Dutch industrialist Tiede Herrema by Eddie Gallagher and Marion Coyle in 1975.

22 In December 1972 the Ulster Defence Association (UDA) exploded two car bombs in Dublin, killing two people. In May 1974 the Young Militants Association exploded car bombs in Dublin and Monaghan which left 33 dead.

23 The first operation in Britain in the current "troubles" was an Official IRA bomb in Aldershot in February 1972, in retaliation for the killing of 13 civilians at a civil rights march in Derry the previous month. The Aldershot bomb killed seven people. Although the Provisional IRA were active in Britain in 1973, killing two people with separate bombs, it was 1974 before they launched a major and sustained wave of attacks. For example, in February 1974 a bomb on a bus that was carrying soldiers and their families killed twelve in Yorkshire; in October two pubs used by soldiers in Guildford were bombed, leaving seven dead; and in Birmingham in November two pub

Bill Rolston

bombs killed 21 people. Each year after that saw some military activity, with high points which included the INLA assassination of Airey Neve, Tory MP, in March 1979; the IRA bombs in Regent's Park and Hyde Park in July 1982, which left 11 soldiers dead; the bombing of Harrods in December 1983, when six died, in an attack which the IRA said was unauthorized; and the attempt to kill Margaret Thatcher at the Tory party conference in Brighton in October 1984, in which five died. After that the next death through IRA activity in Britain was when a soldier was killed in a bomb explosion at Mill Hill barraks in London in August 1988.

In February 1989 a bomb virtually demolished Tern Hill barracks, near Shrewsbury in Shropshire; 60 soldiers narrowly escaped. In the same month a parcel bomb damaged a British army recruiting office in Halifax. September 1989 saw the largest loss of British army personnel in any one incident in Britain when eleven Royal Marines were killed by a bomb at Deal in Kent. In November 1989 a car bomb at Goojerat barracks, Colchester, left a staff sergeant critically injured, and the commander-in-chief of the UK land army, Lt General David Ramsbottom, escaped when a bomb was discovered under his car in London. The activity continued into 1990, with a narrow escape in February for some soldiers when a bomb fell from under their vehicle and exploded in Leicester, extensive damage in May from a bomb at the Institute of British Army Education in London, and the death of a sergeant in a van bomb, also in London. June 1990 saw: the death of two soldiers by shooting in Lichfield; a bomb at the headquarters of the artillery regiment in London; a bomb at the stately home recently owned by top Conservative Party financier Lord Colin McAlpine in Hampshire; a bomb at the Conservative Party's Carlton Club in central London; and a bomb at RAF Stanmore Park in London. In July 1990 an IRA bomb blasted the London stock exchange, and Conservative Party MP and close friend of Prime Minister Margaret Thatcher, Ian Gow, was killed by a car bomb at his home in Sussex.

24   C. Scorer and P. Hewitt, *The Prevention of Terrorism Act: The Case for Repeal* (National Council for Civil Liberties, 1981), p. 66.

25   Colville Report, *Report on the Operation in 1988 of the Prevention of Terrorism (Temporary Provision) Act 1984* (Home Office, January 1989), p. 4.

26   See C. Mullen, *Error of Judgement: The Truth about the Birmingham Bombers* (Poolbeg Press, 1987); G. McKee and R. Franey, *Time Bomb: Irish Bombers, English Justice and the Guildford Four* (Bloomsbury, 1988); P. Hill, *Stolen Years: Before and After Guildford* (Doubleday, 1990); G. Conlon, *Proved Innocent: The Story of Gerry Conlon of the Guildford Four* (Hamish Hamilton, 1990).

27   Colville Report, p. 21.

28   See B. Rolston and M. Tomlinson, " 'The Challenge Within:' Prisons and Propaganda in Northern Ireland," in M. Tomlinson, T. Varley, and C. McCullagh (eds), *Whose Law and Order?* (Sociological Association of Ireland, 1988), pp 167–92.

29   Three Irish republican prisoners in Britain are currently serving life with a

recommendation of 30 years minimum. Paul Hill, one of the Guildford Four, released when their sentences were quashed in 1989, had been serving a "recommended natural life" sentence.

30 IRA statement, cited in the British daily newspaper the *Independent* (March 7, 1988).

31 The first major IRA operation on the continent was in March 1979, when the British ambassador to Holland, Sir Richard Sykes, was shot dead. But the bulk of such operations have been more recent, and have been aimed primarily at British service personnel. A 300-pound bomb was exploded at the British army headquarters in West Germany, at Rheindahlen, in March 1989. In April 1988 three servicemen were killed in two incidents in Holland on the same day. In August 1988 another serviceman was shot dead in Belgium. A British army corporal was killed by a car bomb in Hanover, West Germany, in July 1989. In September 1989 two soldiers were critically injured in a shooting in Munster, West Germany, and the wife of a British army sergeant was killed in another shooting in Dortmund. The following month saw the death of an RAF sergeant and his infant daughter in Wildenrath, West Germany. In May 1990 two Australian civilians, mistaken for off-duty British soldiers, were shot dead in Roermond, Holland. A British army major was shot dead in Dortmund, West Germany, in June 1990. (The above list excludes a number of actual and attempted bomb attacks on British security personnel and bases in West Germany).

32 There are currently 21 IRA prisoners in jails outside of Britain and Ireland: 12 in the US, six in France, three in Holland, two in West Germany, and one in Belgium (figures from Sinn Fein Prisoner of War Department). Note that these figures do not include people from other republican organizations, nor innocent people accused of being IRA members.

33 M. Farrell, *Sheltering the Fugitive? The Extradition of Irish Political Offenders* (Mercier, 1985).

34 Evelyn Glenholmes, the subject of an extradition attempt by Britain, was released by a Dublin court on March 22, 1987, on the grounds that the extradition warrant was invalid. But she was pursued through the streets by police and detectives who expected a further warrant to arrive and did not want to lose sight of her in the meantime. After the police opened fire on Dublin's main street, she was rearrested, but re-released on the grounds that she had been arrested prior to the arrival of the extradition warrant. By the time the warrant arrived, Glenholmes was on the run, and has been ever since.

35 Britain's record of violations of the European Convention on Human Rights has been greater than that of any other signatory of the Convention. Britain has been found guilty of violation by the European Court of Human Rights 19 times; the closest competitor is Austria, with 11 violations. As regards rulings by the Committee of Ministers, Britain has been judged in violation more times than all other signatories together: 37 times versus 14 times. See the *Independent* (November 10, 1988).

36 *An Phoblacht/Republican News* (June 23, 1988).

37 P. Bishop and E. Mallie. *The Provisional IRA* (Heinemann, 1987), p. 330.

175

38 The *Independent* (March 10, 1988).
39 Thus, speaking to the Association of American Correspondents in London in 1988, Secretary of State Tom King referred to the IRA as "a dedicated group of extreme Marxist republican terrorists, now receiving their only real support from Gaddafi. The IRA have as their ambitions to destroy the government in Dublin and to establish a Marxist revolutionary government in a 32-country republic" (Northern Ireland Information Service press release (May, 13 1988)).
40 Northern Ireland Information Service press release (November 18, 1986).
41 C. Dobson and R. Payne, *The Weapons of Terror* (Macmillan, 1979), p. 32.
42 C. Sterling, *The Terror Network* (Weidenfeld and Nicolson, 1981), p. 169.
43 J. Lodge, "Introduction – Terrorism and Europe: Some General Considerations," in J. Lodge (ed.), *The Threat of Terrorism* (Wheatsheaf, 1987), pp. 1–28.
44 P. Wilkinson, "Terrorism: International Dimensions," in W. Gutteridge (ed.), *The New Terrorism* (Mansell, 1986), p. 48.
45 Ibid., pp. 38–9.
46 Sterling, *The Terror Network*.
47 C. Hewitt, *The Effectiveness of Anti-Terrorist Policies* (University Press of America, 1984), p. 20.
48 Sterling, *The Terror Network*, p. 152.
49 *Belfast Telegraph* (January 20, 1988).
50 On the latter, see Gaddafi's statement, quoted in the *Irish News* (April 12, 1988): "It is a just fight and we will support it."
51 In March 1973 the *Claudia* was captured off the coast of Ireland with 5 metric tons of arms and ammunition on board. In November 1987 the *Eksund* was captured off the coast of France. It contained 150 metric tons of arms and ammunition, including 20 surface-to-air missiles. Both consignments were shipped from Libya.
52 Foreign Office, *Libya and Irish Terrorism*, briefing (June 1984).
53 Quoted in the *Irish News* (August 9, 1988).
54 Baldy, *Battle for Ulster*, p. 61.
55 A. Guelke, *Northern Ireland: The International Perspective* (Gill and Macmillan, 1988).
56 There is some slight evidence of PLO involvement in training of IRA personnel in the early 1970s. However, by the 1980s the PLO's new-found respectability led it to distance itself from the IRA: "We have no relations with the IRA and I would challenge anybody who can dare to say anything about it. The British government have full information about this" (Yasser Arafat, quoted in the *Irish News* (September 15, 1988)). Interestingly, not everyone was in full agreement with the PLO's new image. When British Ambassador to Israel Mark Elliot drew a distinction between the IRA and the PLO – "The IRA use, as a matter of regular practice, lethal weapons against a civilian population and the police force. By contrast, the PLO is not engaged, as a matter of regular practice, in terrorist activities within Israel" – the Israeli

paper *The Nation* was quick to respond, listing PLO attacks on civilians within Israel. See the *Irish News* (December 15, 1988).

57 Guelke, *Northern Ireland: The International Perspective*, p. 15.

58 Sterling, *The Terror Network*.

59 R. Clutterbuck, *The Media and Political Violence* (Macmillan, 1981), p. 91.

60 E. O'Ballance, "IRA Leadership Problems," in P. Wilkinson (ed.), *British Perspectives on Terrorism* (Allen and Unwin, 1981), pp. 73–82, esp. p. 81.

61 M. Tugwell, "Politics and Propaganda of the Provisional IRA," in P. Wilkinson (ed.), *British Perspectives on Terrorism* (Allen and Unwin, 1981), pp. 13–40; Clutterbuck, *The Media and Political Violence*.

62 P. Wilkinson, "Terrorism versus Liberal Democracy: The Problems of Response," in W. Gutteridge (ed.), *The New Terrorism* (Mansell, 1986), p. 17.

63 B. H. Reid, "The Experience of the British Army in Northern Ireland," in Y. Alexander and A. O'Day (eds), *Ireland's Terrorist Dilemma* (Martinus Nijhoff, 1986), pp. 249–60, esp. p. 255.

64 Kitson, *Low Intensity Operations*, p. 49.

65 Wilkinson, "Terrorism versus Liberal Democracy," pp. 17–18.

66 R. Evelegh, *Peace-Keeping in a Democratic Society: The Lessons of Northern Ireland* (Hurst and Co., 1978), p. 54.

67 C. C. O'Brien, *Herod: Reflections on Political Violence* (Hutchinson, 1978), p. 36. While Minister for Posts and Telegraphs in 1973, O'Brien had a chance to ensure that republicans had no chance to express themselves on public airwaves. Section 31 of the Broadcasting Act, introduced by O'Brien, banned republicans from the state-monopolized radio and television networks in the South of Ireland.

68 Wilkinson, "Terrorism versus Liberal Democracy," p. 17.

69 Hewitt, *Effectiveness of Anti-Terrorist Policies*, pp. 37, 97.

70 A. Schmid, *Political Terrorism* (North Holland Publishing Co., 1984).

71 Wilkinson, "Terrorism versus Liberal Democracy," pp. 4, 29.

72 J. A. Sluka, "Hearts and Minds, Water and Fish: Support for the IRA and INLA in a Northern Irish Ghetto," unpublished Ph.D. thesis, University of California, Berkeley, Cal., 1986.

73 The distinction between state propaganda and the counterinsurgency expert's writing is often difficult to ascertain. Thus, Chris Dobson published two articles in the *Irish Independent* of May, 2 1988, and the *Daily Telegraph* of May, 3 1988, linking a number of people, such as Liz Curtis (see L. Curtis, *Ireland: The Propaganda War* (Pluto Press, 1989)), to the IRA. What he "forgot" to add was that much of his information was lifted verbatim and unacknowledged from a Foreign Office "background brief" entitled *The Provisional IRA: International Contacts Outside the United States* (London Foreign and Commonwedlth Office, January 1988).

74 Ironically, Official Secrets legislation introduced in March 1990 in Britain outlawed the publication of many of the criticisms of counterinsurgency experts, despite their pro-state stance.

75 Social Democratic and Labour Party (SDLP), *"Justice" in Northern Ireland*, discussion paper (SDLP, June 1985), p. 9.

Bill Rolston

76 SDLP leader John Hume, quoted in *Belfast Telegraph* (November 16, 1985).
77 The New Ireland Forum estimated that between 1969 and 1982 the direct costs to the South of security arising out of the Northern conflict were £901 million, and the indirect costs £938 million (New Ireland Forum Report).
78 K. Boyle and T. Hadden, *Ireland: A Positive Proposal* (Penguin, 1985).
79 P. Macrory, T.E. Utley, J. Biggs-Davison, N. Budgen, and P. Lloyd, *Britain's Undefended Frontier: A Policy for Ulster – The Report of an Independent Study Group* (Institute for European Defence and Strategic Studies, 1984), p. 29.
80 Both Guelke (*Northern Ireland: The International Perspective*) and Holland (J. Holland, *The American Connection: US Guns, Money and Influence in Northern Ireland* (Viking, 1987)) provide detailed accounts of the intricate lobbying by Irish and Irish-American groups in the US. The Irish National Caucus, a broadly republican pressure group in the US, persuaded presidential candidate Jimmy Carter in 1976 to call for an international commission on human rights in Northern Ireland. But when Carter was elected, the Irish government's diplomatic corps under Ambassador Sean Donlan swung into action and turned Carter around. In 1977 Carter issued a statement comdemning the IRA and promising economic aid for Northern Ireland in the event of political progress, a veiled criticism of the British government. Tip O'Neil, one of the Four Horsemen – senior Irish-American politicians strongly influenced by the Irish lobby – stated that "the Irish diplomatic mission is second only to that of the Israelis" (quoted in Holland, *The American Connection . . . in Northern Ireland*, p. 129).
81 N.J. Haagerup, *Report Drawn up on Behalf of the Political Affairs Committee on the Situation in Northern Ireland*, European Parliament Working Documents 1983–1984, Document 1–1526/83 (March 19, 1984). A common factor thoughout is SDLP leader John Hume. He has major influence with the government in the South of Ireland, with the Irish-American political community in the US (and especially the Four Horsemen), and within the European Community in his role as MEP. One theory is that his influence derives from the fact that he is the only real statesman that the North has thrown up (see R. Kearney (ed.), *Beyond the Frontiers: Ireland in the 1990s* (Wolfhound Press, 1989); B. White, *John Hume: Statesman of the Troubles* (Blackstaff Press, 1984)). Others would stress more fundamental factors, such as his long-term friendship with Irish Ambassador to the US Sean Donlon, dating back to their days in Maynooth Seminary together.
82 See B. Rolston, "Alienation or Political Awareness? The Battle for the Hearts and Minds of Northern Nationalists," in P. Teague (ed.), *Beyond the Rhetoric: Politics, the Economy and Social Policy in Northern Ireland* (Lawrence and Wishart, 1988), pp. 58–80.
83 The aid promised by Carter finally materialized under the International Fund for Ireland, President Reagan's response to the Anglo-Irish Agreement. In pledging $85 million over two years, Regan quoted Carter's 1977 promise directly (November 15, 1985: cited in Holland, *The American Connection . . . in Northern Ireland*, p. 115).
84 See M. McKinley, "Lavish Generosity: The American Dimension of Inter-

national Support for the Irish Republican Army, 1968–1983," *Conflict Quarterly*, 7 (2), 1987, pp. 20–42.

85 See Holland, *The American Connection . . . in Northern Ireland.*
86 British opposition to the MacBride lobby, according to Oliver Kearney (in interview), has involved a permanent civil servant seconded from the Northern Ireland Office to the British Embassy in Washington, DC to handle propaganda, the retaining of leading public relations companies in each state where the Principles are being discussed in legislature, and copious cross-Atlantic traffic – of witnesses from Northern Ireland to speak against MacBride at legislative hearings in the US, and of US politicians and journalists to flavour Northern Ireland directly.
87 The *Irish News* (February 18, 1989). The intensity with which the US administration, taking the lead from the British, has opposed the MacBride Principles in mysterious to many Americans, as Patrick Doherty, assistant to New York City Comptroller Harrison Goldin states; the Principles "embody traditional American principles of equality and mirror US affirmative action programmes which have gained wide acceptance over the last twenty years" (see Doherty, "MacBride Effort: US Map Keeps on Getting Darker," *Fortnight*, 264 (July/August 1988), p. 12.
88 Guelke, *Northern Ireland: The International Perspective*, p. 20.
89 "We have signed an Agreement in which the Prime Minister of the Republic of Ireland has in fact accepted for all practical purposes and into perpetuity that there will never be a united Ireland" (Secretary of State Tom King, quoted in the *Sunday Independent* (December 8, 1985)).
90 General Sir James Glover, quoted in *Belfast Telegraph* (March 1, 1988).
91 Sinn Fein President Gerry Adams, quoted in the *Irish News* (August 24, 1988).
92 Quoted in *Belfast Telegraph* (November 11, 1987).
93 See *Belfast Telegraph* (November 11, 1987).
94 Quoted in *Belfast Telegraph* (March 9, 1989).
95 There have been twelve national opinion polls in Britain since 1971 which have raised the question of British army withdrawal from Northern Ireland. In nine of these polls those in favour of withdrawal were in excess of 50 percent (between 53 percent and 64 percent). In two polls those supporting withdrawal made up 50 percent. And in only one poll, held in November 1987, did a minority favour withdrawal: 40 percent. In none of the polls did a majority oppose withdrawal (source: Information on Ireland, a London-based agency).
96 Baldy, *Battle for Ulster*, pp. 97–8.

8

Indonesia: Mass Extermination and the Consolidation of Authoritarian Power

Carmel Budiardjo

1 Introduction

The military regime which came to power in Indonesia in 1965 has perpetrated numerous acts of terrorism against its own people and against the people of West Papua and East Timor. In the six months from October 1965 to March 1966, as General Suharto consolidated his control over the Indonesian state, hundreds of thousands of people were slaughtered in massacres initiated and organized by the Indonesian army, in a drive to eliminate the Indonesian Communist Party (PKI). After West Papua was handed over to the Indonesian state in 1963, massacres of villagers and organized bands of resistors to Indonesian rule led to heavy loss of life; estimates of casualties vary from tens of thousands to 150,000, more than 10 percent of the population. In the first four years of Indonesia's war to annex East Timor, from December 1975 till 1979, it is estimated that up to 200,000 people, nearly a third of the population, were killed in aerial bombardments or from war-related starvation and disease.

Other, smaller-scale massacres have occurred. Fisrt there was the slaughter in Purwodadi, Central Java, of more than eight hundred captured communist suspects, who were clubbed to death by their captors in November and December 1968. Then came the murder, by army death squads, of about 4,000 people during 1983, in a so-called clampdown on crime. In September 1984, many dozens, perhaps more than a hundred people, attending a rally in Tanjung Priok, Jakarta, pressing for the release of four local mosque officials, were shot dead, and in February 1989, many dozens of villagers were slain when troops attacked a village that had become the centre of a rebellion prompted by the expropriation of their land.

Not one of these well-documented acts of state terrorism has been condemned by any state power, West or East. There have been no UN resolutions calling Indonesia's rulers to account, no international commissions of inquiry to examine the facts and help establish more accurately the number of victims. The only public outcry in the US against the bloodthirsty crimes of Indonesia's military rulers in 1965–6 was when members of a militant, left-wing organization, Youth Against War and Fascism, unfurled banners condemning the massacres in the public gallery of the UN General Assembly in New York when Indonesia was readmitted to the UN in 1967. In Britain, the lone voices raised in outraged protest against these massacres were those of the Labour MP, Stan Newens, the historian, Malcolm Caldwell, and the Movement for Colonial Freedom. Stan Newens told the author he had no idea, from what he read in the British press in late 1965, that any massacres had taken place. His only impression for months was that some "left-wing officers" had gunned down a group of generals. It was not until he read an article by John Hughes in the *Christian Science Monitor* and, not long after, an article by Lucien Rey entitled "Dossier of the Indonesian Drama" in the *New Left Review* of March–April 1966 that he realized what had happened, then started protesting and asking questions in the House of Commons about the massacres.

In Indonesia itself, no one has been charged or tried for participating in any of these massacres, indeed, many generals have publicly bragged about their exploits during the 1965–66 massacres, without fear of being charged for murder.

The world's media has shown a singular lack of interest in the terrorist activities of the Indonesian state, reflecting the attitude of governments and multinational corporations which regard Indonesia under its present-day rulers as the best possible safeguard for "business as usual." Richard Nixon expressed this unashamedly when he wrote, in 1967, with the Suharto regime firmly in power in Jakarta: "With its one hundred million people and its three thousand-mile arc of islands containing the region's richest hoard of natural resources, Indonesia constitutes the greatest prize in the Southeast Asian area."[1]

2 Washington's Role in Promoting Anti-Communism in Indonesia

Formerly the Dutch East Indies, Indonesia provided the raw materials which fuelled Dutch commercial and industrial expansion from the seventeenth century to 1942. The southward drive of the Japanese Imperial Army in the 1940s was prompted primarily by the need to gain access to

Indonesia's natural resources, particularly petroleum. After the defeat of Japan in 1945, the US intervened repeatedly to prevent the restoration of Dutch colonial power in Indonesia, while at the same time supporting the Indonesian army and right-wing politicians in their drive against the Indonesian left. Following an army offensive against the left in Madiun, East Java, in September 1948, which left thousands of people dead, the Truman administration hailed the government of Vice-President/Prime Minister Mohamad Hatta as "the only government in the Far East to have met and crushed an all-out communist offensive."[2] Once Hatta had proven his anti-communist credentials, Washington proceeded to compel the Dutch to abandon their military operations against republican forces and enter into negotiations with the Republic for the transfer of sovereignty in 1949. The negotiations in the Hague took place under the patronage of US diplomat Merle Cochrane, who lobbied tenaciously to iron out disagreements and prevent Dutch obstinacy from sabotaging US objectives.

However, US relations with the new Republic, which received international recognition in December 1949, were far from smooth. Washington had to contend with an archetypal nationalist state leadership in postcolonial Indonesia. In the first 15 years, the Republic pursued a "free and active" foreign policy, shunning alliances with the West. It also became embroiled in an anti-colonial confrontation with the Netherlands over the status of Western Papua New Guinea, a territory that had been excluded from the 1949 settlement between Jakarta and the Hague. This led Indonesia to adopt militant anti-Western postures at a time when it also emerged as a leading power in the non-aligned movement of the 1950s.

During the period of parliamentary democracy from 1950 to 1957, the Communist Party of Indonesia (PKI) made a remarkable political recovery, winning 18 percent of the votes and taking fourth place in Indonesia's first – and only – free and democratic parliamentary elections in 1955. In the following decade, the PKI grew to become the largest left-wing party outside the Eastern bloc. By 1965, it claimed a membership of three million, supported by trade unions, a peasants' organization, and other mass organizations, with a combined membership of around fifteen million. As the communist-led movement gained in mass support, the armed forces were initially seriously split in their approach towards the leftward shift in Indonesian politics. In the regions, some army commanders took the path of rebellion against the centre, partly in protest against the growth of the left and partly to take control of locally produced natural resources. But the army leadership at the centre was no less anti-communist.

The outbreak of regional rebellions in North Sulawesi and West Sumatra in 1956, spearheaded by local army commanders with the support of pro-Western politicians, led to the declaration of martial law in March 1956. The army leadership at the centre, under General Nasution, opted for an alliance with the populist President Sukarno in order to combat regionalism. For his part, Sukarno used the communist-led masses to balance his alliance with the armed forces and began to give them his encouragement and protection, in exchange for their backing of his populist policies.

It was the alliance between Sukarno and Nasution, however, that dominated state policy and paved the way for authoritarianism. The shift towards authoritarianism quickened when parliamentary democracy was discarded and replaced by Guided Democracy in 1957. This system eroded the independence of the political parties, allotting to them the role of mass mobilization in exchange for firm pledges to uphold state ideology and support government policies. It was during the period of Guided Democracy that confrontation with Holland intensified, and Indonesia assumed the role of an anti-colonial power still engaged in revolutionary struggle, in the forefront of the non-aligned movement that was beginning to take shape. These policies had the support not only of most political parties and especially the PKI, but also of the central army leadership.

It was a mixture that was unpalatable for John Foster Dulles and the CIA, leading them to intervene on the side of the regional insurrectionists as the most effective way to stem the spread of communism in Indonesia. CIA support for the rebel government set up in West Sumatra proved to be a major setback for the agency. The rebellion was easily crushed by army forces from Java, commanded by officers who had received their training in the US. Still worse, a US pilot on a bombing sortie over Ambon was shot down and captured in February 1958, giving conclusive evidence of CIA involvement and forcing Dulles to distance himself publicly from the rebel movement, and leading to a major reappraisal of US policy towards Indonesia.

The turnabout in US policy was to some extent the work of the newly appointed ambassador, Howard Jones, who urged Washington to stop plotting the downfall of Sukarno and revise its assessment of Nasution. "The army is gathering power both in the political and economic spheres," he wrote, referring among other things to the army's control over Dutch enterprises that had been taken over in 1957 as part of Indonesia's confrontation with Holland. "The army does not regard the struggle with the rebels as a battle between communists and anti-communists since the army leadership in Jakarta is as strongly anti-communist as the army leadership on the rebel side."[3]

The new policy of supporting the central army leadership as the most effective force against the PKI had the support of the State Department and the Pentagon. The National Security Council, in two reports issued in January 1959 and December 1960, acknowledged that the key to US efforts to curtail communist influence in Indonesia was the army, attributing the anti-PKI stance of the army to US training of its officers.[4] Although this may have been the view from Washington and the aim of the US policy of support for the Indonesian army, it is wrong to conclude that the Indonesian army regarded the US army as its model. Nor indeed did the Indonesian army ger inspiration solely from the US for its anti-communist fervour. Anti-communism was well established in the Indonesian army long before officers began receiving instruction in Fort Leavenworth, as the army's slaughter of the left in Madiun in 1948 convincingly proves.

A military assistance programme (MAP) for Indonesia was agreed and, during the Kennedy administration, it was the US Civic Action Programme (CAP) that became the cornerstone of US influence. Significantly, CAP "was not a joint US–Indonesia governmental effort as in other countries but rather, a direct US army–Indonesian army effort in accordance with the wishes of General Nasution."[5] Here too, the US was only contributing its bit to a policy that had been established several years earlier by the Indonesian army. Operasi Karya, or Civic Mission, which provided the basis for army units to become involved in road building and general development activity, was a key tool of the army to confront growing PKI support in the rural areas, particularly in Java. Even after 1963, when Indonesia's policy of confrontation with the Dutch over West Papua (which the Dutch ceded to Indonesia under pressure from Washington) was replaced by confrontation with the UK over the creation of Malaysia, leading among other things to the takeover of US oil companies, CAP remained intact. And it did so notwithstanding the passage of the Broomfield Amendment to the Foreign Assistance Act adopted in July 1963, stipulating that no aid to Indonesia could be granted without a presidential determination that this was in the national interest.[6] Even after Sukarno, in 1964, publicly denounced US efforts to use aid as the means for exerting pressure on Jakarta to abandon confrontation over Malaysia, when he told the US at a rally attended by the US ambassador to "go to hell with your aid," the Indonesian army was still receiving aid and equipment under CAP. When the General Accounting Office conducted an inquiry into military aid for Indonesia, the Department of Defense added a comment to its findings, stressing the political nature of this aid and acknowledging the role the army was assuming in government affairs and its emergence as a major force to combat communism. "Therefore, Indonesia's MAP was not based on external defense but on a policy of assisting and influencing the armed forces to retain a non-communist posture."[7]

According to a CIA report of October 1966, approximately 2,800 Indonesian officers had been trained in US service schools, the bulk of them in the period from 1960 to 1964. US military manuals were being widely used and programmes of instruction in Indonesian army branch schools were almost identical with their US counterparts. "In spite of the Indonesian government's anti-American posture, US training and equipment was still highly valued by Indonesian military officers."[8] One unit strongly influenced by this US training was the army paras regiment, known originally as the RPKAD (now called Kopassus), the mobile strike force which the army needed in order to impose its will throughout the archipelago. The RPKAD became a well-trained, airbone elite unit due largely to the efforts of General Yani, one of the earliest beneficiaries of training at Fort Leavenworth. This was the unit that in late 1965 spearheaded the anti-communist massacres, under the command of Lieutenant Colonel Sarwo Edhie, a graduate of the US army's Infantry School at Fort Benning, Georgia, where the US army's ranger and airborne courses are located. Ten years later, the RPKAD led the way in Indonesia's invasion of East Timor, and it has since become notorious among the Timorese, who call them *nanggala* or "knife-wielding killers."

3 Integrating Military and Economic Aid

In the late 1950s, US policy-makers were becoming increasingly convinced that for the countries of the Third World it was necessary to integrate military and economic aid and to promote the military as the leading political force. In his first foreign aid message in 1961, President Kennedy made it clear that "military assistance will in the future more heavily emphasize the military security, civil works and economic growths of the nations thus aided."[9]

A key adviser on policy towards Indonesia during this period was Guy Pauker, a Rand Corporation consultant who was widely believed to be on the CIA's payroll. He had established excellent contacts among anti-communist army generals and advised the US Congress, in the so-called Conlon Report of 1959, to help provide them with "administrative and managerial skills."[10] Pauker was also chairman, from 1959 to 1963, of the Centre for South and Southeast Asian Studies at Berkeley University, which trained a number of economists from Indonesia, disciples of Professor Sumitro Djojohadikusumo, former dean of the Faculty of Economics at the University of Indonesia and one of the politicians who threw in his lot with the West Sumatra-based rebel movement of 1956. Some of the Center's graduates returned to Indonesia to teach part-time at the army's Staff and Command school (SESKOAD). After 1965, they were the technocrats who helped run the Indonesian economy during the first two decades of General Suharto's rule, and came to be known as the Berkeley Mafia.

By 1959, the PKI was able to mobilize such huge support that it was generally agreed that, had the second parliamentary elections been held as scheduled, an overwhelming communist victory would have been inevitable. At this time, Pauker wrote: "Communism is bound to win in Southeast Asia . . . unless effective countervailing power is found in some groups who have sufficient organizational strength, goal-direction, leadership and discipline . . . Those best equipped . . . are members of the officer corps as individuals and the national armies as organizational structures. . . . To succeed in the competition with communism, the officer corps will need substantial economic and technical assistance."[11]

Three years later, Pauker was growing impatient with army leaders like Nasution and Yani, who appeared to be trapped in an alliance with the populist Sukarno, leading him to complain that "the officers have not assumed full responsibility" and the officer corps had failed to use its capabilities for reform and progress. The army "accepts the role of partners or even instruments of a group of emotional, radical nationalists."[12] A year later, Pauker's optimism had waned even further, leading him to call for a fascist-type solution:

> Were the communists to lose Sukarno as a proctector, it seems doubtful that other national leaders, capable of rallying Indonesia's dispersed and demoralised anti-communist forces, would emerge in the near future. Furthermore these forces would probably lack the ruthlessness that made it possible for the Nazis to suppress the Communist Party of Germany a few weeks after the elections of March 5, 1933, an election in which the Communist Party still won five million votes, almost 13 percent of the total. The enemies of the PKI, including the remnants of the various rightwing rebellions, the suppressed political parties and certain elements in the armed forces, are weaker than the Nazis, not only in numbers and in mass support, but also in unity, discipline and leadership.[13]

But the ruthlessness for which Pauker yearned and for which Washington had been laying the foundation was not long in coming.

4 Creating the Myth

The events of October 1, 1965, were traumatic in their impact on Indonesian political life. They brought the army to power under General Suharto, led to the extermination of the PKI, and resulted in the downfall of Sukarno.

It all started with an operation launched by middle-ranking army officers to kidnap seven army generals, including the army commander,

General Yani, ostensibly to force them to account to President Sukarno for their covert plans to depose him. This was the operation that paved the way for Major General Suharto, as he then was, to take over command of the army and seize power.

Suharto did not appear at the time to be a contender for power, nor was he recognized as being involved in either of the two rival factions within the armed forces centred on General Nasution and General Yani. Suharto obtained his early military training and experience in Peta (Defenders of the Motherland), the Indonesian armed corps set up by the Japanese Imperial Army during the Pacific War. Like so many Indonesian officers who later took over the leadership of the republican army, he imbibed the warrior spirit nurtured by the Japanese militarists. He had always been fiercely nationalistic, dedicated to the centralized, Java-based control of the farflung empire Indonesia inherited from the Dutch colonialists, and proved himself to be a commanding officer of great ruthlessness against opponents of the Indonesian state. He had never attended military school in the US. From his time as commander of the Diponegoro Division in Central Java in the mid-1950s, he surrounded himself with a loyal team of intelligence officers and attached great importance to the army's strike force and airborne troops. By 1965, he was commander of the Army's Strategic Command, KOSTRAD, in Jakarta, and it was from this base that he launched his successful bid to seize power. By this time, he also had wide-ranging economic interests in businesses run by his army cronies or by Chinese entrepreneurs, whom he patronized and promoted.

The plotters who planned and executed the October 1, 1965, kidnaps were led by Lieutenant Colonel Untung, who had for years been Suharto's subordinate. His main co-plotter was Colonel Latief, also a longtime subordinate and close family friend of Suharto; Latief had a secret meeting with Suharto at the army hospital in Jakarta, only a few hours before the kidnap gangs set out on their missions at the crack of dawn on October 1. Although the plotters all insisted in their trials that the plan was to kidnap the generals, it resulted in the murder of six generals and a junior army officer. The seventh officer targetted, General Nasution, escaped, but his adjutant was kidnapped by mistake.

By taking D.N. Aidit, the chairman of the PKI, to their operational base, the plotters succeeded in implicating the PKI, giving Suharto the pretext to order the physical destruction of the party and the left-wing movement.

Suharto's own role in planning the alleged "coup attempt" has been well documented by many writers.[14] Apart from Suharto's midnight meeting with Latief, there is the fact that although the Untung plotters seized control of several strategic points in the capital, they conveniently forgot to occupy Suharto's KOSTRAD headquarters, leaving him free to launch his counterattack, paralyzing and dispersing the Untung plotters within hours. Suharto was in command of the RPKAD paras, who were easily able to regain control of the streets of Jakarta as the Untung forces showed themselves to be hesitant, poorly led, and ill prepared for an armed seizure of power. At his headquarters, Suharto also possessed the only up-to-date telecommunications system in the country, delivered to the unit from the US earlier that year.

On October 4, the corpses of the murdered generals and the adjutant which had been dumped down a well in an airforce base on the outskirts of Jakarta, were exhumed in the full glare of publicity, with Suharto in charge. He used the highly charged atmosphere to accuse the PKI of full responsibility for the murders. On the same day, *Berita Yudha*, the army newspaper (all non-army newspapers had been banned), launched a campaign of vilification against the PKI, focusing on the dead generals and the alleged mutilation of their bodies before the corpses were thrown down the well. Since responsibility for the kidnappings could not be pinned on the PKI, as army squads had carried out the missions, the army press began to publish statements extracted from young girls who were members of the left-wing women's organization, Gerwani, and the youth organization, Pemuda Rakyat, "confessing" that they had slashed the genitals of the generals and gouged out their eyes. Before the bodies were buried on October 5, autopsies were conducted on the instruction of Suharto, but their findings were never made public in Indonesia, although Sukarno referred to them in several speeches in the last quarter of 1965, suggesting that they had produced no evidence of mutilations.

More than twenty years later, the mystery of the autopsies was solved with the translation by Ben Anderson of seven autopsies carried out on October 4 and 5, 1965, by doctors acting on Suharto's instructions. Anderson had discovered the autopsies when glancing through the verbatim report of one of the military tribunal trials held in the late 1960s. Publication of these documents finally exploded one of the most outrageous propaganda myths created during the Suharto operation against the PKI.[15] The autopsies show, with reasonable certainty, he wrote, "that the victims died by gunfire (the case of Harjono, who died in his own home, remains puzzling), and that if their bodies suffered other violence, it was the result of clubbing with the butts of the guns that fired the fatal bullets, or of damage likely to occur from a 36-foot fall down a stone-walled well." As for claims that their genitals had been slashed, the autopsies failed to confirm any such thing. On the contrary, they found all the victims' penises to be intact, recording that four of the men were circumcised and three were uncircumcised.

The autopsies were completed early on October 5, the day when the bodies were buried. There can be no doubt that Suharto knew of their findings, yet even so the two army dailies, as well as *Api Pancasila*, the journal of the army-sponsored party IPKI, published reports alleging, for example, that "General Suprapto's face and skull had been smashed by savage terrorists,"[16] that "Lieutenant Tendean had knife wounds on his left chest and stomach, his neck had been mutilated and both his eyes had been gouged out,"[17] that some of the generals "had their genitals cut off as well as other inhuman horrors,"[18] and that "the eye-gouges used on the generals had been discovered by anti-communist youths ransacking Communist Party buildings in the village of Harupanggang, outside Garut."[19] Later, in a report about the "confessions" of one woman, Mrs Djamilah, said to have been a three-month pregnant, 15-year-old Gerwani member from Patjitan, it was alleged (according to a story circulated to the whole press on November 6 by the armed forces information service) that she and her associates at Lubang Buaya "had been issued penknives and razors by armed members of the 30 September Movement. They then, all one hundred of them, following orders from the same men, proceeded to slash and slice the genitals of the captured generals." Summing up, Anderson wrote:

> In these accounts, which filled the newspapers during October, November and December, while the massacres of those associated with the Communist Party were going on, two features are of particular interest here. The first is the insistence that the seven men were subjected to horrifying tortures – notably eye-gouging and castration; the second is an emphasis on civilians in organizations of Communist affiliation as the perpetrators.[20]

According to Ralph McGehee, a former CIA agent, the campaign of deception which paved the way for the massacres was largely the work of the CIA. Referring to the fabricated horror stories about events at Halim, he wrote:

> This cynically manufactured campaign was designed to foment public anger against the communists and set the stage for the massacre . . . To conceal its role in the massacres of those innocent people, the CIA concocted a false account of what happened (later published by the Agency as a book, *Indonesia - 1965: The Coup That Backfired*). At the same time . . . it also composed a secret study of what really happened. [One sentence deleted by the CIA.]
> The Agency was very proud of its successful [one word deleted by the CIA] and recommended it as a model for future operations (one half sentence deleted by the CIA].[21]

Although McGehee never worked for the CIA in Indonesia, he later explained that, as the CIA's East Asia division representative to the

International Communism Branch, he was custodian of the Branch's studies describing CIA operations against various communist parties. "Its study about the Agency's operation in Indonesia in 1965 was so heinously fascinating that I read it many times. It boastfully outlined how a simple covert action had been decisive in destroying the PKI."[22]

The inflammatory reports of alleged PKI atrocities led immediately to demonstrations in the capital calling for the party to be banned. Within days, party property and the homes of PKI members were being looted and burnt and the party's organization was virtually smashed. Although a nationwide ban was not declared until March 1966, the Jakarta military commander suspended the PKI and its many mass organization at the beginning of October and ordered its functionaries to register themselves with their local military commands. Thousands of people were arrested. By October 7, the army had produced its master slogan, calling Untung's coup the Gestapu, an acronym for Gerakan September Tiga-Puluh, September 30 Movement. (The syntax is not correct in Indonesian as dates are always written in reverse, e.g. "tiga-puluh September".) Using a Nazi, German-sounding acronym is very much at odds with Indonesian political terminology and suggests an external source of inspiration. One cannot help wondering whether Guy Pauker may have been the source. The campaign to expurgate the PKI and communist ideology from Indonesia had begun.

5 The Bloodbath

With the entire press closed down except for army-run newspapers, no one could challenge the sensational claims. The "confessions" had been extracted by means of intimidation and torture. None of the women was brought to trial and most retracted their statements later, after spending years in detention without trial. But these were the stories that helped set alight a wave of anti-communist fervor, leading to the massacres that swept the country.

Although the PKI and its many mass organizations were not officially banned until March 1966, when Suharto forced Sukarno to surrender all his powers, the message that the PKI had to be crushed was conveyed informally, leaving local commanders to decide the means to be used.[23] Some military commanders knew what was expected of them even without waiting for the murdered generals' bodies to be exhumed. Brigadier General Kemal Idris, a battle command commander in North Sumatra, later boasted to a US journalist: "I told my men to seize members of the Communist Party even before I had any authority to do so. Their initial orders were to clean up communists within a five-mile radius of their posi-

190

tions. But they completed the assignment so fast that they spread out-wards, still farther afield."[24] A source close to Kemal Idris said that "the army killed 20 percent of the rubber plantation workers in the Medan area, in those days of bloody retaliation."[25]

In Aceh too, the bloodletting started early. The military commander, Brigadier General Ishak Djuarsa, claimed that "Aceh was the first region to be cleansed of counter-revolutionary G30S [read: PKI] elements," and by December 1965, he said that "the PKI is no longer a major problem for Aceh because the region has been purged in a physical sense of PKI elements."[26] General Nasution gives details of many anti-PKI and anti-unionist actions taken in the early days of October throughout Sumatra. The directors of state plantation companies in North Sumatra banned the activities of the PKI and its mass organizations in the plantation sector on October 19. The West Sumatra regional assembly adopted a decision, without any of its PKI members present, to condemn the G30S (read: the PKI). This led to the destruction of the premises of the PKI and affiliated organizations and to a call for the PKI and associated organizations to be banned. It was the presence of several KOSTRAD brigades in North Sumatra, Nasution wrote, that made possible "speedy and correct" actions against the PKI. Seven local branches of political parties set up an "Action Front to Crush the G30S," in order to "annihilate all elements and supporters" of the G30S.[27] This was the kind of language used at the time to incite people to murder anyone suspected as a left-wing activist.

On October 19, the military commander of West Kalimantan, Major General Amir Mahmud, issued an instruction temporarily banning the PKI and all its mass organizations. Two days earlier, a public meeting in the capital, Pontianak, had "vehemently condemned the ungodly actions of the G30S," and called on the president to ban the PKI and all associated organizations.[28] In Central Java, the PKI's biggest strong-hold, the extermination campaign against the PKI needed outside intervention to get it started. It was only in Central Java that the Untung operation had inspired a local attempt to take control of the Diponegoro Division in the province and set up a revolutionary council, giving Suharto the excuse to send in outside troops to "restore order." The division was hardly in a state to initiate its own PKI extermination campaign. Well aware of the political complexities of the situation in Central Java, Suharto decided that, once the Halim air-base had been retaken, he would dispatch his elite para-commando regiment, the RPKAD, under its US-trained commander, Colonel Sarwo Edhie, to take charge of the crackdown in Central Java. After staging a massive show of strength in the provincial capital, Semarang, on October 19, which triggered attacks on PKI property and the homes of left-wing activists, RPKAD troops

191

moved southwards to take control of the major cities, while Diponegoro battalions were sent off to North Sumatra "to take part in confrontation with Malaysia."

Railway workers in Central Java had called a strike in an attempt to obstruct troop movements and, in some parts of the province, members of the PKI youth organization, Pemuda Rakyat, had cut down trees to set up barricades against advancing troops. These isolated efforts were soon quelled with a great amount of bloodshed. As Anderson and McVey point out: "The struggle was completely one-sided as the local PKI had never been trained for combat and had virtually no arms."[29]

It soon became clear that there were not enough RPKAD troops to mount operations in so many places at once, so Sarwo Edhie began training and arming vigilante bands of nationalist and Islamic youths to scour the villages for those suspected of communist sympathies. John Hughes quoted Sarwo Edhie: "In Solo, we gathered together the youth, the nationalist groups, the religious organisations. We gave them two or three days' training, then sent them out to kill communists".[30] Another writer described the operations as follows:

> In each village, members of the communist organisations were rounded up and taken away. After quick interrogation, those considered to be activists were killed and passive supporters were placed under detention in camps and jails. During the following weeks, similar operations spread through all of Central Java. In general, the operations remained under army control and were directed mainly at PKI activists, but in some areas, such as Banyumas, it was reported that the army authorities stood aside and permitted the Muslim and nationalist youths to select their own victims, with the result that many thousands, who would have been merely arrested in areas where the army exercised close control, were killed.[31]

Many of those placed in camps and prisons were later taken out and shot, beheaded, or killed in other ways.

There was a grim logic to Suharto's decision to deal directly and decisively with Central Java. Central Java is the most densely populated region of Indonesia and it was here that the PKI had its largest following.

In East Java, the wave of terror was initiated by black-shirted, Muslim paramilitary youth groups, who had been beating up PKI or peasant union members since before the October events, to obstruct unilateral actions to implement the 1960 land reform law. They were faster off the mark in the crusade against communist suspects than the troops. Religious fanaticism played a particularly important part in the East Java massacres. The writer of the following account was a schoolboy in Kediri, East Java, in October 1965 and was caught up in the anti-PKI violence:

Not only the NU (Muslim party) masses but also those of the PNI (Nationalist Party) joined in. The army didn't get much involved. First to be raided were workers' quarters at the sugar factory . . . It was done like this: a particular village would be surrounded by squads of nationalist and religious youth (Muslim and Christian [Protestant] for example in Pare). A mass of village youth would be brought in. . . . On average about 3,000 people would be involved. The expectation was that, with the village surrounded, no communist elements would be able to escape.

. . . Each day as [I] went to or returned from school, [I] always saw corpses of communists floating in the River Brantas. The thing was that the school was located to the west of the river. And usually the corpses were no longer recognisable as human. Headless. Stomachs torn open. The smell was unbelievable. To make sure they didn't sink, the carcasses were deliberately tied to, or impaled on, bamboo stakes. And the departure of corpses from Kediri region down the Brantas achieved its golden age when bodies were stacked together on rafts over which the PKI banner proudly flew. . . .

It was evident that the Kediri area was unsafe for communists (strangely enough, except in one instance, they made no move to offer any resistance). So most of them tried to flee to Surabaya or sought protection at the Kediri town *Kodim* (district military command). But even in jail they were not safe. Too many of them sought safety there, and the jail could not take them all in. In the end the army often trucked them off to Mt Klotok. . . . Who knows what the army did with them there – what was clear was that the trucks went off fully loaded and came back empty.[32]

From East Java, the killings spread across the straits to Bali, where the army played on the conflicts that had festered below the surface between the PKI and the PNI. Here, the massacres were conducted "with an intensity that was second only to what happened in Aceh."[33] According to Hughes, Bali erupted in a frenzy of savagery worse than Java's after a soldier was killed in a clash between troops and communists in the western part of the island in early December. When the local commander asked for instructions from his superior in Den Pasar, he was told to "behave as a commander should." Without further prompting, the troops were unleashed against the communists:

But military forces in Bali were slender and, as the death toll in the two ensuing weeks mounted through the thousands, it was civilians who were mainly killing communists. In the forefront were black-shirted bands of PNI shock-troopers called Tamins. Working in teams they went through village after village, checking off names against communist party lists, accepting the words of informers, and putting their victims to death. Usually, the execution was by knife or sword. Men marked for death would either have their throats cut or be decapitated.[34]

A time came when Suharto felt that things in Bali "were getting out of hand" with the killings "becoming indiscriminate [sic]", so he ordered Sarwo Edhie's troops "to restore order:"

> This did not mean that communists were no longer to be killed. It meant that the para-commandos were to halt looting, prevent anarchy and see that innocent [sic] people were not harmed. But the execution of communists was to go on in orderly fashion. As Sarwo Edhie remarked to one leading Balinese, "In Java we had to egg people on to kill communists. In Bali we have to restrain them, make sure they don't go too far."[35]

From then on, Hughes quotes one official as saying, "the killing was coordinated. The military and the police got together with civilian authorities and made sure that the right people were being executed." Hughes says that "responsible" Balinese believe that 40,000 people had by then met their deaths in the purge.

Estimates of the numbers killed in the six-month period from October 1965 vary from half a million to a million. A fact-finding commission set up by Sukarno in late 1965 visited only four districts, Central and East Java, Bali, and North Sumatra, and came up with the figure of 78,000. But the credibility of that exercise was shattered by the comments of a commission member who, when asked by Hughes whether he thought that figure was correct,

> laughed merrily. "Oh dear me, no," he said. "That was nowhere near the right figure." Then what did he believe to be the correct figure? "My own view," he replied unblinkingly, "is that about ten times as many people as that were killed."
>
> Taken aback, I asked him to spell that out again. Was he really saying that although the commission had reported 78,000 people killed, he himself believed the figure to be 780,000? "Yes, that's right," he assured me.[36]

6 Washington and the Final Solution

Since the beginning of 1965, the US embassy had been passing on to Washington reports of coup plans by those in charge of the army, and of the establishment of a secret group which came to be called the "Generals' Council," set up to consider what to do if Sukarno, known to be ailing, became incapacitated or died. Typical of this traffic is a cable from the embassy, dated January 21, 1965, based on information from a source described as "excellent," which reported that:

[the] army is developing specific plans for takeover of government [the] moment Sukarno steps off stage. . . . [Name deleted] said that although planning was being done on contingency bases [sic] with an eye to [the] post-Sukarno era, strong sentiment existed among important segment [of] top military command for takeover prior to demise [of] Sukarno. Conflicting pressures were building up to such a pitch that in his own opinion [the] army might be forced to take action within the next 30 to 60 days to offset PKI moves.

The embassy added the following comment: "Department will recognize this report as kind which has in past frequently appeared only to prove [a] mirage. Nevertheless, source is excellent and there are growing signs [of] concern and discontent among army leaders and reports and rumours of this kind are on [the] increase."[37]

Although much of the cable traffic between the embassy and the State Department during 1965 has now been declassified, Gabriel Kolko, whose latest book[38] forms the basis for the following paragraphs, says that:

the documents for the three months preceding 30 September and dealing with the convoluted background and intrigues, much less the embassy's and the CIA's roles, have been withheld from public scrutiny. Given the detailed materials available before and after July–September 1965, one can only assume that the release of these documents would embarrass the US government. . . . and that Washington's involvement in the terrible events of late 1965 was far greater than it has been willing to admit.[39]

No later than October 3, 1965, the embassy thought the crucial issue was whether the army under Suharto would "have the courage to go forward against [the] PKI."[40] Basing his account on a study of the cable traffic, Kolko writes that the embassy clearly informed key Indonesian officers of the need to destroy the PKI "and the latter had similar thoughts even though they too believed the degree of PKI culpability was still very much a question."[41]

The CIA reports that on October 5, the army made the decision to "implement plans to crush [the] PKI."[42] The next day, the embassy cabled Washington that the army could move against the PKI, stating that "it's now or never."[43] Three days later, the US ambassador Marshall Green, who had taken over the post from Howard Jones in June 1965, was still worried about the army's "determination" to stand up to Sukarno. On October 14, Green was getting more confident: "We do think [the] army will go on trying, possibly not always as directly as we would like, to keep matters moving in [the] direction we would wish to see. . . . Their success or failure is going to determine our own in Indonesia for some time to come."[44]

As the embassy well knew by the latter part of October, the army was already coordinating a wave of destruction against the PKI. Kolko's account continues:

> Washington received all the details the embassy possessed on the army's support for the massacres and it took consolation that the army had resisted Sukarno's belated efforts at the end of October to stop the slaughter. The cleanup task would go on, Green told Rusk on October 28, and the next day, the secretary of state cabled back that "the campaign against PKI" must continue and that the military "are [the] only force capable of creating order in Indonesia" which they had to continue doing "with or without Sukarno". Meanwhile, the generals could expect United States help for a "major military campaign against PKI."[45] A week later Green reported back that while the army was aiding the Muslim youth in Java to take care of the PKI, it was assuming the task directly in the outer islands, and it was contemplating a military state in the future. We have "made it clear that embassy and USG [are] generally sympathetic with and admiring of what army [is] doing."[46] The army was wholly engaged, as Green described it several days later, attacking the PKI "ruthlessly" and "wholesale killings" were occurring.[47]

But Washington, guided on an almost day-to-day basis by the US embassy under Marshall Green, was not merely watching and cheering on the sidelines as the slaughter continued. It responded to a request from the army early in November for equipment "to arm Moslem and nationalist youths in Central Java for use against the PKI." As most were using knives and primitive means, communications gear and small arms would expedite the killing.

> Since "elimination of these elements" was a precondition of better relations, the United States quickly promised covert aid, dubbed "medicines" to prevent embarrassing revelations.[48] At stake in the army's effort was the "destruction," as the CIA called the undertaking, of the PKI, and "carefully placed assistance which will help army cope with PKI" continued, as Green described it, despite the many other problems in Indonesian–US relations that remained to be solved.[49]

As Kolko states, the extermination of the PKI in 1965–66 "surely ranks as a war crime of the same type as those the Nazis perpetrated. . . . No single American action in the period after 1945 was as bloodthirsty as its role in Indonesia, for it tried to initiate the massacre, and it did everything in its power to encourage Suharto, including equipping his killers, to see that the physical liquidation of the PKI was carried through to its culmination."[50]

BRITISH LABOUR GOVERNMENT IS UNMOVED

As for the role of the UK, it is far more difficult to discover how the Labour government under Harold Wilson, which was in power in late 1965, responded internally to the events in Jakarta. Government and Cabinet papers are kept secret for thirty years, and in some cases, highly sensitive documents can been shrouded in secrecy for a hundred years. It goes without saying that the takeover by Suharto was welcomed by Whitehall; at last, the intransigent spokesman of anti-colonialism and non-alignment, Sukarno, for long despised by the British establishment, had been removed and British investors could heave a collective sigh of relief about the future of their extensive interests in Indonesia. Indonesia's stubborn opposition to the creation of the Federation of Malaysia had resulted in the outbreak of military operations between British and Indonesian troops along the border between Indonesian Kalimantan and the British colonial territories in North Borneo. Labour's foreign secretary at the time of the massacres, Michael Stewart, spared not a thought for the hundreds of thousands of victims of Suharto's butchers. Dealing in his autobiography with this period of his term as foreign secretary, he did not so much as mention the slaughters that attended Suharto's rise to power:

> When that country was afflicted by drought, we made a large and uncondi-
> tional gift of food. This was criticised by some newspapers as strengthening
> those who were fighting against British soldiers but I believe it helped
> encourage those in Indonesia who wanted peace. It would not have been
> effective by itself but there was growing dissatisfaction with Sukarno in his
> own country. In 1966 he was pushed into the background and the suc-
> ceeding government decided to stop the confrontation. I was able in the
> summer of that year to visit Indonesia and reach a good understanding with
> the Foreign Minister, Adam Malik. He is a remarkable man who, without
> wealth or military background, rose to his position by personal ability and
> was evidently resolved to keep his country at peace. The present Indonesian
> Government is like Sukarno's, harsh and tyrannical; but it is not
> aggressive.[51]

6   Indonesian Aggression and Terror in East Timor

On the afternoon of December 7, 1975, a Darwin radio post heard an appeal of great desperation from the radio transmitter of Fretilin (Revolu-tionary Front for the Independence of East Timor) in Dili:

197

Carmel Budiardjo

The Indonesian forces are killing indiscriminately. Women and children are being shot in the streets. We are all going to be killed. I repeat, we are all going to be killed. . . . This is an appeal for international help. Please do something to stop this invasion.[52]

It was an appeal that was to go unheeded in the West, except for the response of small solidarity groups that had sprung up in many countries, having become acutely aware of Indonesia's intentions to invade the former Portuguese colony.

The horror of the atrocities visited upon the population of Dili by the invading Indonesian troops did not become fully known until a former Australian consul in Dili, James Dunn, who is fluent in Portuguese, visited Lisbon in January 1977 and was able to piece together the ghastly events from East Timorese refugees who had lived through the nightmare. The following extracts come from the account in his book, *Timor, A People Betrayed*:

The attack on the Timorese capital, much of which was uncontested, turned out to be one of the most brutal operations of its kind in modern warfare. Hundreds of Timorese and Chinese were gunned down at random in the streets of Dili. In one such incident, a large number of Apodeti [pro-Indonesia party] supporters, who had just been released from internment by Fretilin, went out to greet their liberators, to be gunned down in the street for their trouble. A number of executions were carried out by Indonesian troops, with some of the condemned being selected at random, and others with the help of collaborators.

One of the most bizarre and gruesome of these atrocities occurred within 24 hours of the invasion and involved the killing of about 150 people. This shocking spectacle began with the execution of more than 20 women who, from various accounts, were selected at random. Some had young children who wept in distress as the soldiers tore them from the arms of their terrified mothers. The women were led out to the edge of the jetty and shot one at a time, with the crowd of shocked onlookers being forced at gunpoint to count aloud as each execution took place! . . .

Similar killings were carried out in other parts of the capital before the senseless rampage was to subside. About thirty supporters of the pro-integration party (Apodeti) were shot outside the former Portuguese Military Police barracks. This party of Timorese had been sent to the barracks and ordered to remove weapons and ammunition from it. According to a survivor of this killing, the Indonesian soldiers then asked the men which party they belonged to. They all answered "Apodeti", but the Indonesians fired on them with machine guns (which the witness believed were M16s). Most of the group died in the first volley of shooting but the Indonesians then walked around firing at bodies that showed signs of life. Five Timorese are believed to have survived this massacre, one (now a resident

198

in Perth) by placing his injured hand over his head, lying still, and letting the blood from the wound seep over his head.

A group of Chinese community leaders who, it seems had come out into the street to offer some kind of welcome to the vanguard of the "new order" were gunned down. The Chinese who had been studiously neutral in East Timor's political conflicts . . . and who were probably more disposed than any other section of the population to come to terms with integration, were to die by the hundreds in the aftermath of the invasion. In some cases the men were separated from their families and then shot. . . .

There were many other random killings of Timorese and Chinese in the streets and in houses. Apparently faced with the orgy of indiscriminate kill-ing, many of the residents of the capital retreated into their homes but this was to afford them little protection. Indonesian soldiers broke into the houses, especially those displaying Fretilin or even UDT flags or symbols, and in some cases shot whole families. In the suburbs near the airport, soldiers resorted to hurling grenades through the doors or windows of houses crowded with frightened people, causing heavy loss of life. . . .

With the battle against Fretilin raging to the south and west of the city, the orgy of killing was reported to have continued for about a week. Accor-ding to a Catholic priest who was in Dili after the invasion, as many as 2,000 citizens of the capital, some 700 of them Chinese, were killed in the first few days of the Indonesian invasion. In a letter smuggled out of Timor some months after the invasion, an elderly Chinese who had been in the territory during World War 2 wrote that the Indonesian excesses were far worse than anything he had experienced during the Japanese occupation.[53]

Gruesome facts about Indonesian atrocities in Dili and other East Timorese towns during the first years of the war also became available from letters smuggled out to refugees living in Lisbon and from reports by journalists who succeeded in breaching the information blackout imposed by the Indonesian army. Much of this information was reproduced in a book published by TAPOL, the Indonesia Human Rights Campaign, in 1979.[54]

Extremely high casualty figures were already becoming available early in 1976. In February 1976, an Indonesian client, Lopez da Cruz, who had been appointed deputy chair of the "Provisional Government" of East Timor set up by the forces of occupation, asserted that 60,000 Timorese had already died.[55] In September 1976, a report by Indonesian Catholic Church officials who visited East Timor to conduct relief operations con-tained the following statement:

According to reports, sixty thousand people had been killed during the war. We found this figure rather high because it means ten percent of the total population of East Timor. But when we asked, two fathers in Dilli [sic] replied that according to their estimate, the figure of people killed may reach one hundred thousand.[56]

With evidence mounting of a horrendous death toll in East Timor in the first year of Indonesia's war of aggression, the Indonesian foreign minister, Adam Malik, pressed by foreign journalists to confirm or deny the reports, said: "Fifty thousand people or perhaps eighty thousand people might have been killed during the war in Timor. . . . It was [sic] war. Then what is the big fuss?"[57]

But worse was still to come for the people of East Timor. In the first year of the war, most of the population were living in the interior, many having fled there as Indonesian troops gained control of the towns and the coastal plains. From 1977 to 1979, the Indonesian armed forces, reinforced by bombers and counterinsurgency aircraft supplied by the Carter administration in 1977 – "taking time off," as Noam Chomsky has remarked on several occasions, "from its human-rights-based foreign policy" – mounted a huge encirclement and annihilation campaign to isolate and crush the Fretilin resistance and force the population down from the mountains into army-controlled strategic villages. By the end of 1979, the death toll had reached an estimated 200,000, meaning that nearly a third of the population had lost their lives in three years of Indonesian war and occupation.[58] President Carter's decision to supply Indonesia with the aircraft it needed to establish control over East Timor was in continuation of the policy of support for the takeover pursued by Gerald Ford and Henry Kissinger.

Washington has made little attempt to conceal its support for Indonesia's aggression against East Timor. When President Ford arrived in Hawaii on the day after the invasion and was asked for his reaction, he "smiled and said: 'We'll talk about that later.' "[59] In a December 12, 1975, seminar at Berkeley University, the US Ambassador to Indonesia David Newsom said that Washington had "not disapproved" of the invasion,[60] and not long after, a State Department official was quoted as saying: "We regard Indonesia as a friendly, non-aligned nation – a nation we do a lot of business with. In terms of bilateral relations between the US and Indonesia, we are more or less condoning the incursion into East Timor."[61]

It is well established that the Western powers most directly concerned, the US, Australia, and the UK, had already decided to give Indonesia a free hand months before the invasion was launched. Cable traffic flowing between embassies and their capitals in July and August 1975 shows that they had decided on a policy of condoning an act of aggression against East Timor. On August 17, 1975, Richard Woolcott, Australian ambassador in Jakarta, cabled the Foreign Affairs Department in Canberra:

The situation in Portuguese Timor is going to be a mess for some time. From here, I would suggest that our policies should be based on disengaging ourselves as far as possible from the Timor question. . . . [and] if and when Indonesia does intervene, act in a way which would be designed to minimise the public impact in Australia and show privately understanding to Indonesia of their problems.

[US] Ambassador Newsom told me last night he is under instructions from Kissinger personally not to involve himself in discussions on Timor . . . The State Department has, we understand, instructed the [US] embassy to cut down its reporting on Timor . . . [Newsom's] somewhat cynical comment to me was that if Indonesia were to intervene, the US would hope they would do so "effectively, quickly, and not use our equipment".[62]

As Newsom knew only too well, this would not have been possible, considering that 90 percent of the weapons used by the Indonesian army at the time were supplied by the US.

British diplomats adopted the same attitude of indulging Indonesian aggression. In a confidential letter to the Foreign Office dispatched in July 1975, Sir John Ford, the British ambassador in Jakarta, wrote:

The people of Portuguese Timor are in no condition to exercise their right to self-determination. . . . The territory seems likely to become steadily more of a problem child, and the arguments in favour of its integration into Indonesia are all the stronger. . . . Certainly as seen from here, it is in Britain's interest that Indonesia should absorb the territory as soon and as unobtrusively as possible, and that if it should come to the crunch and there is a row in the United Nations, we should keep our heads down and avoid taking sides against the Indonesian Government.[63]

Washington, Canberra, and London certainly knew very well what was happening militarily in the months that preceded Indonesia's all-out invasion on December 7, 1975. Several months before the invasion, which was launched the day after Ford and Kissinger completed a state visit to Jakarta, the CIA was monitoring Indonesian army operations along the border between West Timor and East Timor. The details of this monitoring, undertaken by the CIA, its military counterpart the Defense Intelligence Agency, the National Security Agency, and the State Department, were reproduced in two special supplements entitled "The Timor Papers," published in mid-1982 by the Sydney-based weekly, *The National Times*.[64] These revelations passed virtually unnoticed in the world's press.

The CIA's *National Intelligence Daily*, a news sheet which was published daily by the director of the CIA for an elite, specially cleared audience in Washington and which was on the president's desk every morning, recorded on August 29, 1975:

> Indonesia's preparations for an invasion, originally discussed by Suharto and his military commanders on 8 August, now are expected to be complete by 31 August. The plan calls for a three-pronged attack on the north coast of the island. Two battalions are to launch a combined assault against Dili. The larger force of some 6,000 infantry will land in Atapupu in Indonesian Timor and then drive north into the Portuguese half of the island. . . . The Indonesians expect some stiff resistance, but are confident they will be successful.[65]

Although plans for the invasion were ready in August, Suharto, always a man of caution, delayed things for three months, preferring to proceed carefully, testing the reaction of the Western powers on whom he relied for virtually all of his military equipment. Early in September, the CIA reported: "Suharto is concerned about the impact on Indonesia's bilateral relations with Australia and the US. In both cases, he is worried about the loss of military assistance which he badly wants, to improve Indonesia's outdated equipment."[66]

From mid-September 1975, repeated armed incursions took place across the border from West Timor, closely monitored by Western intelligence agencies, as revealed in "The Timor Papers." Perhaps the most crucial test of Western reaction to the crimes Indonesia was perpetrating was the murder by Indonesian troops on October 16, 1975, of a team of five television journalists from Australia in the town of Balibo, not far from the border with West Timor. Although this incident led to widespread international outrage, there was no protest, not even a call for an inquiry, from the Australian government, leading to greater confidence in Jakarta that Western supporters had no intention of making a fuss about an Indonesian invasion.

7 Western Diplomatic Support and Arms for an Aggressor

On December 12, 1975, five days after the Indonesian invasion, the UN General Assembly adopted a resolution which "strongly deplored the military intervention of the armed forces of Indonesia in Portuguese Timor" and called on the Security Council to "take urgent action to protect the territorial integrity of Portuguese Timor and the inalienable right of its people to self-determination." Even though it was abundantly clear that Indonesia had violated the United Nations Charter, the voting was 72 votes in favour, 10 against, and 43 abstentions. Among the abstainers were the US, the UK, and most of Europe. Fretilin's representative to the UN, José Ramos Horta, explains that, even though the word "deplores" was used instead of the more forceful "condemns," most Western powers could not bring themselves to vote against their Indonesian ally: "The western abstention on East Timor was based on two considerations: a desire not to offend the pro-western regime of General Suharto, and at the same time, not to offend their lesser European ally, Portugal. The Timorese people themselves and their rights did not enter into the equation."[67]

As Lord Avebury, chair of the Parliamentary Human Rights Group, was later to say: "If at the time of the Indonesian invasion there had been anything like the outcry in the west which greeted the Soviet invasion of Afghanistan, Indonesian aggression might well have been halted. Western countries, after all, give Indonesia massive economic, military and diplomatic support."[68]

The equivocal position adopted by many UN members gave the signal to Indonesia that although this was the first time that "a leading member of the anti-colonial bloc in the UN found itself the target of attack,"[69] it could rest assured that its western allies would "keep our heads down and avoid taking sides against the Indonesian Government." It could also rest assured that the supply of much needed weapons would not dry up.

The outcome of the crucial December 12 vote was due largely to the manoeuvres of the US representative, Daniel P. Moynihan, who had no scruples later about explaining his achievement in his memoirs: "The United States wished things to turn out as they did and worked to bring this about. The Department of State desired that the United Nations prove utterly ineffective in whatever measures it undertook. This task was given to me and I carried it forward with no inconsiderable success."[70]

Pressed by many people to explain why it had done so little on East Timor, the British Labour government actually tried to take credit for UN decisions on East Timor, so as to portray itself as a defender of peace and justice in East Timor. Labour's foreign minister, Dr David Owen, claimed that his government "played a leading part in efforts to reach an internationally acceptable settlement in East Timor. We were in the chair at the United Nations Security Council when it called for the withdrawal of Indonesian troops . . . on December 22, 1975."[71] In fact this Security Council resolution, and a later one which Britain also voted in favour of on April 22, 1976, were acknowledged to be watered down and weakly worded, and led to no effective action to compel Indonesia to withdraw its troops from East Timor: the *New York Times* remarked that "the language was considered ineffectual . . . and many delegates and some United Nations officials said privately that the rather bland language of today's Security Council document practically meant that Indonesia was given leeway to consolidate its hold on the former Portuguese colony."[72] Moreover, Dr Owen conveniently forgot to explain why, on December 12 at the General Assembly, the UK had abstained on the first East Timor resolution. As for Washington, the *New York Times* noted that Indonesia's position at the Security Council had "the discreet backing of the United States,"[73] which, along with Japan, abstained in the voting.

The UN Security Council December 22, 1975, resolution, which had called for "a special representative [to go to] East Timor for the purpose of making an on-the-spot assessment of the existing situation and of establishing contact with all parties in the territory," resulted in a three-day visit by a UN official to three Indonesian-occupied towns, not venturing out of Dili, Manatuto, or Baucau, even though most of the country was still firmly in the hands of Fretilin. The official's somewhat feeble attempts to visit Fretilin-held territory were sabotaged by the Indonesian authorities, backed by Canberra.[74]

Meanwhile, as fighting and widespread atrocities continued in East Timor, another charade was being played out over weapons supplies. As was widely acknowledged, 90 percent of the equipment used by the Indonesian army was supplied by Washington. By using these weapons, Indonesia had violated a 1958 agreement prohibiting the use of US arms for external aggression. At the time, it was claimed by a State Department official that the Ford administration had "secretly stopped processing new requests for arms" for Indonesia during the six-month period after the invasion, although US weapons on order had continued to be delivered.[75]

In July 1976, Indonesia asserted that it had integrated East Timor. This claim was based on a stage-managed act of self-determination performed in wartorn Dili by a "people's assembly" composed of Indonesian-appointed puppets, an act which the UN refused, and still refuses, to acknowledge. But, to the satisfaction of the Carter administration (still insisting that human rights was the "soul" of its foreign policy), it could now be said that Indonesia was "defending its own territory." The Congressional Sub-Committee, chaired by Donald Fraser, which investigated the unlawful use by Indonesia of US-supplied weapons, learned at a hearing in February 1978 that the Indonesian government had never been told that the US had "secretly stopped processing new requests for arms" because the policy had never been put into effect. Congressman Fraser concluded that the "suspension" reminded him of "the Cheshire cat in *Alice in Wonderland*: all we have left is the grin."[76]

The chief witness to appear before the Fraser Sub-Committee at its hearing in March 1977 was James Dunn, who had two months earlier heard the shocking testimony of refugees in Lisbon about Indonesian atrocities. Without making any attempt to check up on Dunn's account, a State Department spokesman alleged that reports of Indonesian atrocities had been "greatly exaggerated," and claimed that "there is no useful purpose" in questioning Indonesia's claim to East Timor.[77]

In late 1977, it became apparent that the Indonesian armed forces, at the end of the second year of their war of aggression against East Timor, were fast exhausting their supply of weapons and were sorely in need of ground-attack aircraft to implement the strategy of encirclement and annihilation, and to end resistance once and for all. In February 1978, Washington announced the sale of 16 sophisticated F-5 fighters to Indonesia, followed on April 4, 1978, with an announcement by British Aerospace of a deal to supply Indonesia with eight Hawk ground-attack aircraft. In May, the US agreed to supply 16 A-4 bombers and to license the construction of a factory in Indonesia to manufacture M-16 rifles. These deals greatly enhanced Indonesia's capacity to bring to its knees the determined resistance in East Timor, still in control of some 80 percent of the territory, and materially contributed to the mounting death toll. In the history of the war, 1978 has gone down as the most difficult year in the struggle of the Timorese people: "The deliberate campaign of starvation, the relentless aerial bombardments, the destruction of the agricultural system brought untold suffering for the Timorese people. . . . the steady onslaught from land, sea and air brought most of the country under Indonesian military control."[78]

During the course of that year, the Labour government in Britain was under intense pressure to cancel the Hawks deal, but Foreign Secretary Owen stoutly defended it, alleging that the aircraft supplied "cannot be used in East Timor."[79] However, the British government refused to give any assurances that the planes supplied, said to be only the trainer version, would not be modified for a combat role, even though British Aerospace hailed its product as "an aircraft with worldwide market potential" which offers "full ground attack capability."[80] As the savagery continued in East Timor, Dr Owen stated in November 1978 that "we believe that such fighting as still continues [in East Timor] is on a very small scale."[81] The day after this statement was made, a key Fretilin base in the Matabian mountain range, where some 30,000 people were gathered, fell to the Indonesians, causing huge loss of life among civilians as well as resistance fighters. In December, Natarbora, where 60,000 people were hemmed in, was overrun by Indonesian troops:

> By this time, the food situation was desperate and sickness was widespread, so the encircled population had no alternative but to surrender. Many guerrillas were captured and killed during the mopping up operations that lasted until March 1979. There was a great slaughter of Fretilin Central Committee members and activists. . . . The death toll among the people herded into camps in conditions of great distress was very high indeed.[82]

By late 1979, armed resistance in East Timor was almost at an end. Virtually the entire Fretilin leadership had been captured, been killed, or surrendered under a presidential amnesty, only to be killed as well. Several hundred thousand Timorese who survived the terror and destruction of the previous two years had been herded into strategic villages, where they still remain today. These strategic villages have dramatically restricted the food-producing activities of the Timorese; much of the fertile land is now out of bounds to the farmers and there is no freedom of movement, even for the purposes of tilling land just outside the perimeters of the villages.

It seemed as if Indonesia, substantially aided by its Western allies, had indeed brought resistance to an end. But 1980 turned out to be a year when surviving Fretilin fighters remustered their forces, devised a new strategy of struggle, created links with the population now being held in Indonesian-occupied territory, and again challenged Indonesia's hold on the country. In 1981, Indonesia was forced to conduct a nationwide fence-of-legs operation, using tens of thousands of troops and many more tens of thousands of Timorese civilians to sweep the countryside with a gradually diminishing human circle to capture guerrillas. The operation had little effect on the resistance, though it intensified the shortage of food because so many men had been forced to leave their villages for months.

In December 1982, a set of army intelligence documents was captured by Fretilin guerrillas and smuggled abroad.[83] The documents gave a unique insight into Indonesia's efforts to consolidate its control over the population already herded into the strategic villages by isolating the people from the armed resistance. One of the documents, entitled "Established Procedure for the Interrogation of Prisoners," provided a rare glimpse of the practices of totalitarian regimes in the handling of captives.

> If it proves necessary to use violence, make sure that there are no other people around (members of TBO, Hansip, Ratih or other people [these are paramilitary Timorese units]) to see what is happening so as not to arouse other people's antipathy. . . . Avoid taking photographs showing torture in progress (people being photographed at times when they are being subjected to electric current, when they have been stripped naked, etc.). Remember not to have such photographic documentation developed outside, in Den Pasar, which could then be made available to the public by irresponsible elements.
>
> It is better to make attractive photographs, such as shots taken while eating together with the prisoner, or shaking hands with those who have just come down from the bush.[84]

As with all major documents relating to the war in East Timor, these documents created hardly a stir, except in East Timor solidarity circles, even though Amnesty International publicly accused Indonesia of officially condoning the use of torture.

After an informal, six-month ceasefire in 1983, armed forces commander in chief General Benny Murdani announced a new all-out offensive. The armed forces would, he said, show "no mercy" for the resistance fighters and would "use all the forces at our disposal" to destroy them. In 1983, Indonesia created a special military command to handle military operations, and since then it has annually launched major offensives, employing up to 15,000 troops against the armed resistance, in addition to thousands of territorial troops permanently in East Timor to supervise and terrorize the population.

Meanwhile, East Timor is still on the agenda of the UN General Assembly. However, since 1982, when a resolution scraped through by 50 votes in favour with 46 against (including the US and Australia) and 50 abstentions (including the UK and most Western nations), calling on the UN Secretary-General to "initiate consultations with all parties directly concerned [to achieve] a comprehensive settlement," the Assembly has not voted on the question of East Timor. Meanwhile in a different forum, the Western powers meet every year in the international aid consortium known as the Inter-Governmental Group on Indonesia, agreeing on a never-ending upward spiral of grants and loans. There appears to be no limit to the beneficence and generosity which the West is ready to bestow on Suharto's terrorist regime. Excluding special assistance, Indonesia benefited to the tune of $3.15 billion in 1987, $4.01 billion in 1988, and $4.297 billion in 1989.

A "comprehensive settlement" appears to be as far from achievement as ever, primarily because Western powers studiously ignore the long-drawn-out tragedy that has befallen the people of East Timor. Horta's bitter complaint still rings true – they do not want to offend the pro-Western regime of General Suharto, but hesitate to offend their lesser European ally, Portugal. To this day, the Timorese people and their rights do not enter into the equation.

In February 1989, Bishop Carlos Filipe Ximenes Belo, head of the Catholic church in East Timor, abandoned his silence on the crucial matter of East Timor's right to self-determination, which Indonesia brutally violated in 1975. He made a passionate plea to the UN for a referendum to be held in East Timor:

> Hitherto, the people have not been consulted. Others speak in the name of the people. Indonesia says that the people of East Timor have already chosen integration, but the people of Timor themselves have never said this. . . . And we continue to die as a people.[85]

Carmel Budiardjo

Not one single Western government has responded to this plea, even though the international climate today seems to favour negotiation and the peaceful resolution to conflicts like that still raging in East Timor. While resistance still continues in East Timor, and solidarity groups, including many church-based organizations, have stepped up their pressure for Indonesian troops to leave East Timor and for the people to be allowed to decide their own future, General Suharto can still bask in the confidence that terror pays.

Notes

1 Richard Nixon, "Asia After Vietnam," in *Foreign Affairs* (October 1967).
2 Acting Secretary of State, Lovett, quoted in Robert J. MacMahon, *Colonialism and Cold War: The United States and the Struggle for Indonesian Independence 1945–49*, Cornell University Press, Ithaca and London, 1981, p. 266.
3 Howard Jones, *The Possible Dream* (Harcourt Brace Jovanovich, 1971), p. 127.
4 Bryan Evans III, "The Influence of the United States Army on the Development of the Indonesian Army (1954–1964)," in *Indonesia*, Cornell Modern Indonesia Programme (April 1989), pp. 42–3.
5 Ibid., pp. 34–5.
6 Ibid., p. 36.
7 Ibid., p. 36, footnote 69.
8 Ibid., pp. 40–1, and see table on p. 44.
9 Quoted in Peter Dale Scott, "Exporting Military-Economic Development: America and the Overthrow of Sukarno, 1965–7," in Malcolm Caldwell (ed.) *Ten Years's Military Terror in Indonesia* (Spokesman Books, 1975), p. 221.
10 Ibid., p. 221.
11 Guy J. Pauker, "Southeast Asia as a Problem Area in the Next Decade," in *World Politics* (April 1959), pp. 339–42, quoted in Scott, "Exporting Military-Economic Development," pp. 227–8.
12 Guy J. Pauker, "The Role of the Military in Indonesia," in John J. Johnson (ed.), *The Role of the Military in Underdeveloped Countries* (Princeton University Press, 1962), pp. 221–3, quoted in Scott, "Exporting Military-Economic Development," p. 230.
13 Guy J. Pauker, *Communist Prospects in Indonesia* (The Rand Corporation, November 1964), p. 22, quoted in Scott, "Exporting Military-Economic Development," p. 231.
14 Benedict Anderson and Ruth McVey, *A Preliminary Analysis of the October 1, 1965, Coup in Indonesia* (Cornell University Press, 1971); Peter Dale Scott, "The United States and the Overthrow of Sukarno, 1965–1967," in *Pacific Affairs*, 58 (2), Summer 1985; Gatot Lestaryo, defense statement delivered before the Blitar District Court (December 26, 1975); Coen

Holtzappel, "The 30 September Movement: A Political Movement of the Armed Forces or an Intelligence Operation?," in *Journal of Contemporary Asia* 9 (2), 1979; "Suharto and the 1965 Affair," in *TAPOL Bulletin* 78 (December 1986); W.F. Wertheim, "Whose Plot? New Light on the 1965 Events," in *Journal of Contemporary Asia* 9 (2), 1979.

15 See Ben Anderson, "How Did the Generals Die?" in *Indonesia* 43 (April 1987).

16 *Berita Yudha* (October 9, 1965).

17 *Ibid.*

18 *Berita Yudha* (October 10, 1965).

19 *Api Pancasila* (October 20, 1965).

20 Anderson, "How Did the Generals Die?," p. 111.

21 Ralph W. McGehee, "Foreign Policy by Forgery: The CIA and the White Paper on El Salvador," in *Nation* (April 11, 1981).

22 Letter from Ralph W. McGehee, published in *Harper's* (December 1984).

23 Harold Crouch, *The Army and Politics in Indonesia* (Cornell University Press, 1978), pp. 141–2.

24 John Hughes, *The End of Sukarno* (Angus and Robertson, 1967), p. 141.

25 *Ibid.*, p. 142.

26 Crouch, *Army and Politics in Indonesia*, p. 143, quoting Ulf Sundhausen, "The Political Orientation and Political Involvement of the Indonesian Officer Corps, 1946–1966: The Siliwangi Division and the Army Headquarters," unpublished Ph.D thesis, Monash University (1971), p. 630.

27 Abdul Harris Nasution, *Memenuhi Panggilan Tugas: Jilid 6, Masa Kebangkitan Orde Baru [Responding to the Call of Duty: Volume 6, The Birth of the New Order]* (Gunung Agung, 1987), p. 328.

28 *Ibid.*, p. 330.

29 Anderson and McVey, *A Preliminary Analysis*, p. 63.

30 Hughes, *The End of Sukarno*, p. 151.

31 Crouch, *Army and Politics in Indonesia*, p. 151.

32 Pipit Rochijat, "Am I PKI or Non-PKI?," in *Indonesia* 40 (October 1985), pp. 43–4, 45.

33 Crouch, *Army and Politics in Indonesia*, p. 152.

34 Hughes, *The End of Sukarno*, p. 179.

35 *Ibid.*, p. 181.

36 *Ibid.*, pp. 185–6.

37 Cable of January 21, 1965, Control No. 16607, from *Indonesia*, 3, Box 246.

38 Gabriel Kolko, *Confronting the Third World: United States Foreign Policy, 1945–1980* (Pantheon Books, 1989).

39 *Ibid.*, footnote on p. 177.

40 Marshall Green to Dean Rusk, October 3, 1965, R:607E. See also CIA, report, October 7, 1965, 75:53D; cited in Kolko, *Confronting the Third World*, chapter 14.

41 Kolko, *Confronting the Third World*, p. 180.

42 CIA, report, October 8, 1965, R:29A; cited in, Kolko, *Confronting the Third World*, chapter 14.

43 Green to Department of State, October 5, 1965, R:608E; cited in Kolko, *Confronting the Third World*, chapter 14.
44 Green to Rusk, October 14, 1965, R:609A; cited in Kolko, *Confronting the Third World*, chapter 14.
45 Rusk to Green, October 29, 1965, R:612C. See also Green to Rusk, October 17, 1965, R:609C; Green to Rusk, October 28, 1965, R:612A; cited in Kolko, *Confronting the Third World*, chapter 14.
46 Green to Rusk, November 4, 1965, second of two cables, 79:434E; cited in Kolko, *Confronting the Third World*, chapter 14.
47 Green to Rusk, November 7, 1965, R:613A; November 8, 1965, R:613E; cited in Kolko, *Confronting the Third World*, chapter 14.
48 US embassy, Bangkok, to Rusk, November 5, 1965, R:612G. Kolko adds the note: "To maintain secrecy, much of the negotiations regarding such aid were done in Bangkok." See also Rusk to embassies, Bangkok and Jakarta, November 6, 1965, R:613B; Green to Rusk, November 7, 1965; embassy, Bangkok to Rusk, November 11, 1965, R:614E; all cited in Kolko, *Confronting the Third World*, chapter 14.
49 Ibid., p. 181. The quotes are from CIA memo, November 12, 1965, R:30A; Green to Rusk, November 19, 1965, R:615D.
50 Kolko, *Confronting the Third World*, p. 181.
51 Michael Stewart, *Life and Labour: An Autobiography* (Sidgwick and Jackson, 1980), p. 149.
52 *The Age*, Melbourne (December 8, 1975).
53 James Dunn, *Timor: A People Betrayed* (Jacaranda Press, 1983), pp. 283–5.
54 Arnold Kohen and John Taylor, *An Act of Genocide: Indonesia's Invasion of East Timor* (TAPOL, 1979).
55 *The Age*, Melbourne (February 14, 1976).
56 See James Dunn, "Notes on East Timor," in Dunn, *East Timor, From Portuguese Colonialism to Indonesian Incorporation* (Parliament of Australia, Legislative Research Service, 1977), p. 108.
57 Hamish MacDonald, *Sydney Morning Herald* (March 31, 1977).
58 See Carmel Budiardjo and Liem Soei Liong, *The War Against East Timor* (ZED Books, 1984), pp. 49–51, for an analysis of the death toll figures.
59 *Boston Globe* (December 8, 1975).
60 Kohen and Taylor, *An Act of Genocide*, p. 97.
61 *The Australian* (January 22, 1976).
62 G.J. Munster and J.R Walsh, *Documents on Australian Defence and Foreign Policy 1968–75* (Munster and Walsh, 1980), pp. 199–200. Publication of this book, which contained a number of confidential cables, proved so embarrassing to the Australian government that it was immediately impounded and withdrawn from circulation.
63 Ibid., pp. 192–3.
64 "The Timor Papers," in the *National Times* (May 30–June 5 and June 6–12, 1982).
65 Ibid., (May 30–June 5, 1982).
66 Ibid., (May 30–June 5, 1982).

67 José Ramos Horta, *Funu: The Unfinished Saga of East Timor* (Red Sea Press, 1987), p. 107.
68 Letter from Lord Avebury to *The Times* (July 7, 1980).
69 Horta, *Funu*, p. 107.
70 Daniel P. Moynihan (with Suzanne Weaver), *A Dangerous Place* (Little, Brown, 1978), pp. 245-7.
71 Letter from David Owen to Sir Harold Wilson (June 22, 1978).
72 Paul Hoffman, "UN Calls on Indonesia to Leave Eastern Timor," *New York Times* (April 23, 1976), quoted in Alexander George, *East Timor and the Shaming of the West* (TAPOL, 1985), p. 34.
73 Ibid.
74 For a detailed account of the abortive mission of Vittorio Winspeare Guicciardi, Director General of the UN office in Geneva, see Horta, *Funu*, pp. 113-18.
75 *Washington Post* (March 18, 1977); *Human Rights in East Timor and the Question of the Use of US Equipment by the Indonesian Armed Forces*, Hearings before the Congressional Sub-Committee on International Organisations of the House Committee on International Organisations on 23 March 1977, pp. 11-13.
76 Quoted in Kohen and Taylor, *An Act of Genocide*, p. 47.
77 *Human Rights in East Timor*, March hearings, pp. 11-13.
78 Budiardjo and Liem, *The War Against East Timor*, p. 34.
79 Letter from David Owen to Sir Harold Wilson (June 22, 1978).
80 *British Aerospace Information* (April 5, 1978).
81 Letter from David Owen to Moss Evans (November 21, 1978).
82 Budiardjo and Liem, *The War Against East Timor*, p. 33.
83 The nine documents are reproduced in ibid., pp. 169-244.
84 Ibid., pp. 236-7.
85 Letter from Bishop Belo to Peres de Cuellar, Secretary-General of the UN (February 6, 1989).

9

The Reagan Doctrine and the Destabilization of Southern Africa

Sean Gervasi and Sybil Wong

1 Introduction

History will record that in the 1980s South Africa and the United States jointly waged a terrible but almost invisible war against the innocent peoples of Southern Africa. The war, it will be remembered, engulfed much of the subcontinent and was of almost unprecedented barbarity.

It is certain that this war, whose effects will be felt for decades to come, will be bitterly remembered, not just in Africa, but in the entire world. The war has already left terrible scars: a million and a half or more dead, millions displaced from their homes, whole economies in ruins, and millions facing starvation and disease.

Worst of all, the war may be far from over. It continues today. This is a fact which must not be lost sight of.

It may be, of course, that we are nearing the moment when apartheid will be dismantled. The struggle within South Africa has moved to a new stage, at once promising and very dangerous. Afrikanerdom is fighting a rearguard action to preserve white power and privilege, but it is increasingly beleaguered. Namibia, having achieved formal political independence, is at least on the way to true independence and freedom. We may, therefore, not be very far from that fundamental shift in power within South Africa which will truly mark the beginning of the end of apartheid.

When that change takes place, when the oppressed people of South Africa hold the reins of government and can end the system of indirect forced labor called "apartheid," peace may well descend upon the subcontinent – unless, of course, foreign powers intervene to prevent fundamental change, as they have been doing covertly for decades.

It is clearly impossible to say at this point when such a fundamental shift of power might take place, or even, considering the complexity of today's circumstances, to describe exactly what might produce such a shift in the foreseeable future, or what the response in the rest of the world might be.

This paper will not attempt to speculate on the future course of events in Southern Africa, whether, in the front-line states or in South Africa itself. It would require a book even to begin such a task. The present paper is instead an effort to look backward and to reflect upon the nature and meaning of the war which has been waged against the front-line states. It attempts to shed light on two issues. Firstly, it raises the question of what ten years of "destabilization" and "unconventional war" have done to be peoples of Southern Africa. Secondly, it tries to fix the responsibility for the terrible suffering and costs which the war has entailed.

A certain amount is known about the first question, although public opinion in many countries seems quite indifferent to the tragic drama which has taken place in the subcontinent. Little more than the obvious is known about the second issue. It is generally recognized that South Africa has been attacking the front-line states, using every means available to undermine and weaken them. What is not recognized is that the United States Government has played a key role in assisting South Africa. US actions, of course, have been carefully veiled. And when they have been public, they have been carried out under a barrage of propaganda which has apparently succeeded in misleading even the public at home.

It would be wrong, however, to give too much credit to the propagandists of the two Reagan administrations – and to the present Bush administrations. If the world is unaware of the US role in destabilizing a subcontinent, the fault lies as much in ourselves as in the cleverness of propaganda. It was possible to know what the US was doing in Southern Africa. Information was available. And careful investigation could have uncovered the whole, ugly secret alliance between the US and South Africa; an alliance which, after all, has been fairly visible since Kissinger's National Security Study Memorandum on Southern Africa was made public in 1974.[1]

The fact is, however, that journalists, academics, Congressmen, and many others have steadfastly refused to look carefully at the issue. For years, efforts to look into the role of the US in Southern Africa's "unconventional wars" were met with blank stares and determined evasiveness. It seemed that people were afraid to speak of the issue. And the excuse which was most frequently heard was that too little was known about the matter. However, evidence has now been accumulating for ten years. And today more than enough is known for us to insist upon serious public discussion of the issue.

We cannot attempt here to provide a comprehensive account of US actions in Southern Africa over the last decade. We can show, however, that the US has played a major role in the region by its active, if often secret, intervention in support of South Africa and against the front-line states. It has therefore played a major role in the devastation of an entire subcontinent.

Members of the first Reagan administration were quite clear about what they were going to try to do.[2] In May 1981, the then assistant secretary of state designate for Africa, Chester Crocker, wrote to Secretary of State Haig to prepare him for a meeting with the South African foreign minister. In a guarded internal memorandum, Crocker stated that the United States and South Africa, "despite their differences,' might together ensure "constructive internal change" in South Africa and a "new era of co-operation, stability and security in the region." Crocker stated that the US had a role in "rebuilding security in southern Africa." And to be very clear about the importance of that role, he said *"that is a shared goal they cannot reach without us, and they cannot go it alone"* (italics added).[3]

In retrospect, it is quite clear that "stability and security" meant the retreat of the front-line states from their support for the struggle against apartheid, and that the phrase even embraced the forced retreat of Angola and Mozambique from socialism. Furthermore, despite his bland terminology, Crocker made it clear in his memo that he understood pursuit of these goals would involve the destabilization of the front-line states. And, only a few weeks earlier, the secretary of state had given his implicit approval to South Africa's first cross-border raid outside Angola.[4]

Looking back, it seems fair to say that US officials must have understood that the path to what they called "stability and security" would be strewn with the bodies of hundreds of thousands of innocent people.

2 South Africa's Aims in Southern Africa

To understand the war in Southern Africa, it is necessary to consider South Africa's situation in 1980 and the strategy which it adopted in the hope of preserving apartheid. This strategy, it should be plain, could only have led to war; war, of course, of a very particular kind, "unconventional war," as it is called in the Pentagon.

Throughout the period since World War II, South Africa has been the dominant power in the Southern African region. The surrounding states, some of which attained independence only fifteen years ago, are in varying degrees economically dependent upon it. South Africa is a semi-industrial country, much wealthier than its neighbors. Moreover, it controls many of the region's transportation lines and outlets to the sea.

And South Africa has built, since the late 1960s, a powerful, modern, military machine.

In 1980, however, despite its weight, South Africa was uneasy. The struggle against apartheid had intensified steadily through the 1960s and the 1970s. Angola and Mozambique, previously secure colonial buffer states, had become independent and had committed themselves to the elimination of apartheid; the liberation struggle in Namibia had intensified sharply during the 1970s; and South Africa found itself under growing pressure from the United Nations to leave the territory. Then, in 1980, Zimbabwe succeeded in winning its independence, after a long armed struggle in which South Africa had aided the losing side, the Smith regime. Suddenly, South Africa found itself surrounded by independent states strongly opposed to apartheid, many of them professing socialism and receiving aid from countries of the socialist bloc. South Africa thus faced three problems simultaneously: growing internal unrest, growing international criticism and the risk of isolation, and strong regional opposition to apartheid, including support of various kinds for the African National Congress.

In the 1960s and the 1970s, South Africa had sought to maintain control of the region through the pursuit of various schemes designed to reinforce its hold on neighboring countries. The idea of a constellation of states which it would dominate was one of these. These schemes, however, had all failed. Consequently, in 1980, South Africa faced the prospect of a simultaneous increase of internal and external pressure. Its leaders feared, in particular, that neighboring states would at that point increase their support for the ANC and that the country would be subjected to a rising wave of sabotage and cross-border raids.

South African leaders in 1980 would not contemplate reforms which would move the country towards the elimination of apartheid. Nor would they enter into serious negotiation with the African National Congress about the future of the country. The alternative was to adopt a "total strategy" which would mobilize all of South Africa's resources – including its allies – to resist change. This "total strategy," conceived in the late 1970s, would seek to use South Africa's economic and military power to bend its neighbors to its will.

In a paper commissioned by the Institute for Strategic Studies of the University of Pretoria in 1981, Deon Geldenhuys, a leading South African strategist, described the specific objectives of South Africa's strategy in the Southern African region:

"Neighbouring states are not to be used as springboards for guerrilla or terrorist attacks."[5] South Africa wanted undertakings to this effect and assurances they would be effectively implemented.

215

Sean Gervasi and Sybil Wong

Soviet bloc powers were not to "gain a political and least of all a military foothold in the Southern African States."

"Existing economic ties with states in the region should be maintained or even strengthened." That would permit "the strategic application of economic relations," that is, the use of economic pressure.

"Black states" were not "to support calls for sanctions against South Africa."

Lastly, "Black States in Southern Africa" would have to "display some moderation in expressing criticism of the republic's domestic policy and in suggesting solutions."

In short, South Africa wanted the front-line states to accept greater dependence on it, to refuse aid from the socialist bloc, and to end, or substantially reduce, support for the liberation struggles in South Africa and Namibia.

In the conditions prevailing in Southern Africa in 1981, it is hard if not impossible to believe that South Africa could possibly have expected the independent states of the region to accept these demands voluntarily. So the publication of the Geldenhuys article, at the very moment that "unconventional war" was beginning, was seen not so much as an invitation to negotiations as an open threat that South African power was to be used to force their acceptance.[6]

3 Pretoria Launches an "Unconventional War"

In the tense situation which existed after Zimbabwe achieved independence, it seemed likely to knowledgable observers that South Africa would use its power to press its demands on the front-line states,[7] and that only a concerted, forceful intervention by the major Western powers could have held South Africa in check.

At the same time, South Africa had to proceed carefully. It could not openly attack its neighbors militarily or publicly use its full economic weight against them. Such action would have greatly intensified international opposition to South Africa policies. It could have isolated South Africa at a dangerous moment; and it might have precipitated large-scale military assistance from socialist bloc countries.

South Africa therefore chose to mount a clandestine attack on its neighbors which would make it possible to deny any responsibility for its actions. The front-line states, of course, would know that South Africa was the attacker. But the important point was to be able to deny responsibility to the world outside Southern Africa.

This attack has been widely referred to as the "destabilization" of the front-line states, a term which normally refers to covert action by intelli-

216

gence agencies in which pressure is brought to bear on a "target" country by diplomacy, propaganda, and political and economic means, often supplemented by paramilitary action such as sabotage and assassination. In Southern Africa, however, South Africa mounted what would more accurately be described as all-out unconventional war. Pretoria set out to impose mounting human and economic costs on the front-line states as the price of resisting its demands. This meant isolating the front-line states internationally, disrupting their trade routes, disrupting production, especially of food and export commodities, terrorizing the rural populations, sabotaging key installations, using "surgical military strikes" to pressure governments, creating internal political chaos, and, in one case, occupying large areas of a country militarily. South Africa would use every instrument of modern power in this "unconventional war," but especially direct economic pressure, surrogate forces, special operations forces and conventional military units. Pretoria would also be assisted in various ways by some of the major Western powers.

The attack was launched in mid-1980. South Africa invaded southern Angola in June, deploying three infantry brigades there.[8] There were also scattered threats, pressures, and special operations directed against Lesotho, Mozambique, Swaziland, and Zimbabwe. A 200-man force of mercenaries attempted a coup d'etat against President Kaunda in Zambia, but Zambian security forces defeated it.

Tension in the region mounted. It was not until 1981, however, that the war really began to gather momentum. In January, South African commandos raided Maputo, the capital of Mozambique, killing several members of the African National Congress. A few hours earlier, Secretary of State Haig had declared that "the war against international terrorism" was a priority of the new administration's foreign policy. In June, South Africa mounted yet another plot to overthrow President Kaunda in Zambia. The plot failed. South African agents also carried out assassinations in Zimbabwe and sabotaged the Inkomo barracks in Harare, destroying the Zimbabwe Army's first-line ammunition. In August, Pretoria mounted a major invasion of Southern Angola, deploying 11,000 men there and several armored columns. There was fierce fighting in Kunene province, and 80,000 people were forced to flee their homes.

More ominously, South Africa had embarked upon a major effort to disrupt the economies of several front-line states, notably Angola, Lesotho, Mozambique, and Zimbabwe. "Unconventional war" is not waged against the military forces of an adversary. It is waged primarily against the population of an adversary. It aims at disrupting and even destroying an adversary's economy and at sowing terror among the population. The effects of economic destruction and terror mutually reinforce each other.

Even a popular government is likely to find that, if it cannot protect people from economic loss and terror, it will lose its support among the population. By its very nature, therefore, "unconventional war" aims at creating widespread suffering and death among "target" populations.

During 1981, South Africa was training, arming, and deploying covert surrogate forces, or "pseudo-insurgencies," in various parts of Southern Africa in order to wage this war. Its invasion of Angola was part of an effort to implant the National Union for the Total Independence of Angola (UNITA) once again in the southern and central parts of that country, where it could disrupt road transport and food production, terrorize the population, and ensure the closure of the Benguela railway, which would deny Angola, Zambia, and Zaire outlets for their exports. The latter part of 1981 saw a significant escalation of "low intensity war" in Angola.

In Mozambique, South Africa was expanding and deploying the so-called Mozambique National Resistance (MNR), which it had taken over from Rhodesian Military Intelligence the year before. It consisted of some Mozambican dissidents, former Portuguese colonial troops, and large numbers of pressganged Mozambican workers who had been in South Africa. The MNR was assigned to attack roads, railways, bridges, and other economic targets and to assassinate officials, terrorize the rural population, etc. By the second half of 1981, the MNR had been deployed in large areas in the central provinces of Manica and Sofala and had made transport between Zimbabwe and the Indian Ocean port of Beira exceedingly dangerous.

MNR actions brought considerable economic pressure to bear on Zimbabwe. In particular, they threatened important supplies of oil which came through the pipeline from Beira. South Africa itself intensified the pressure on Zimbabwe by refusing to lease it locomotives and by slowing the return of freight cars. The result, by the autumn, was a major transport crisis and the loss of tens of millions of dollars in foreign exchange revenue from exports.

At the same time, the International Monetary Fund (IMF), prodded by Britain and the US, began to press Zimbabwe for substantial cuts in government expenditure, insisting on the reduction of key social expenditures. And, at the very moment that MNR groups were beginning to carry out raids inside the eastern border, the IMF also demanded a large cut in the defence budget.[9]

There was also considerable sabotage inside Zimbabwe in the latter half of 1981. At the end of the year, a bomb blast nearly destroyed Zimbabwe African National Union (ZANU) headquarters in the middle of Harare, killing six people and wounding many others.[10] South African commandos attacked port facilities and power plants at Beira. They also blew

218

up bridges over the Pungwe river in central Mozambique, cutting road and rail bridges to Zimbabwe, as well as the oil pipeline from Beira to Zimbabwe. While the Mozambique Army began to react with some effect against the MNR in the latter part of 1981, the scale of South African operations was very large and difficult to cope with. Almost nothing could be done to prevent sabotage by South African special forces.

The pressures went on increasing throughout the next year. The fighting continued and spread inside Angola and Mozambique. UNITA moved further north inside Angola and intensified its attacks. In Mozambique, the MNR greatly intensified its operations and began conducting attacks further south in Inhambane and Maputo provinces.

South Africa also sent surrogate forces into action elsewhere. In Zimbabwe, in addition to carrying out raids with its own commandos, South Africa began to assist "dissident" bands in Matabeleland, seeking to inflame ethnic differences in the country. In one spectacular raid, a South African sabotage team destroyed a large part of the Zimbabwe Air Force's first-line aircraft. In Lesotho, a "Liberation Army," backed by South Africa, resumed a low-level guerrilla war against the government. In December, South African commandos flew to Maseru, the capital, by helicopter and raided houses inhabited by South African refugees. Forty-two persons were killed. On the same day, South African commandos, aided by British and Portuguese intelligence operatives, attacked and destroyed the oil depot in the Mozambican port of Beira. Supplies of oil to Zimbabwe were cut, creating some panic in Harare.

However, by the end of the year, it was becoming clear that these military attacks were far less important than the continuous destruction and disruption sown by UNITA and the MNR. South Africa was clearly bent upon the total disruption of everyday life in Angola and Mozambique, and that posed the serious threat of widespread starvation.

The direct effects of the war were disastrous enough. Thousands were being killed and wounded. Tens of thousands more had to flee their homes and could no longer engage in productive work. In Angola and Mozambique, and to a lesser extent in Zimbabwe, whole provinces were paralyzed as bridges, roads, power lines, port facilities, schools, health stations, and food storage depots were destroyed. War, systematic sabotage, bombing from the air, and attacks on the population were destroying the infrastructure and the economies of several countries. At the beginning of 1981, Southern Africa was already suffering from the effects of the world recession and from drought. After nearly three years of undeclared war, however, the region was in crisis.

The net result was what relief organizations, aid agencies, and the United Nations called an unprecedented "humanitarian crisis" in Southern Africa. By the first months of 1983, starvation, destruction, and the mass flight of refugees presented major problems. The dimensions of the "humanitarian crisis" were becoming well known, at least to observers in the region. What was not well known was that the crisis was in large part manmade and planned in detail – the result of a calculated policy on the part of South Africa to inflict as much destruction and suffering as it could on the front-line states, and particularly on Angola and Mozambique.

4 The Reagan Doctrine

When the Reagan administration took office in 1981, it began to fashion a new foreign and military policy, one which went well beyond the traditional policy of "containment" of the Soviet Union. This policy, which remained secret until the spring of 1985, has come to be known as "the Reagan Doctrine." It is under the terms of the Reagan Doctrine that the United States, during the 1980s, became involved in covert operations, proxy wars, counterinsurgencies, and "stability operations" around the world.

From 1981, the Reagan Doctrine shaped US policy in every region of the globe; and it was within the framework of the Reagan Doctrine that a new policy towards Southern Africa was formulated. Unfortunately, scholars and journalists have paid insufficient attention to the influence of the Reagan Doctrine on regional policies. This has been particularly true with respect to Southern Africa.

It need not have been so. For while the existence of a Reagan Doctrine remained a tightly held secret through the whole of the first Reagan administration, there were early public clues that the conservative Republicans of the New Right had embarked upon an extraordinarily aggressive foreign and military policy. These clues should have been pursued by those seeking to understand Reagan's policy towards Southern Africa.

The general thrust of the Reagan Doctrine was being discussed in detail within the foreign policy and military establishment in early 1981. By the summer, the broad lines of the new policy had been set. In July, Secretary of Defense Weinberger gave an account of the Reagan Doctrine to a select Washington audience, which was clearer than many of the summaries published years later. This account was contained in his keynote address, "US Military Strategy for the 1980s," to the annual conference on National Security Affairs held at the National Defense University at Fort McNair.[11]

The tone of Weinberger's speech was somewhat alarmist. The substance was new, and harsh. It was very much in keeping with the views of the New Right. "The United States," the secretary said, "is, and always should be, a global power, with global concerns and responsibilities" which were vital to its interests. The job of the government was "to protect those interests wherever they are assailed, and, in view of our global role," it had to "defend and support a stable, peaceful international system." In the recent past, Soviet military power had grown hugely, and "we must assume some rationale behind the Soviet Union's enormous allocation of resources to the military at the expense of other basic needs. In fact, we have clear evidence of aggressive Soviet military activity around the globe." Soviet military power, which included "the training and support of terrorists" and "the use of military assistance and proxies," was "the most immediate, significant and dangerous threat to the national security of the United States." "Soviet gains," the Secretary stated, "and the growing perception that they and their proxies can act with impunity" had gone "unchallenged in recent years by the United States." The Carter administration, in short, had failed to prevent the spread of Soviet influence and power. This had undermined "the credibility of the United States as a defender of freedom." The new Administration would not permit this situation to continue. A US military strategy for the coming decade "must begin with our national interests, recognize the threat and be designed to counter it."

Weinberger then referred to the national security objectives of the United States, as described in his recently issued Defense Guidance. The list included the usual aims of foreign and military policy: protecting US interests, supporting allies and friends, maintaining access to resources, etc. However, there were two notable departures in his list of objectives from the usual formulations.

The first had to do with the goal – fourth in Weinberger's list of five – which has given the policy of containment its name. This is usually described as being "to contain Soviet expansion." Secretary Weinberger, however, proposed a reformulation. In his words, the United States had to oppose "the geographic expansion of Soviet control and military presence worldwide, particularly where such presence threatens our geo-strategic position." This was a definite hardening of previous formulations. For, among other things, it implied active measures to prevent change or revolution which might threaten US interests and which might be supported – or be thought to be supported – by the Soviet Union.[12]

Even more striking, however, was the statement of an entirely new aim, that of intervening in areas that the United States deemed to be part of "the Soviet empire." In Secretary Weinberger's words: "We will encourage long-term political and military *changes within the Soviet empire* that will facilitate building a more peaceful and secure world order" (italics added). Thus, a senior Cabinet officer was saying that the United States

221

was preparing to intervene in the internal affairs of countries which it regarded as Soviet dependents or as having close relations with the Soviet Union. Weinberger's "objective" was a barely veiled threat to use force, to destabilize or overthrow foreign governments.

In retrospect, it is clear that the Reagan Doctrine explains the extensive, systematic, and aggressive interventionism of the US government in the Reagan era, and especially its intervention in many parts of the non-industrial world. The logic of the Reagan Doctrine suggests that the US would be sorely tempted to intervene in Southern Africa, and to assist South Africa in its efforts to "stabilize" the region, particularly if its intervention could be kept secret. This will become clear in the next section.

In Angola, the Reagan Doctrine was openly implemented after Savimbi's visit to Washington at the beginning of 1986.[13] And UNITA was spoken of openly as one of the groups of "freedom fighters" that the Doctrine was meant to assist.[14]

Three questions remain. Was the Reagan administration aiding UNITA secretly from 1981, in defiance of the Clark Amendment, which had barred US aid to UNITA? And did the Reagan Administration also embark upon a policy of destabilizing the socialist regime in Mozambique at the same time? In short, did the Reagan Doctrine lead to a secret policy allying the Reagan administration with South Africa to wage unconventional war against the front-line states?

5 The 1981 Southern Africa Policy Review

The answer to all these questions turned out to be "yes."

In 1981, the Reagan foreign policy team was aware that South Africa was on the brink of an explosion. However, they saw the prospect of radical change there as threatening what they considered vital Western interests in the entire Southern African region. They believed that American power could and should be used to prevent further upheaval in Southern Africa. This view was stated clearly in a major article in *Foreign Affairs* at the end of 1980 by Chester Crocker, who was to become Assistant Secretary of State for Africa under Reagan and who was the architect of Southern Africa policy until very recently.[15]

Crocker's article set out the broad lines of the policy of "constructive engagement," which was to determine US actions in Southern Africa for almost a decade. Crocker's starting point was that there was still time to "forestall revolutionary violence" in South Africa. The United States could not afford to let this time slip by. It had to become actively involved in the region in order to ensure that change would move in the right directions. "Constructive engagement," as outlined at the time, was based essentially on two ideas. Firstly, change in South Africa had to be "white-led." It had to be controlled. Secondly, the region had to be made "stable" in order to allow time for controlled change.

In practice, the first idea was that the US had to force the pace of change in South Africa, while guiding it towards goals which would be compatible with Western interests. Therefore, a future Republican government would have to ensure that the Afrikaners remained in control in South Africa. It would have to work through a "modernizing group" which would drag a reluctant Afrikaner establishment towards reforms. Eventually, as Africans attained some power in local governments and trade unions, they could begin to negotiate with the Afrikaners for a share of power at the national level. Through compromise, the demands of the majority would be gradually modified and then accommodated. Crocker never posed the question of whether the interests of the non-white majority could really be reconciled with those of the Afrikaners. He simply seemed to assume that everyone could be made happy by moving South Africa towards a "non-racial liberal democracy."

The main problem was with Crocker's second idea. Southern Africa was in turmoil, and a confrontation between the front-line states and South Africa loomed. How was the region to be "stabilized" so as to buy the time which was needed to implement, or even to try to implement, Crocker's theoretical reforms in South Africa? South Africa was already embarked on a policy of using force and pressure to "stabilize" the region. Crocker was perfectly aware of what was happening in the region, and of South Africa's plans.[16] An active US role in "stabilizing" the region, in parallel with South Africa, had to involve the use of force and pressure.

That, of course, could not be said in an article in *Foreign Affairs*. But it was said in the deliberations of the National Security Planning Group, which discussed the lines of a new policy towards Southern Africa in 1981. It was even broadly hinted at in various public pronouncements in the months which followed the final formulation of that policy.

The 1981 Southern Africa Policy Review was carried out in the National Security Council by an interdepartmental committee which included senior representatives of the Department of State, the Central Intelligence Agency and the Department of Defense. It resulted in a policy paper offering the president a number of alternative courses of action in Southern Africa. By the summer, the president had "signed off" on an option which was to carry the US into a tacit alliance with South Africa in its war against the front-line states.[17]

Both the National Security Council's policy analysis and the President's Directive are classified. However, it is possible to reconstruct the basic lines of the policy ultimately decided upon from publicly available evidence, from various official speeches after mid-1981, and from the known facts of US policy actions in the last decade.[18] What follows is such a reconstruction. The language in quotations is taken from the speeches of senior US officials.

President Reagan decided upon a general posture which would be supportive to South Africa. The United States would seek "to encourage peaceful evolutionary change" in order "to forestall mass revolutionary violence" within South Africa. Beyond South Africa's border, the US would seek "to counter Soviet influence in the region." In particular, US policy would seek "to help bolster the security of South Africa," that is, "to foster regional security" by means which would meet South African needs.

In pursuit of these objectives, President Reagan decided upon the following lines of action:

South Africa
- to move towards closer and more supportive relations with the government of South Africa
- to encourage the government of South Africa to move towards a "nonracial liberal democracy" by moderate reforms of apartheid.
- to support, politically, financially, and by other means, "those elements inside and beyond the Republic which foster peaceful and evolutionary change there"
- to assist South Africa in resisting internal efforts to isolate it, especially at the United Nations

Namibia
- to help "end the guerrilla warfare that has continued in northern Namibia and southern Angola for 15 years"
- to seek the removal of Cuban troops from Angola
- to seek a "peaceful solution" of the Namibia question, which would allow South Africa to retain control of the territory and yet be acceptable internationally

Southern African region
- to seek to end "the dangerous cycle of violence in the region" and to direct "the impetus toward change into peaceful channels"
- privately to encourage South Africa "to pre-empt any armed threat – guerrilla or conventional – from its neighbors" and "to use its military superiority for that end"
- to apply strong pressure, with others, against Angola and Mozambique and eventually to seek radical changes in the internal political balance in those countries

- to apply pressure against the government of Tanzania, Zambia, and Zimbabwe and gradually to draw them close to the West
- to cooperate closely with South Africa in mounting pressure on the front-line states
- to use US diplomacy "to help establish the rules of the game that will limit and discourage the application of outside force" in the region

Public relations (cover)
- to maintain strict secrecy about active collaboration in support of South Africa
- to maintain strict secrecy about certain actions taken against the front-line states
- to mount an extensive campaign of political action and propaganda in Africa, Western Europe, and the United States to ensure that the actions of the US government would remain invisible or be accepted by public opinion.

The policy of constructive engagement fashioned in 1981 thus pushed the Reagan administration into an invisible alliance with Pretoria in its attack on the front-line states.

6 Coercive Diplomacy

The Reagan administration, in a major shift of policy, thus began extensive overt and covert collaboration with South Africa within weeks of taking office. Its aim was to assist South Africa in "defeating" the threat to apartheid, that is, to assist it in reversing change in the front-line states and blocking change in South Africa itself.

The US and South Africa together developed a joint strategy. This was essentially an extension of the military doctrine of coercive diplomacy. According to this doctrine, a nation can sometimes achieve limited political objectives by combining carefully measured doses of military force with diplomacy. Selective force is used against an adversary who resists one's demands, while one "negotiates" with the adversary about ceding to those demands. In some cases, inducements of aid or other incentives may be offered. The idea is that an adversary may be "persuaded" to accept one's demands when enough military pressure has been applied, and when suitable inducements have been offered.[19]

US and South African officials were meeting to work out a common strategy for "stabilizing" the Southern Africa region while the National Security Council review was still under way, and cooperation on some projects seems to have begun before the review was completed.[20] By the summer of 1981, the US and South Africa were working jointly to apply increasing military, economic, political, diplomatic, and other pressures against the front-line states. They reasoned that this was the best way to "close down" the liberation movements in the region. The front-line states had access to and influence over the liberation movements, and the liberation movements were dependent on their hosts. By applying pressure on the front-line states, the Reagan administration expected to force them to cease their support for the anti-apartheid struggle. And that, they thought, would be the end of the struggle, which they saw in large part as "Soviet-sponsored" intervention in South African affairs.

Coercive diplomacy requires a very close coordination of military force and diplomacy. For political reasons, the United States could not openly make use of its military power in Southern Africa, and, again for political reasons, South Africa had very little diplomatic credibility anywhere in the world. There was therefore an obvious division of labor. South Africa would use its military power against the front-line states; it would also use its considerable economic power in the region to bring pressure to bear on them; and it would use such other means of waging war as sabotage, subversion, and assassination. The United States would concentrate on diplomacy, although it would also make use of its power – its economic power in the Southern Africa region was substantial and could be used to good effect. The US would, in addition, use various other means both to strengthen South Africa and to undermine its adversaries.

The diplomatic side of this systematic coercion, however, would be the focus of its public policy. As the pressure on the front-line states increased, the United States would assume the role of "mediator" between South Africa and the victims of their joint attack. By steps, using its authority and its worldwide network of diplomatic contacts, the US was to edge the front-line states closer to conceding South Africa's demands.

7 Covert Collaboration

Despite the so-called Iran–Contra scandal, it is not generally understood that, from 1981, the foreign policy of the United States was conducted without any effective supervision by Congress; for, under the Reagan administration, the execution of foreign policy became, in large measure, covert. As one US official put it in 1986, "A trademark of this Administration is that it has effectively substituted covert action for foreign policy."[21]

One cannot understand the US role in Southern Africa in the 1980s without taking into account the very substantial expansion of covert action and special operations.[22] Secret operations, in the broad sense of the term, became a major component of foreign and military policy, and particularly with respect to Angola and Mozambique. At the same time, it was not at all easy for the public to grasp the importance of the expanding capability of the US for waging unconventional war. For, as it was increasing this capability, the Reagan administration was also reorganizing the entire covert action–special operations establishment; and the purpose of the reorganization was to remove the execution of policy from the public arena.

Two changes were of special importance. Firstly, the Reagan administration, under Executive Order 12333 of 1981, put the National Security Council (NSC) in charge of all "national foreign intelligence, counterintelligence and special activities." The NSC thus became a "super-CIA," outside the reach of Congress.[23] Secondly, the Reagan administration also carried out a pseudo-privatization of many secret operations, creating a vast network of private and proprietary corporations, banks, consulting and management firms, and public relations companies within which "detailees" and others executed policy on orders from the NSC. "The Enterprise," which surfaced in the Iran–Contra hearings and was run by Oliver North, Richard Secord, and Albert Hakim, was exactly that network. The use of the Enterprise by William Casey, director of the CIA, made secret operations much more difficult to see and unravel than they would otherwise have been.

It took some time, of course, to reorganize the intelligence–special operations establishment. But, from 1981, operations were being set in motion as the changes were being made.

US involvement in the attack on the Front-line States appears to have originated in a memorandum written by William Casey to President Reagan in early 1981. Casey's idea was that there should be a common front of various anti-communist movements around the world and that the United States should actively aid these movements.[24] Angola and Mozambique were specifically targeted as countries in which the United States should secretly intervene.

The major problem, as always in large-scale secret operations, was to move money and arms secretly. Casey's "freedom fighters' bureau" was well funded. Significant funding was arranged through a secret provision of the 1981 agreement to sell US AWACS radar planes to Saudi Arabia.[25] Casey proposed that the US and the Saudis should make equal contributions to a secret fund based in Geneva. He met with Saudi Arabia's King Fahd in 1981 and succeeded in obtaining his agreement.[26] The Swiss bank account in which the money was kept contained between $1 billion and $2 billion.[27]

The *New York Times* wrote in 1987 that the disclosure of the 1981 agreement "demonstrates that the Reagan Administration used covert means to fund resistance groups such as the contras *years earlier than had been publicly known before*" (italics added).[28] Funds from the Swiss account, and others, were used to pay for arms, equipment, logistical support, and other costs incurred by UNITA in Angola and the MNR in Mozambique. The *New York Times* reported in 1987 that, according to a reliable source, the Saudi Ambassador in Washington had acknowledged Saudi assistance to UNITA.[29] Confidential documents obtained by *Africa Report* indicate that the Reagan administration was providing covert political, financial, and military support to UNITA "since at least 1982."[30] A secret meeting to arrange support for UNITA took place in Kinshasa in 1983, in which US officials met with representatives from South Africa, Israel, Zaire, and UNITA. In November of that year, the US Navy delivered arms shipments for UNITA to the ports of Boma and Matadi in Zaire.[31]

The Enterprise was also used to deliver arms by air to bases in Zaire for transhipment to UNITA in Angola. Such operations appear to have been run by the CIA but used St Lucia Airways and possibly other proprietary airlines.[32] St Lucia Airways was often chartered by companies in the Enterprise network. Arms came from Spanish and Portuguese companies and were flown to Zaire via Morocco. Some of the arms came from Egyptian stocks of captured socialist-bloc weapons.

Money to support the MNR, which was also funded by South Africa, came from the US–Saudi "black op" slush fund and from private sources, which may have sent funds through organizations in the Enterprise. The funds were channelled to the MNR through the Bank of Credit and Commerce International (BCCI), a $20-billion holding company owned by powerful Middle East families, including Sheikh Kamal Adham, the former head of Saudi Arabian Intelligence.[33] The BCCI's Monte Carlo branch was used by the Enterprise to channel millions of dollars to help finance the secret sale of TOW missiles from the United States to Iran in the mid-1980s.[34]

Arms destined for the MNR were shipped from a secret CIA base in Oman to the Comoros Islands in C-130 transport aircraft. Some of these bore Omani markings, and others bore no markings at all. The arms were flown from the Comoros in smaller aircraft and parachuted to the MNR in Mozambique. There was, especially in the beginning, some resistance in the CIA and the Department of Defense to the idea of aiding the MNR. However, the CIA director and the Saudi Arabian government insisted that such aid should be a priority. The Saudis and the Omanis were antagonistic to Mozambique, because FRELIMO, the governing party there, had expelled from the country a number of Muslims who later found favor with them.

This description of the US operations in aid of UNITA and the MNR is far from being comprehensive. But it will suffice to indicate the broad lines of US policy towards Angola and Mozambique from late 1981. There is additional supporting evidence for this outline, which, for lack of space, cannot be cited here. It seems clear from the evidence cited, however, that this outline of the programs is more or less accurate; but obviously, a proper evaluation of US covert policy towards the front-line states must await the results of a full investigation.

8 Coercive Diplomacy: The Road to Nkomati

From early 1982, as has been indicated, South Africa steadily escalated its covert war against the front-line states and, with the aid of the major Western powers, steadily pressed its political demands. Despite the considerable economic and military pressure brought to bear on them, however, the front-line states continued to resist, rebuffing South African and US "diplomatic approaches" repeatedly, and especially rebuffing efforts to persuade them to accept "linkage" of the Cuban presence in Angola to the decolonization of Namibia. The response to this resistance was to escalate the war and to try to force through a grand "regional security settlement;" that is, a "settlement" in which the front-line states would end their support for the liberation movements, and even for the liberation struggle. The objective, in effect, was partially to rebuild a *cordon sanitaire* of buffer states around South Africa by neutralizing the newly independent states of Angola, Mozambique, and Zimbabwe.

In September 1982, shortly after the front-line states had repulsed President Reagan's approach on "linkage" to their chairman, President Nyerere of Tanzania, William Casey flew to Southern Africa, visiting a number of countries including Mozambique, Zambia, Zimbabwe, and South Africa.[35] CIA sources explained to Congressional aides that this was a "familiarization" trip, with no particular political purpose. This is not true. Casey went to Southern Africa, and particularly to South Africa, to begin implementing a grand design for rebuilding a *cordon sanitaire* around South Africa.

A few press reports at the time made it clear that South Africa and the US would demand that the front-line states cease or reduce their support for the South West Africa People's Organization (SWAPO) and the African National Congress (ANC), or face an escalation of military, economic, and other pressures. The London *Sunday Times*, for instance, reported that the director of the CIA had flown to South Africa on a secret visit to meet with the South African prime minister and other high officials and to discuss what it called a "US plan" for "the creation of a *cordon sanitaire* on the border of South Africa's northern neighbors to end ANC infiltration."[36] The *Sunday Times* made it clear that the US would play an important role in securing a "regional settlement" and that the "settlement" would have to be accepted if the front-line states were to escape further attacks. As its correspondent put it: "The United States is launching a diplomatic offensive in southern Africa aimed at speeding up a Namibia settlement, curbing sabotage raids into South Africa by the African National Congress (ANC) and ending South Africa's alleged campaign of 'destabilization' of neighboring states which give backing to the ANC."[37]

The *Washington Post* also reported that CIA Director Casey had made "an unpublicized visit to Africa" in September.[38] According to that paper, the US was undertaking "a series of high-level diplomatic contacts designed *to salvage its southern Africa policy*" (italics added).[39] The *Post* reported that South Africa rather than the US had suggested broadening the "negotiations" in the region "to encompass the issue of infiltration across its borders by the African National Congress."[40] And its reporter underlined the fact that the front-line states faced a serious threat of escalation if they refused to accept the demands that would be put to them: "In exchange fo a ban on an ANC guerrilla presence in surrounding countries – including Angola, where the movement has important training facilities – South Africa hinted it would curb its own military actions against neighboring states, US sources said."[41]

Casey's discussions with South African officials apparently resulted in an agreement on implementing the next phase of coercive diplomacy in Southern Africa. Pressures on all the front-line states would be increased. The demand for an end to support for the liberation movements would be stated more openly and more persistently. The US would intensify its diplomatic efforts, acting as "mediator" between South Africa and its adversaries, and coordinate its actions even more closely than it alrady had with South African actions against the front-line states.

One important implication of the planned new offensive should be noted. From late 1982 on, Mozambique was to bear the brunt of the attack against the front-line states. South Africa and the United States had found Angola too difficult to crack. In late 1982, they shifted their sights to weaker countries, and particularly to Mozambique, where they hoped they could "score a diplomatic success." State Department sources in a private conversation at the time described Mozambique as "the most vulnerable country" in Southern Africa. In a sense, it was. Just across the Transvaal border from South Africa and with modest military forces and little foreign assistance, Mozambique was both more exposed and less able to resist South African and US pressures.

From the beginning of 1983, South Africa began to carry out paramilitary and military attacks almost openly. In May, it sent its air force brazenly over Maputo to bomb residences and a factory, killing several Mozambican civilians.[42] US diplomatic activity in the region was being intensified at the same time. Writing in the *New York Times* in the beginning of 1983, Anthony Lewis could apparently see the outlines of coercive diplomacy. The South African government, he wrote, had "had a year of remarkable successes."[43] "Externally," Lewis observed, "the last year has seen South Africa use its military power both covertly and overtly in neighboring black-governed states." And it had done so "without any significant political penalty," although, he thought, "the United States has privately urged restraint on South Africa." Still, "South Africa's neigbors have in effect been told, without subtlety, that they can have peace and a chance for economic development only on South African terms."[44]

Lewis also saw that US diplomatic efforts were closely tied to South African actions. The US, he said, was engaged in "an intricate and ambitious diplomatic venture, one that could affect all of southern Africa."[45] And the US and South Africa were "*acting separately but in close co-ordination*" (italics added) in seeking solutions to a number of regional problems, including that of Namibia. However, he praised what he called a "bold African diplomacy," describing it as an "extraordinarily complex design in which the United States has invested so much."[46] In short, the cooperation between the Reagan administration and South Africa was becoming increasingly visible.

During 1983, economic warfare against the front-line states, most of which was covert, continued, and several countries found themselves facing unprecedented difficulties. They could not export their goods. They could not attract foreign capital. They could not purchase essential commodities, and particularly adequate supplies of food. They lacked the means to sustain domestic production of needed goods. And foreign aid projects had to be shut down, often for security reasons. By mid-1983, drought, war, and a variety of external pressures had begun to make a difficult situation desperate. US analysts predicted that the front-line states would soon "be on their knees."[47]

The situation which existed by the end of the year in most parts of the region is hard to describe. In Zimbabwe, millions of people were receiving emergency food aid. South Africa was again intensifying its efforts to produce chaos in the province of Matabeleland. It had mounted a further large-scale invasion of Angola, sending its troops nearly 200 miles into the country. While Angola offered strong resistance, this third invasion was a harsh blow to a country already suffering from drought, a partial economic blockade, and the dislocation and damage caused by previous attacks. South Africa's UNITA surrogates, furthermore, were extending their military actions in the center of the country.

Mozambique faced the gravest economic situation it had known. The drought had continued, further reducing food production. There was insufficient foreign exchange to purchase the needed food imports. The war in the central provinces had spread south and north. MNR attacks had greatly aggravated economic problems which might otherwise have been coped with. Emergency food supplies could not reach those who needed them. More than 100,000 Mozambicans had fled to Zimbabwe in search of food. In Inhambane province, where the war was especially intense, the lack of food had caused the death of tens of thousands of people, and possibly as many as 100,000, in 1983 alone.

As the war escalated in 1983, and as the situation of several of the frontline states grew increasingly difficult, US diplomats pressed hard for a series of "non-aggression" agreements. They concentrated their attention on Angola and Mozambique. Behind their diplomatic overtures, however, there was the threat of South African power being used even more harshly, and implicitly of further US economic pressure. US diplomats said they were trying to help bring "peace" to the region. However, a South African official quoted in the *New York Times* made it clear what kind of peace they were offering: "We want to show that we want peace in the region, we want to contribute and we can help a lot. But we also want to show that if we are refused, we can destroy the whole of southern Africa."[48] US officials, of course, were for the most part more circumspect about expressing such views. The Reagan administration could not openly link its proposals to the frontline states to such crude threats. But the linkage was there nonetheless, and the front-line states understood this. In late 1983, in an inteview with the South African magazine *Financial Mail* Charles Lichtenstein, the Deputy US Ambassador to the United Nations, made it abundantly plain that the United States and South Africa were working to the same plan. In as clear a threat as any American official had made publicly, Lichtenstein said that, "destabilization will remain in force until Angola and Mozambique do not permit their territory to be used by terrorists to attack South Africa."[49]

In the first months of 1984, Angola and Mozambique were forced to agree in part to the terms pressed upon them by South Africa and the United States. In mid-February, Angola agreed to form a joint commission with South Africa to monitor the "disengagement" of South African troops from the southern part of its territory. A month later, Mozambique signed the Nkomati accord with South Africa, in order to obtain a respite from South African attacks. Under the terms of this accord, in return for a South African promise to cease its support for the MNR,

Mozambique agreed to prohibit any military activity on its territory by the ANC.

The Reagan administration was widely praised for bringing long-time adversaries to the negotiating table, and Crocker's policy of "constructive engagement" was described as the key to peace in a region wracked by conflict. *Time* magazine wrote in the third week of March that the "winds of peace were sweeping through" Southern Africa. The new developments "were a sorely needed foreign policy victory for the Reagan Administration." "The US policy of 'constructive engagement,' of soft-spoken diplomacy with South Africa," it said, "appeared to be vindicated."[50] Joseph Kraft, writing in the *Washington Post*, pushed praise, it seemed, as far as one could; declaring "Southern Africa provides the most striking foreign policy gain so far achieved in the Reagan Administration."[51] Inasmuch as few, if any, gains had been made, this seemed overly effusive, but Kraft meant that the administration had taken "a historic step toward the safe dismantling of the most explosive racial powder keg in the world."

Such comments reveal starkly the utter blindness of the press and the rest of the media in the United States. And they go some way towards explaining how the Reagan administration could collaborate in a policy of covert war against whole populations with impunity.

9 From "Destabilization" to Permanent War

The Nkomati accord was a victory for South Africa and the United States. It did not, however, bring peace to the region. South Africa was really far from achieving the objectives of its regional policy. The Afrikaner regime still felt insecure, for it faced determined opposition to apartheid in the front-line states, primarily from the governments of Angola, Mozambique, and Zimbabwe.

South Africa was intent on objectives beyond Nkomati. To "stabilize" the region, it needed other agreements with its principal adversaries, modelled on Nkomati.[52] It also wanted to engineer political changes within Mozambique, and if possible in Angola, which would weaken their existing governments. Some South African strategists wanted to force a FRELIMO–MNR coalition in Mozambique; and some wanted to overthrow the FRELIMO government outright, as did senior members of the Reagan administration. There were disagreements in South Africa on how far to press in Mozambique. But everyone seems to have been in agreement that it was necessary to press the Maputo government harder; and greater pressure on Mozambique would, of course, keep the pressure on Zimbabwe. The insecurity of the Beira corridor would force Harare to depend upon South African transport routes, with all the consequences which followed. In the case of Angola, South Africa never hesitated for a moment about escalating the war there, despite the Lusaka accord signed with Luanda shortly before Nkomati. Thus, even in the weeks immediately after Nkomati, when many observers thought peace was at hand, the logic of the situation indicated that South Africa would continue to escalate the war.

Events in South Africa itself may even have increased the internal pressures to strike out against the front-line states. In the summer of 1984, the anti-apartheid struggle in South Africa entered a new phase. The ANC, the United Democratic Front (UDF), the other opponents of the regime organized a mass mobilization to protest against the new constitution. This led to harsh and more or less continuous confrontations between the anti-apartheid forces on the one hand, and the government and the security forces on the other. By 1985, it was clear that this mass mobilization had altered the internal balance of forces. Given the psychology of the Botha regime and the views of the military on the front-line states, it was almost inevitable that the regime would return to the attack.

It was soon clear, in fact, that South Africa had no intention of abiding by the Nkomati accord. The Directorate of Special Tasks sent 1,000 fully armed MNR men into Mozambique in the very month that the accord was signed. It had also provided the MNR with large stocks of weapons to continue waging the war. In 1985 and 1986, the MNR greatly intensified its attacks inside Mozambique. The war spread into large parts of Zambesia and Tete provinces, and even into Niassa in the north. From new bases in Malawi, very large MNR forces penetrated far into Zambesia, in an apparent effort to reach the sea, and possibly in an effort to capture an administrative center and to install a "government."[53] This created pressure on Zimbabwe. The Beira corridor was being rehabilitated, and traffic from Zimbabwe to Beira was increasing. Large-scale MNR attacks in areas near the corridor forced Zimbabwe itself to respond. It had to send increased numbers of troops to aid Mozambique in repelling the attacks.

South Africa never really implemented the Lusaka accord in Angola. Its troops never withdrew from the southernmost strip of the area it had agreed to evacuate. In the summer of 1985, it resumed cross-border raids. By early 1986, it was carrying out attacks in many parts of southern Angola, and aid to UNITA had been greatly increased. Pretoria mounted large-scale military operations repeatedly to prevent UNITA being routed by FAPLA, the Angolan armed forces. Two years after the Lusaka accord, the war in Angola was more intense than ever. Air and commando raids throughout the region resumed. In January of 1986, South

Africa mounted an economic blockade of Lesotho, demanding that all members of the ANC residing in the country be expelled. In the face of this pressure, the military carried out a coup and installed a government that was prepared to comply. South Africa then lifted the blockade. Later in the year, Pretoria sent its commandos to attack ANC targets in Gaborone, Harare, and Lusaka.

Statistics make the escalation of the war after Nkomati very clear. One indication of the growing devastation may be found in the statistics recently prepared by the United Nations Children's Fund (UNICEF) on deaths among infants and children under five in Angola and Mozambique. These show that the number of such deaths in the two countries rose from 25,000 in 1981 to 105,000 in 1984 and to 147,000 in 1988. the last year for which statistics were available. (See table 9.2.) The Southern Africa Development Co-ordination Conference (SADCC) has also estimated the direct economic costs of the war in the region on a year-by-year basis. For the period 1980–4, the average annual cost in overall damage was approximately $2,000 million. In 1984, the cost must have been of the order of $5,000 million. By 1986, the cost of damage had risen to $8,000 million, and by 1988, it had risen to $10,000 million per year. (See table 9.5.) Despite the fact that the economic estimates contain a component for cumulative output losses, the meaning of these statistics is clearly that the war was increasingly destructive.

What was South Africa trying to achieve? The answer seems to be that, in the face of continuing resistance to its demands from the front-line states, South Africa was trying to create a cordon of increasing instability on its borders to ensure that its neighbors remained dependent upon it, and even to force them to become more dependent. In effect, South Africa was attempting to recolonize the region by force. It is also possible that, encouraged by the Reagan administration, it was pushing towards the eventual overthrow of the governments of Angola and Mozambique. This is quite clear in retrospect, and Western diplomats at the UN at the time were discreetly declaring their intentions to selected journalists.[54]

Whatever its precise motives, and those of the Reagan administration, the front-line states found themselves facing a permanent war.

10 Specific US Actions

The following is a summary of selected US actions taken against the front-line states or on behalf of South Africa. It is far from being more than suggestive of the direction of policy towards Southern Africa under the two Reagan administrations. It does, however, help to show how US actions supported and reinforced South African military attacks and covert action mounted against the front-line states.

1 From 1981, the US orchestrated a campaign of political and economic pressure against Tanzania, demanding persistently behind the scenes that Tanzania abandon socialist economic policies. This campaign succeeded in depriving Tanzania of needed credit, investment, and aid, thus contributing to the "economic failure" which the Reagan administration decried.[55]

2 In 1981, Zambian security forces thwarted a plot by "dissidents" and South African commandos to assassinate President Kaunda and seize power. It was reported at the time that agents of the CIA had recruited Zambians in an effort to examine "the possibility of an alternative leadership in the country."[56] According to African sources, William Casey flew secretly to Lusaka and threatened sanctions against Zambia if the role of the CIA were exposed.[57]

3 In 1981, the Reagan administration blocked the implementation of the UN plan for a Namibian settlement by linking it for the first time to the withdrawal of Cuban troops from Angola. While the US continued to state its support for the UN plan, Secretary of State Haig wrote the South African foreign minister late in the year that "the United States would not press South Africa to settle the Namibian question unless Cuban troops were withdrawn from Angola."[58]

4 While the US and South Africa were applying various pressures against Angola, including substantial and overt military pressure, General Vernon Walters, a former deputy director of the CIA and then a US special envoy, made numerous trips to Luanda to persuade the Angolan Government to agree to the withdrawal of Cuban troops.[59]

5 In 1981, after South Africa had mounted a large-scale invasion of Angola and occupied a large area in the southern provinces, the US vetoed a Security Council resolution condemning its actions.[60]

6 In the same year, the US vetoed the candidacy of Salim Salim, the foreign minister of Tanzania, for the post of secretary-general of the United Nations. It had been expected that the next secretary-general would be an African, and Mr Salim was the choice of the Organization of African Unity for the post.[61]

7 During 1982, US officials worked successfully to secure a loan of $1.1 billion for South Africa from the IMF, although that country did not appear to qualify for such a loan.[62] The South African government uses a substantial amount of foreign exchange to purchase oil and arms and to finance covert operations.

8 In August 1982, during a major military effort by South Africa to

236

extend its control over southern Angola, President Reagan sent a letter, classified "secret," to President Nyerere of Tanzania, the chairman of the front-line states, urging him to accept the "linkage" of a Namibian settlement to the withdrawal of Cuban troops from Angola. Reagan suggested that if "linkage" were not accepted soon, the US would cease to press for implementation of the United Nations plan for a Namibian settlement.[63]

9   Throughout this period, the US used diplomatic and political pressure behind the scenes to prevent South Africa from being condemned for its destabilization of neighboring countries.[64] To take one example, the US intervened to prevent South Africa from being named in a Security Council resolution condemning an attempt to mount a coup against the government of the Seychelles in late 1981.[65] It was later learned, during a series of trials in South Africa, that the attempted coup had been officially authorized.

10   In 1983, the US which was displeased with Zimbabwe's voting in the Security Council, cut assistance to that country by almost half. US officials stated that Zimbabwe's sponsorship of a resolution condemning US intervention in Grenada and its abstention on a US-sponsored resolution after the Korean airliner incident "played a bit part" in its decision.[66]

11   In 1983, when large numbers of Mozambicans faced starvation and when tens of thousands had already died from lack of food, the Reagan administration deliberately held back food aid to that country, just as it was seeking to "persuade" it to sign a non-aggression pact with South Africa. Mozambique had repeatedly refused to agree to South Africa's demand that the ANC be expelled from its territory. Mozambique began 1984 facing the most serious food shortages it had known and with a deficit of well over 100,000 tons of cereals.[67]

12   In September 1984, Mozambique gave way to US pressures, which had been insistent since 1981, for it to join the IMF and the World Bank. Shortly thereafter, when destabilization and malnutrition threatened the health of growing numbers, the IMF pressed for reductions in health expenditures.[68]

13   In the summer of 1985, after a not inconsiderable lobbying effort by the Reagan administration, the Congress repealed the Clark Amendment, which had barred US aid to UNITA in Angola. The Clark Amendment had long been ignored by the CIA and the National Security Council (NSC), but its repeal cleared the way for UNITA to join the group of "resistance fighters" publicly sponsored and financed by the US under the Reagan Doctrine.[69]

14   From the early years of the Reagan Administration, US intelligence

agencies provided South Africa with extensive intelligence on the front-line states and on the ANC. This intelligence, among other things, assured the provision on a routine basis of top-secret communications intelligence from the National Security Agency. A former senior official in the Reagan administration said of the provision of intelligence that "Our interests require helping the South Africans."[70]

15 In early 1986, the Reagan administration virtually declared open war on Angola. In a major public relations campaign to garner support for UNITA, the Reagan administration brought Jonas Savimbi to Washington, where he talked to influential groups and met with President Reagan. It was later reported that the US had agreed to give UNITA some $15 million in arms and equipment, but the amount was, in fact, substantially higher.[71]

16 Samora Machel, the president of Mozambique, was killed in an airplane crash on the South African border with Mozambique in October, 1986. Machel's death was a terrible blow to Mozambique, to the front-line states and to the Non-Aligned Movement. The crash was not accidental. South Africa used sophisticated electronic equipment which caused the instruments on Machel's aircraft to malfunction. The highly classified equipment had come from the United States.[72]

17 In the summer of 1986, a Zimbabwe minister, speaking at a public function, sharply criticized the US for its refusal to enact adequate economic sanctions against South Africa. Former President Jimmy Carter, who was present, walked out. A few days later, the Reagan administration suspended – and later withheld – more than $13 million in aid to Zimbabwe.[73]

18 It was revealed in 1987 that the Agency for International Development (AID) in Washingtion, DC, was engaged in rebuilding 3,000 miles of dirt roads in the Shaba province of Zaire. Shaba borders on Angola and is one of the base areas from which UNITA guerrillas operate. In 1986, the AID had rebuilt 600 miles of roads running roughly parallel to the Angola border and some 50 miles inside Zaire. These roads are part of the infrastructure for waging unconventional war against Angola.[74]

11 The Human and Economic Consequences

Scholars and journalists are aware of South Africa's aggression in Southern Africa, even if the general public outside Africa is not. Articles on the subject can be found in academic journals and books, and occasionally in magazines and newspapers. And there has been periodic discussion of South Africa's actions in the region even in the United Nations, where the agenda is increasingly dominated by the foreign policy requirements of the US and its more fervent allies.

Yet journalistic and scholarly commentary on events in Southern Africa reveals two weaknesses. The first, already referred to, is that it almost never mentions, and certainly never analyzes, the role of the United States in the destabilization of the front-line states. The other, equally serious, is that such reviews and comments are superficial, confining themselves to little more than "accounting for skirmishes" and other actions. The approach has been to report what has been happening as if destabilization were some kind of battle. It is not; it is much more than that. So the typical reportorial approach does not tell us very much. It certainly has not helped us to understand the impact of external aggression on the peoples of the region. Yet that is the real issue. What has ten years of continuous unconventional war done to the countries and to the peoples against whom it was directed?

The answer has begun to emerge as a result of two recent UN studies, both from peripheral agencies of the UN system. The first is *Children on the Front Line*, published by UNICEF, which examines the impact of apartheid, destabilization, and warfare on children in Southern and South Africa.[75] The second, entitled *South African Destabilization*, is published by an interagency task force of the Economic Commission for Africa (ECA). It examines the economic and human costs of the war waged by South Africa – and its allies – against the front-line states.[76]

The ECA study rightly observes that the effects of South African aggression "are almost impossible to comprehend on a rational or emotional level."[77] Using a variety of statistical techniques, the study does nonetheless succeed in providing a rough description of the economic and human price which the front-line states have had to pay for their opposition to apartheid. This consists essentially of estimates of deaths resulting directly and indirectly from the war, and of the economic losses which the region has suffered because of the war.

Deaths resulting from the war have been astonishingly high. They were caused by famine, when food was unavailable as a result of the security situation, or as a result of that and drought; they were caused by a combination of malnutrition and disease when rural health stations had been destroyed; and they were the direct result of war and terrorism. The data on war-related fatalities in the Southern African region are set out in table 9.1.

By the end of 1988, according to the ECA study, the total number of war-related deaths in the region had reached 1.5 million. Sixty percent of these deaths occurred among children under five and were the result

Table 9.1 War-related loss of life in the SADCC region, 1980–8

Country	Infants/young children	All deaths
Mozambique	494,000	900,000
Angola	331,000	500,000
Zambia	50,000	50,100
Tanzania	25,000	25,060
Malawi	25,000	25,000
Zimbabwe	–	500
Lesotho	–	500
Swaziland	–	250
Botswana	–	50
Total	925,000	1,501,460

Source: UNICEF *Children on the Front Line*, "Children in Southern Africa," and estimates from *South African Destabilization: the Economic Costs of Frontline Resistance to Apartheid*, Inter-Agency Task Force/Africa Recovery Program (United Nations, 1989), pp. 15–17.

of the destruction of health services or starvation caused by the war. The vast majority of fatalities occurred in Angola and Mozambique, which were the principal targets of external aggression. Zambia, Tanzania, and Malawi together accounted for some 100,000 deaths. Fatalities in Zimbabwe, Lesotho, Swaziland, and Botswana were relatively low and came to something less than 1,500 over the nine-year period.

One point of some political significance should be noted. It seems fairly clear *that there was a steady increase in violence and destruction in Southern Africa during the whole of the last decade.* Year-by-year data for total fatalities in the region have not been published. But the UNICEF study presented annual data for war-related deaths among infants and young children in Angola and Mozambique, and they show a steady increase, from 25,000 per year in 1981 to 105,000 in 1984 and to 147,000 per year in 1988 (see table 9.2). Figures for non-fatal casualties in the war are not available at this time. However, it should be clear from the data on fatalities that the number of wounded and those made ill by the war must run in the millions.

Apart from these casualties, external aggression has completely disrupted ordinary life. In non-industrial countries, where the vast majority of people work the land to produce food, this is a threat to a country's very survival. As the authors of the ECA study put it: "Rural terrorism has had the effect of keeping the rural population in Angola and Mozambique on the move, unable to settle down or to restore production. This has resulted in massive food shortages, even in fertile areas."[78] The ECA study provides some data suggesting the extent of this disruption of food

Table 9.2   Death of infants and children under five in Mozambique and Angola from war-related causes 1980–8

Year	Angola	Mozambique	Total
1980	0	0	0
1981	10,000	15,000	25,000
1982	20,000	30,000	50,000
1983	31,000	46,060	77,000
1984	42,000	63,000	105,000
1985	55,000	82,000	137,000
1986	56,000	84,000	140,000
1987	58,000	86,000	144,000
1988	59,000	88,000	147,000
Total	331,000	494,000	825,000

Source: UNICEF, *Children on the Front Line.*

production. In the first half of 1989 in Angola and Mozambique, at least 6 million people had been displaced from their homes and were unable to resume farming. Another 1.5 million Angolans and Mozambicans had become refugees in neighboring countries. In addition, a further 45 million urban dwellers were deprived of the normal rural surplus and had great difficulty securing food.[79]

Allen Isaacman has provided data on the decline of cash crop production in one country, Mozambique, and his figures may serve to indicate the likely magnitude of the decline in food production there. With Isaacman's data, taken from the Mozambique National Planning Commission, we can show the declines in value of cash food crops between 1980 and 1985, the last year for which data are available. (See table 9.3.) Isaacman's figures obviously reflect the effects of drought as well as those of war. However, the drought in Southern Africa had more or less ended by 1984. Yet production continued to decline.

The ECA study attempts to calculate the broader economic costs to the region of the war inflicted upon it. It uses two different approaches to do this, both of which shed valuable light on what has happened.

The first method is to calculate the direct costs of the war. These include: direct war damage, extra defense spending, higher transport costs, the cost of refugees and displaced persons, the effects of boycotts and embargoes, export losses, etc. The difficulty with this method is that it can involve double counting. Nonetheless, the figures are good indications of orders of magnitude, especially when adjusted. (See tables 9.4 and 9.5). It will be seen from table 9.5 that the direct costs of the war *have escalated steadily* through the 1980s. This is partly the result of the escalation of the conflict and of rising defense costs, and partly of

Table 9.3   Declines in value registered by
cash food crops, 1980–5

Food crop	% change, 1980–5
Rice	−59
Maize	−34[a]
Potatoes	−83
Beans	−63
Citrus	−16
Cattle	−61
Pigs	−31[b]
Chickens	−91
Eggs	−30[a]
Milk	−39

[a] 1982–5.
[b] 1981–5.
Source: Allen Isaacman, "Regional Security in
Southern Africa: Mozambique," Survival Inter-
national Institute for Strategic Studies (January–
February 1988)

Table 9.4   Direct cost method of estimating losses to the SADCC region
1980–4

Item	SADCC estimate (current $ million)	Green and Thompson (current $ million)
Direct war damage	1,610	1,610
Extra defense spending	3,060	3,310
Higher transport, energy	970	970
Smuggling, looting	190	190
Refugees and displaced	660	660
Export loss	230	550
Boycotts, embargoes	260	260
Loss of existing production	800	800
Lost of economic growth	2,000	4,000
Trading arrangements	340	590
Total	10,120	12,940

Source: Johnson and Martin (eds), Frontline Southern Africa: Destructive Engagement
(1989)

cumulative output losses and inflation. Despite the fact that the latter factors are of some importance, the data seem to confirm the tentative
conclusion set out above that *the intensity of the conflict in the region
has been increasing more or less steadily.*

Table 9.5 Adjusted estimate of direct war cost to the SADCC region, 1980–8

Year	Adjusted from SADCC estimate ($ million)	Adjusted from Green and Thompson ($ million)
1980–4	10,120	12,940
1985	7,000	7,000
1986	8,000	8,000
1987	9,000	9,000
1988	10,000	10,000
Total at historic prices	44,000	46,940
Total at 1988 prices	53,000	56,000

The sharp increase in 1985 over the 1980–4 average relates to escalation of conflict, the rising defense bill, cumulative output losses, and inflation.

Source: UNICEF, *Children on the Front Line.*

South African Destabilization also calculates the economic costs of the war by a second method, one which estimates the difference between the likely gross domestic product (gdp) in the absence of war and actual gross domestic output in the 1980s. By this method, the costs of the war also appear to be very high. The authors of the study concluded that the war-related loss of gross domestic output in the region between 1980 and 1988 was more than $62 billion. Most of this loss, $45 billion of it, was suffered by Angola and Mozambique. The total gdp loss to the region was the equivalent of 210 percent of the regional gross domestic product in 1988. (See table 9.6.)

Table 9.6 Gross domestic product (gdp) loss in the SADCC region, 1980–8

Country	1988 ($ million in 1988 prices) Loss	% of actual gdp	1980–8 ($ million in 1988 prices) Loss	% of 1988 actual gdp
Angola	4,500	90	30,000	600
Mozambique	3,000	110	15,000	550
Zimbabwe	1,350	25	8,000	145
Malawi	550	30	2,150	133
Zambia	500	20	5,000	200
Tanzania	500	10	1,300	26
Botswana	125	10	500	40
Lesotho	50	7	300	42
Swaziland	30	5	200	33
All SADCC	10,605	43	62,450	210

Source: National data and preliminary 1988 gdp estimates as described in the text.

The question of the economic cost of the war is at this time still an open one. While there is some overlap in what is accounted for by the two methods used in the ECA study, each method also refers to important costs which are quite distinct. It would seem that at some point all the economic costs of the war must be accounted for. So the final estimate for the cost of damage and destruction in the region could well be significantly higher than either of the broad estimates set out in the ECA study. What is already clear, however, is that South Africa and its allies have, in a calculated manner, brought more destruction to the subcontinent than has ever occurred in a single decade in its entire history.

12 Conclusions

We have tried in this paper to examine two aspects of the war in Southern Africa which have so far received little attention: the damage and destruction wrought by unconventional war, and the role of the United States in waging this war along with South Africa. We believe these two aspects of the war are extremely important. Their neglect has prevented the world from understanding what has really been happening in Southern African since the latter part of 1981.

The situation in Southern Africa is far more serious than most accounts suggest, for the war has been more deadly and more destructive than is evident from any chronicle of events. Chronicles do not take account of the cumulative effects of the events they record. At the same time, the war is a much bigger problem than many accounts suggest; it will be very difficult to stop, since the United States is an important protagonist.

The question of damage and destruction in the region is now a matter of public record. Two United Nations agencies have carried out extensive studies on the human and economic consequences of the war, so we have a reliable general picture of what has been done to the region, to its economy, to its infrastructure, to its peoples, and to the social fabric of nations.

It would be hard to disagree with the authors of *South African Destabilization* that the devastation in Southern Africa is almost beyond comprehension. This is, after all, a war in "peacetime," a war waged in the shadows. Until recently wars of this kind, unconventional wars, have been more or less limited in scope. The war waged by the US to frustrate and subvert the independence of Cambodia, Laos and Vietnam was an exception. This war has left at least one and a half million people dead. A "limited" war which has, to much of the world, been almost invisible has left large parts of a subcontinent in ruins.

In early 1988, Roy Stacey, a senior State Department official, told a

United Nations conference of aid donors that the war in Mozambique was "a systematic brutal war of terror against innocent civilians through forced labor, starvation, physical abuse and wanton killing . . . one of the most cruel holocausts against ordinary human beings since World War II."[80] Stacey was quite right. In fact, his eloquent statement was no less valid as a description of the war in other countries of the front line. Yet what are we to make of the specatacle of a senior US official denouncing the nature and consequences of a war which his own government has secretly helped to set in motion?

We do not pretend to know the answer at this stage. It is clear, though, that the United States played an important role in Southern Africa during the 1980s, not in "bringing peace," but in making war. The public declarations and actions of the Reagan administration helped South Africa a great deal. This was partly a question of the US applying political and economic pressure and organizing the diplomatic side of "coercive diplomacy." However, it was also a question of the US applying force covertly under the banner of the Reagan Doctrine. The Reagan administration provided money, arms, logistical support, and probably training to UNITA and the MNR. We do not yet know about everything that the Reagan administration, through the Enterprise, the CIA and possibly agencies and forces of the Department of Defense, actually did in Southern Africa. But we know enough to conclude that its role was far more important than anyone has so far indicated.

Part of this covert role is, after all, quite public. In a bizzarre twist of policy, the Reagan administration more or less openly declared a "covert" war on Angola from the beginning of 1986. The US role in Mozambique has yet to be publicly acknowledged. Yet the evidence indicates that the Reagan administration pursued much the same policy there that it pursued in Angola. It should not be forgotten that the redoubtable Colonel North brazenly hinted at the fact during the Iran–Contra hearings in 1987. He said: "We also worked very hard to unify this [Contra] resistance movement . . . this is the only anti-communist resistance that ever unified . . . We had – didn't succeed in doing that in Angola or Ethiopia, Guinea-Bissau, Mozambique, or other places where resistance movements have grown up to fight communism."[81]

The point is that South Africa was very far from acting alone in Southern Africa during the 1980s. It had important, active assistance from the United States, which wanted "to rid southern Africa of Marxist regimes."[82] In the absence of active assistance from the United States, South Africa would not have been able to press as far as it has against the front-line states. It would not have been able, with "plausible deniability," to unleash large surrogate forces against Angola, Mozambique, and Zimbabwe. It would never have been able openly to use its air

245

force and its army as it has. And it might even have had to use economic pressure and its own special forces much more sparingly.

The Reagan administration, therefore, was in part responsible for the death and destruction which has taken place in Southern Africa. This is a fact which the world, and especially American citizens, must face, if the slaughter which has been going on there is to be stopped. Speaking not long ago of Western indifference to the war of terror against his own country, Mozambique, journalist Carlos Cardoso said: "There is an ever-present risk of conflict escalating into full-scale regional war. We conclude that you people in the West do not care that 500,000 blacks have already died here and that worse may happen. But in 1978 in our capital Maputo there were only eight murders, a city of one million. That is how tranquil Mozambicans are. How can this crime be undone? How many more of us must disappear?"[83]

During the early 1980s, officials in the front-line states, officials from international aid organizations, a few diplomats, and some commentators repeatedly denounced "South African aggression" in Southern Africa. Yet their denunciations had very little effect: certainly they did not stop South Africa. The reason for this was that South Africa had a powerful patron and partner in the United States, which was actively helping it to wage unconventional war against the front-line states. And no one ever confronted the Reagan administration vigorously and effectively. Governments in particular sought to appease the United States. And very few organizations or individuals dared even to try to expose the US role in waging a war which has been as barbarous and almost as murderous as the war in Indochina.

If South Africa has been guilty of genocide in Southern Africa, then the United States has been an accessory to genocide. The time has come to abandon appeasement and to mobilize against a policy which, merely in order to buy time for the reorganization of apartheid, has wreaked havoc in a vast region and left its peoples in poverty and despair.

Notes

This article is an extended and revised version of a paper delivered by one of the authors at the Socialist Scholars' Conference in New York City on April 20, 1984. The authors would like to thank Walter Hättig and Heike Kleffner for their assistance and comments on the draft.

1   "National Security Study Memorandum 39" was produced in the NSC in the course of 1969. It was leaked to academics in 1974 and passages were quoted in the press in that year. In 1976, the text was published by Lawrence Hill and Company in the US under the title *The Kissinger Study of Southern Africa*. The text was accompanied by a commentary by two journalists. The

premise of "Option Two", the option on which the Nixon Policy was based, was that *"The whites are here to stay and the only way that constructive change can come about is through them. There is no hope for the blacks to gain the political rights they seek through violence* (p. 105; italics added).

2   Their intentions, of course, were a closely held secret. But in 1983, journalists were being told more about the goals of policy. The United Nations correspondent of a major US newspaper wrote in that year of "the determination on the part of the Reagan Administration and South Africa to rid Southern Africa of Marxist regimes." See Louis Wiznitzer, "UN Security Council Likely to Be Drawn into Namibia Debate", *Christian Science Monitor* (March 31, 1983).

3   Internal memo from Chester Crocker to the Secretary of State, "Your Meeting with South African Foreign Minister *Botha*, 11:00 a.m. May 14, at the Department – *Scope Paper*" (May 11, 1981).

4   See Daniel Southerland, "US Shifts Terrorism Policy," *Christian Science Monitor* (January 30, 1981). Secretary of State Haig made his statement within hours of the time of the attack. The Reagan Administration later tried to define the liberation movements in the region as "terrorist groups". And the Mozambique government later discovered that CIA agents in Mozambique had collected information about the houses attacked, and their occupants, and passed it to South Africa.

5   The quotes from Geldenhuys are from Robert Davies and Dan O'Meara, "South Africa's Strategy in the Southern African Region: A Preliminary Analysis," paper presented to Southern African Development Research Association Conference, Lesotho (October 1983).

6   Personal conversations with political-military analysts, including government ministers and intelligence officers in Zimbabwe and Mozambique.

7   Zimbabwe at that time was already under siege, with bombings, the sabotage of installations and, in particular, the blocking of the use of railway wagons by the SA Railroads. So Zimbabwe politicians knew, and, therefore, their counterparts in all the front-line states knew, that South Africa was already using its power in this manner.

8   The accounts of this incident and others in this section are taken from Sanctions Working Group, "Major Military, Paramilitary and Subversive Actions against the Front-line States," working paper, 1983). The chronology was constructed from extensive press files, including clippings from the *Financial Times*, *The Times*, *The Guardian*, *The Observer*, the London *Sunday Times*, *Noticias* (Maputo), the *Rand Daily Mail*, the *Star* (Johannesburg), the *New York Times*, the *Washington Post*, the *Christian Science Monitor*, *Le Monde* and *Le Monde Diplomatique*.

9   Interviews with Zimbabwe officials, Harare (October 1981). See also Sean Gervasi, "The Political Economy of Destabilization", Harare, November, 1981, mimeo.

10   According to the Zimbabwe Central Intelligence Organization, the bomb had been planted by South African saboteurs.

11   Caspar W. Weinberger, "US Military Strategy for the 1980s," in *The 1980s: Decade of Confrontation?*, Proceedings of the Eighth National Security

Affairs Conference, (National Defense University Press and the Under Secretary of Defense for Policy, Fort Lesley McNair, Washington, DC, 1981), p. ix. The quotations that follow are taken from pp. x–xi of the address.

12 Weinberger said that "We will prevent the coercion of the United States, its allies and friends."

13 According to CIA sources, the Reagan Administration was supplying assistance to UNITA from 1981, in violation of the Clark amendment. The Clark amendment restrictions were ended by Congress in 1985, and from 1986 the Reagan Administration openly provided arms and money to UNITA.

14 On January 27, 1986, in a report entitled "Now it's US Backing Rebels," *US News and World Report* explained that the Reagan Doctrine was stirring arguments at home, as well as battles abroad. It stated: "A clear test of Reagan's commitment is Angola . . . where UNITA have fought the Soviet-and-Cuban backed regime for more than a decade." A short time later, it was openly announced that the US would resume aid to UNITA.

15 Chester Crocker, "South Africa: Strategy for Change," *Foreign Affairs* (Winter 1980–1).

16 Before becoming Assistant Secretary of State for Africa, Crocker had been a specialist in African affairs at the Center for Strategic and International Studies of Georgetown University, a conservative think tank. In that capacity, he had done government contract work on Southern African affairs, travelled to the region and remained in close contact with officials in South Africa and other countries.

17 There were numerous press accounts from the spring of 1981 to the effect that a formal review of policy towards Southern Africa was under way. See, for instance, Anthony Lewis, "Conservative Reality," *New York Times* (June 11, 1981); Henry Trewhitt, "Reagan Must Juggle a Mix of Ideologies and Politics in Southern Africa," the *Sun*, Baltimore (June 4, 1981).

18 Beginning in August, 1981, Chester Crocker gave a series of speeches bearing on US policy in Southern Africa. Many of these were about regional security. See in particular "Regional Strategies for Southern Africa," *Current Policy*, 308, Department of State, Washington, DC (August 29, 1981); "Communist Influence in Southern Africa", Congressional testimony printed in the *Department of State Bulletin* (June, 1982); "Challenge to Regional Security in Southern Africa: the US Response," *Current Policy*, 431, Department of State, Washington, DC (October 28, 1982); "The Search for Regional Security in Southern Africa," *Current Policy* 453, Department of State, Washington, DC (February 15, 1983).

19 A useful analysis may be found in A. L. George, D. K. Hall, and W. E. Simons, *The Limits of Coercive Diplomacy: Laos, Cuba, Vietnam* (Little, Brown and Co., 1971).

20 According to the *New York Times* of March 15, 1981, five high-ranking South African Defense Force officers, including Lt Gen P. W. van der Westhuizen, met with US officials in mid-March to discuss Southern African problems. Secretary of State General Alexander Haig announced to the press

that he had authorized Jeane Kirkpatrick, then US ambassador to the UN and Cabinet member, to meet with van der Westhuizen. After these meetings, Assistant Secretary of State for Africa Chester Crocker was sent to Pretoria. According to Claudia Wright, writing in the *New Statesman* of November 5, 1982, the Kirkpatrick and Crocker meetings were the "beginning of a US-South African shift on the terms of settlement for Namibia" and were also "the green light for General van der Westhuizen and his fellow generals to widen their military operations in Namibia and Angola and to escalate covert operations against Mozambique and Zimbabwe."

21 Cited in the National Security Archive, "Covert Activity in the Reagan Administration: Areas of Inquiry Suggested by the Iran-Contra Investigation and Press Accounts," Memorandum for the Senate Select Committee on Intelligence, Washington, DC June 24, 1987, p. 2.

22 For useful accounts, see F. Barnett, H. Tovar, and R. Shultz, *Special Operations in US Strategy* (National Defense University Press, 1984); Jay Peterzell, *Reagan's Secret Wars* (Center For National Security Studies, 1984); John Prados, *Presidents' Secret Wars* (Quill-William Morrow, 1986). See also *Covert Action Information Bulletin*, most issues since 1981.

23 Michael Ratner and David Lerner, "A Mini-CIA," *The Nation* (August 15/22, 1987).

24 The National Security Archive, "Covert Activity in the Reagan Administration," pp. 3, 20.

25 Jeff Gerth, " '81 Saudi Deal: Help for Rebels for US Arms,' *New York Times* (February 4, 1987).

26 Interview with a former US official, October 1989.

27 Cited in the National Security Archive, "Covert Activity in the Reagan Administration," p. 3.

28 Gerth, " '81 Saudi Deal."

29 Ibid.

30 "So What Else Is New?," Update in the News, *Africa Report* (May-June 1987).

31 Ibid.

32 The National Security Archive, "Covert Activity in the Reagan Administration," p. 10.

33 Knut Royce, "Bank Busted in Drug Deal," *Newsday* (October 12, 1988).

34 Ibid.

35 Reed Kramer, "US Sends Envoys to Bolster Policy in Southern Africa," *Washington Post*, (November 3, 1982).

36 Eric Marsden, "US Plans a 'Cordon' ", *Sunday Times* (October 10, 1982).

37 Ibid.

38 Kramer, "US Sends Envoys."

39 Ibid.

40 Ibid.

41 Ibid.

42 J. Hanlon and J. Kane-Berman, "South African Air Raids Kill Five in Maputo Suburb Homes," *The Guardian* (May 24, 1983); M. Hornsby and R. Kennedy, "Pretoria Revenge Raid on Maputo, *The Times* (May 24, 1983).

43 Anthony Lewis, "Confident South Africa," *New York Times* January 31, 1983.
44 Ibid.
45 Anthony Lewis, "Bold African Diplomacy," *New York Times* (February 2, 1983).
46 Ibid.
47 Interviews with Congressional sources (April 1983).
48 Flora Lewis, "Pax Afrikaansa," *New York Times* (January 25, 1983).
49 "Charles Lichenstein: the New Right at the UN," *Financial Mail*, Johannesburg November 18, 1983, cited in Jennifer Whitaker, "Africa Beset," *America and the World: 1983, Foreign Affairs* (1983).
50 "Southern Africa: The Winds of Peace," *Time* (March 26, 1984).
51 Joseph Kraft, "Turning Point in Africa," *Washington Post* (March 20, 1984).
52 On the objectives of "destabilization" after Nkomati, see Gerald Braun, "The Afrikaner Empire Strikes Back: South Africa's Regional Policy," in John Brewer (ed.), *Can South Africa Survive?* (Southern Book Publishers, 1989); Robert Davies, "The SADF's Covert War against Mozambique," in Jacklyn Cock and Laurie Nathan (eds), *War and Society: the Militarisation of South Africa* (David Philip, 1989).
53 Allen Isaacman, "Regional Security in Southern Africa: Mozambique," *Survival*, International Institute for Strategic Studies (January–February 1988), p. 27.
54 Wiznitzer, "UN Security Council Likely to Be Drawn into Namibia Debate."
55 Interview with an African ambassador (August 1983).
56 "Foreign Ministry Official on Trial for CIA Links," *Africa News* (July 13, 1981). See also Colin Legum, "Secret Trial Hides CIA Blushes," *Observer* (October 18, 1981).
57 Interviews with African officials (March 1982). Colin Legum reported in *Observer*, London, in late 1981 that "A Zambian Foreign Office official is being tried *in camera* in Lusaka, apparently to spare the American CIA from embarrassment. The request that the trial should not be held in public came from the US Embassy in Lusaka." See Legum, "Secret Trial Hides CIA Blushes."
58 Donald McHenry, "An Assessment of the Reagan Administration at Mid-Term," *TransAfrica Forum* (Spring 1983), p. 12.
59 Interviews with African officials (August 1983 and November 1983). There were press accounts of General Walters's visits to Luanda, but they did not give details of his conversations with Angolan officials.
60 The US veto was reported in the press at the time. See Bernard Gwertzman, "US Doubts Reports that South Africa Hit Angola Again," *New York Times* (September 4, 1981), which also gives the Reagan Administration's stated reasons for the veto.
61 Mr Salim had been chairman of the UN Committee on Decolonization and, as secretary-general, would have been an active advocate of a rapid settlement of the Namibian question.
62 See George Gedda, "IMF Approves Controversial Loan to South Africa,"

Washington Post (November 4, 1982), as well as David Coetzee, "Behind Closed Doors at the IMF," *Africa Now* (March 1983) and "IMF: Calling the Tune," *Africa Confidential* May 25, 1983.

63 Interviews with UN officials (1982). There have been mentions of a Reagan letter in the press, but no details of its contents were given until *Jeune Afrique* published a translated partial text and a photograph of part of the last page. See "L'equation namibienne," *Jeune Afrique* (October 27, 1982).

64 This was generally known among close observers of African affairs. However, there are now numerous public examples, one of the most obvious being the 1981 veto of a Security Council resolution on Angola already referred to.

65 Interviews with African diplomats (May 1982).

66 Jay Ross, "US Slashed Aid to Zimbabwe by Almost Half," *Washington Post* (December 20, 1983).

67 Interviews with Mozambican officials (November 1983) and with congressional sources (January 1984).

68 Cited in William Pomeroy, *Apartheid, Imperialism and African Freedom* (International Publishers, 1986), p. 85. Pomeroy based his account on an article in the *New Statesman*, London, (October 19, 1984).

69 Gordon Winter, a former South African Intelligence agent, stated that "The logistical and propaganda support of Dr Savimbi and his UNITA movement was a mutual relationship between French Intelligence (SDECE), and CIA and South African Military Intelligence to 'keep Savimbi afloat until such time as MPLA is brought down.' " See Gordon Winter, *Inside BOSS* (Penguin, 1982), p. 540. See also John Stockwell, *In Search of Enemies* (Norton, 1978), which contains extensive descriptions of CIA support for UNITA in the mid-1970s.

70 See Seymour Hersh, "US is Said to Have Given Pretoria Intelligence on Rebel Organization," *New York Times* (July 23, 1986).

71 See John Marcum, "Regional Security in Southern Africa: Angola," *Survival* International Institute for Strategic Studies (January–February 1988), p. 8.

72 Interview with former senior US Intelligence officer (January 1987).

73 See the Southern Africa roundup in *Africa News* (January 11, 1981).

74 See James Brooke, "CIA Said to Send Weapons via Zaire to Angola Rebels," *New York Times* (February 1, 1987).

75 *Children on the Front Line: the Impact of Destabilization and Warfare on Children in Southern Africa and South Africa* (United Nations Children's Fund, 3rd edn, 1989).

76 *South African Destabilization: the Economic Cost of Frontline Resistance to Apartheid* Inter-Agency Task Force, Africa Recovery Programme/Economic Commission for Africa (United Nations, October, 1989).

77 ECA, *South African Destabilization*, p. 7.

78 Ibid, p. 15

79 Ibid.

80 Quoted in ECA, *South African Destabilization*, p. 3.

81 Oliver North, *Taking the Stand* (Pocket Books, 1987), p. 219.

82 See Wiznitzer, "UN Security Council Likely to Be Drawn into Namibia Debate." Wiznitzer was explaining that behind the impasse over Namibia was "the determination on the part of the Reagan Administration and South Africa to rid Southern Africa of Marxist regimes."

83 Quoted in Derrick Knight, *Mozambique: Caught in the Trap* (Christian Aid, 1988), pp. 57–8.

Credits

Administration: Bridget Jennings

Commissioning: John Thompson

Co-ordinator: Debbie Seymour

Desk-editing: Tracy Traynor

Indexing: Isobel McLean

Jacket design: M. Kasper

Marketing and publicity: Rebecca Harkin, Clare Moulam

Production: John Keston-Hole

Index

Index

255

Index

Index

Evelegh, R. 165
'evil genius' theory of terrorist
  motivation 166
exclusion orders, Irish people, from
  Britain 158
experts on terrorism 46, 57–62
  counterinsurgency 163–5
extradition arrangements 162
extradition practices 162
  in Northern Ireland 159–61

Fadlallah, Sheikh 26
Farrell, M. 156, 159
FBI (Federal Bureau of
  Investigation) 23, 53
Fenians 155, 158
Fertig, Colonel Wendell 126
Fitzwater, Marlin 3, 4
FMLN (Farabundo Marti National
  Liberation Front) 2
Ford, Gerald 200, 201
Ford, Sir John 81, 201
Foreign Agents Registration
  Act 168, 169
France
  internal security personnel 156
  Irish Brigade in French army 155
  and Northern Ireland 160
  and state terrorism 83–4
Fraser, Donald 204
Fretilin (Revolutionary Front for the
  Independence of East
  Timor) 197–9, 202, 205–6
Freud, Sigmund 7–8

Gaddafi, Colonel 26, 49, 50, 83,
  84, 163–4
Gardiner Report (1975) 157
Garthoff, Raymond 22
Geldenhuys, Deon 215–16
geography as the root of
  violence 102
Germany, terrorist killings 41
Gibraltar, assassination of IRA
  members in 161
Glass, Charles 24
Glenholmes, Evelyn 160

global ascendancy of the United
  States 112
Goodhart, Sir Philip 170
Goodman, Hirsch 32
Gorbachev, Mikhail 117
government ministers propaganda,
  and the IRA 163–4
governments and the terrorism
  industry 52–4, 65, 68
Greece, Ancient, Asian and African
  influence 68–9
Greek National Guard Defense
  Battalions 140
Green, Marshall 195, 196
Guatemala 21, 40, 48, 79, 80, 145
  civil defense organization 141
  and the Reagan administration 48
  terrorist killings 41
  US counterterror in 133, 135
Guelke, A. 164, 169
guerrilla warfare and US
  counterinsurgency 125–6, 128,
  129, 132, 137–8

Hadaad, Saad 49, 62, 65
Hadden, T. 168
Hafez, General Mustapha 25
Haig, Alexander 48, 49, 214, 217, 236
Hailsham, Lord 170
Hakim, Albert 227
Hall, Stuart 64
Hatta, Mohammad 182
Haughey, Charles 160, 167–8
Hegel, G. W. F. 103
Helms, Jesse 5
Henze, Paul 56, 57, 58
Heritage Foundation 55, 56, 60
Hewitt, C. 163, 165–6
Hewitt, P. 158
Higgins, Colonel William 108
Hill, Christopher 85
Hiroshima, atomic bombing
  of 104–5
Holland see Netherlands
Honduras and the UN General
  Assembly Resolution 42/159
  29–30

Index

Index

260

Index

Index

Index

torture of detainees
  in Indonesia 81
  in Northern Ireland 86-7
TREVI 161, 162
Truman, Harry S. 122
Truman administration 182
Tsisis, Dov 29
Tsongas, Senator Paul 17
Tugwell, Maurice 59, 60, 165
Tunis, Israeli bombing of 27, 32-3, 34
Turner, Stansfield 20

UDR (Ulster Defence Regiment) 157
Ulsterization 157
unconventional warfare (UV) 121-2, 125-31, 132, 139, 146
  in Southern Africa 214, 216-20
Unification Church 54, 57, 58
UNITA (National Union for the Total Independence of Angola) 218, 219, 222, 228, 229, 232, 234, 238, 245
United Nations General Assembly Resolution 42/159 29-30
  and Indonesia 81-2, 202-4, 207
United States
  Bush administration 3, 5, 213
  client states 15, 20, 21, 34, 50
  concept of terrorism 13-14
  counterinsurgency 121-47
  and El Salvador 2-5
  and 'the Enterprise' 227, 228
  foreign policy 48, 226
  image 111
  and Indonesia 181, 182, 183-6, 194-6, 200, 201-2, 203-4, 205, 207
  and international terrorism 49-50
  and Irish republicans 159, 160
  model of terrorism 45-6
  and Nicaragua 15-20
  and Southern Africa 212, 213-14, 220-9, 235-8, 246
  and the terrorism industry 53-4, 55-7, 59, 60

terrorist involvement 1-8
and the UN General Assembly Resolution 42/159 29-30
  see also CIA; Reagan administration
Untung, Lieutenant Colonel 187, 190

Vaky, Viron 19
Vietnam syndrome 117
Vietnam War 51
  and counterorganization 133, 138-9, 140
  Operation Phoenix 138
  US counterrevolutionary warfare 116

WACL (World Anti-Communist League) 54, 57, 58
Wall Street Journal 68, 79
Walters, General Vernon 236
Washington Post on Southern Africa 230, 233
Washington Quarterly 57
Washington Times 57
weapons see arms consignments
Weinberger, Casper 220-2
Weizmann, Chaim 28
Wellmer, Albrecht 103, 109
West Germany, internal security personnel 156
Western model of terrorism 43-6
Western Papua New Guinea 182
Western states, terrorist involvement 1-8
White, Robert 79
Whitelaw, William 171
Wicker, Tom 18
Wilkinson, Paul 58, 61, 62, 63
  on the CIA 84, 85
  on counterinsurgency 165
  on El Salvador 77, 78-80
  on the European Community 162
  on the 'excess of democracy' 89-90
  on Indonesia 81, 82
  on Northern Ireland 85-8, 91-2

263